CHELFORD

A CHESHIRE VILLAGE

by

MAVIS AND KEITH PLANT

ROGER J ROYCROFT

JULIA SLATER

A book to celebrate the Millennium

and

The 225th anniversary of the rebuilding of the Church

Supported by Astra Zeneca Pharmaceuticals
Alderley Park, Cheshire

Published by the Authors at 22 Chapel Croft, Chelford, Cheshire.
Tel/Fax: - 01625-860074
E-mail: - Wkeith@Plant30.freeserve.co.uk

ISBN   0 9536123 0 9

Typesetting and Design by: Mavis Plant

Printed in England by:
MFP Design & Print, Longford Trading Estate, Thomas Street, Stretford, Manchester, M30 0JT

Date of issue – October 1999

Mavis and Keith Plant moved to Chelford ten years ago and immediately fell in love with the village. Mavis was a Pensions Officer before she retired and Keith is a Director of a Multi National Engineering Company. In 1996 Keith published a book entitled "History of Chelford in the 19th Century". He also lectures on genealogy.

Julia Slater has lived in the Chelford area all her life and is the daughter of Alan Barber who has been a member of Chelford Parish Council for 50 years, many as Chairman. Julia works as Practice Manager at Chelford Surgery and is also a member of the Parish Council and the Parochial Church Council.

Roger J Roycroft has been one of the village doctors for 37 years. He is a member of Chelford Parish Council, the Parochial Church Council and on the governing bodies of the school and church. Five years ago he published Reflections upon the Chelford Railway Disaster of 22nd December 1894. He is also a warden at Chelford Parish Church.

ACKNOWLEDGEMENTS

The authors would like to express their thanks for the assistance given by various members of the village, past and present, in the preparation of this book. Without their help this book would not have been possible.

Certain information contained in this book has been extracted from the records deposited in the Cheshire County Record Office, Duke Street, Chester and is reproduced with the permission of Cheshire County Council. Where applicable, a description of the records, together with their reference is given.

Thanks are also expressed to the John Rylands Library of Manchester University for permission to use information extracted from the Astle Estate documents deposited in the Library archives.

The picture on the front cover of the book has been reproduced from a painting by Frances Crompton, a former resident. Thanks were expressed to the late Gwenifer Walsh for her permission to use this copy of the painting for the front cover of this book.

Our thanks also to Astra Zeneca Pharmaceutical of Alderley Park, Cheshire for their contribution towards the printing of this book.

~~~~~~~~~~~~~~

This book is dedicated to all members of the village both past and present. It is also dedicated to the Rev. John Ellis to mark his retirement after 18 years of dedicated service to the village and its people. We hope this book will evoke many happy memories in those who have lived there and be an inspiration to those who will come in the new Millennium.

Special thanks are due to the following for information provided in the preparation of this book: -

John & Anne Ellis, Josie Parfitt, Christine Johnston, Edna Pimlott, Prunella Bradshaw, Freda Massey, Mike Shenton, Peter Robertson, Bernard Anniken, Melanie Bouskill, Gwyn Williams (Marshalls Chartered Surveyor), George Brew, Minty Day, Dr Day, Joyce Richardson, Hilda Lowe, Dorothy Bradshaw plus many past and present members of the village who have provided photographs, newspaper cuttings, reminiscences, post cards and other information helping in the production of this book.

~~~ CONTENTS ~~~

The Walsh Family

Gledhill Family

THE NEW SCHOOL AT OAK ROAD

Open September 1999

AERIAL VIEW OF CHELFORD

There is some evidence that the Chelford area had Roman connections. After purchasing Milne House (the site where Astle Hall was subsequently built) in 1749 John Parker carried out extensive alterations to the house and gardens. It was during this work that a number of Roman urns were discovered and recorded by Mr Foote Gower[2]. After stating that there were some discoveries made at Capesthorne, he continues:

'When Mr Parker, of Astle, the early and much valued friend of the author of these pages, was making considerable alterations both in the disposition of his grounds and mansion, a place that had been dedicated to sepulchral uses was fortunately exposed to view. Some of these Roman urns that came to light upon this occasion were esteemed worthy of being deposited in the curious museum of Sir Asheton Lever, and others of them are still preserved at Astle[3] . There were no traces indeed of the station to be found which had supplied the place with these sepulchral relics. But though the appearances were vanished, yet the remembrance of it was retained by tradition having fixed it in the vicinity of the spot where this cemetery was discovered. A line of imperfect barrows marks the track of road from this station to the village of Withington, and it may possibly have proceeded from thence to King Street and the Roman station of Middlewich. Another road after passing the stream at Peover at the ford which has given the designation to the chapelry, may be traced with a little care and attention through the township of Over Alderley to Handforth."

---

2   Foote Gower's MSS, Gough MSS, Bondleian Library, Oxford

3   There is also reference to two urns being found in front of Mr Parker's house. One of them was too rotten to be preserved. Of the other, two thirds was entire indicating that the urn would have been 15" high and 11" wide at its widest point. There was some opinion at the time that this urn could have been of British rather than Roman origin.

There is also some evidence of a Roman road in an Inq. 20 Hen VIII[4] (1535)as to a right of way across a meadow of John Birtles, in the village of Chelford, "to the kings highway called Macclesfield Street". The boundaries described in this Inq. refer to land of Richard Cotton, gent, and William Astyll. The land is referred to as 'a close of land, on the east part following a selion[5] of land called an Hadeland of William Astyll, near the ditch: and so continuing by land of Richard Cotton and entering a close called the Woodhey, following to the kings highway, by le Portway, and following the ancient kingsway to Chelford broke'.

It has been proved that a Roman road existed between Northwich and Rainow where it connected with the road between Manchester and Buxton. It is possible that the area around Chelford lay on the route of this road, though as yet Chelford did not exist.

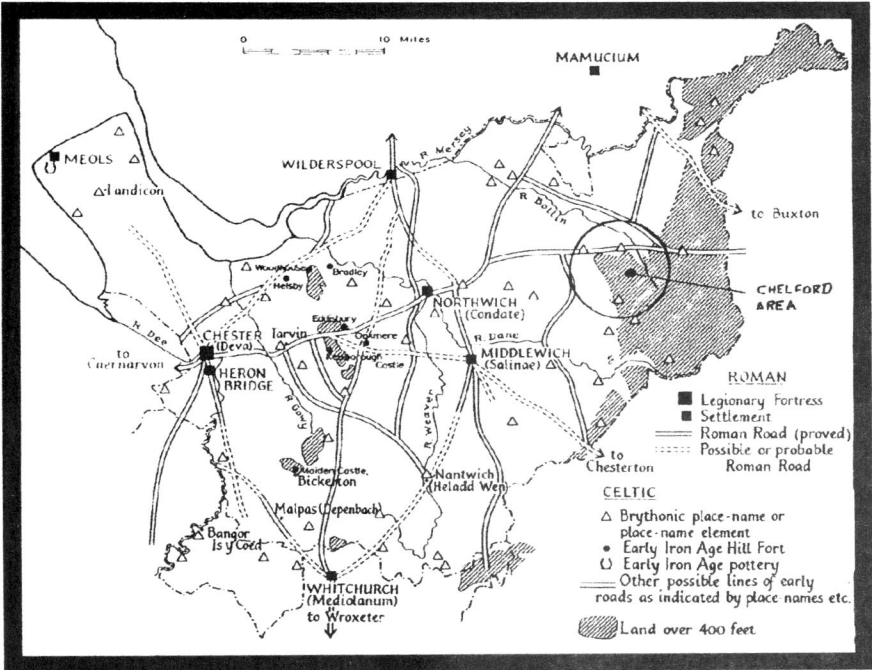

4   Inquisition of 20th year of Henry VIII's reign.

5   A cultivated strip in an open field, consisting of a ridge with a furrow on either side.

The Romans withdrew from England in AD410 and for some 200 years following the withdrawal Cheshire's population consisted largely of short, dark British people who eventually became known as Welsh, speaking a language now known as Primitive or Old Welsh[6]. Peover is a British name, indicating that people now known as British existed in the Chelford area at that time.

For centuries after AD600 Cheshire was invaded by tall, fair people known as the Anglo Saxons. These invaders were basically village-farmer type people who originated in the plains of Northern Germany and Southern Denmark. For at least two centuries they spread over Cheshire, followed in the ninth century by the Vikings, forming settlements at strategic locations throughout the county. There are many examples of place names with Scandinavian origins in Cheshire, notably in the Chelford area, Church Hulme (now Holmes Chapel).

It was during this period, possibly during the ninth century that the name of Chelford originated, according to J. Mc N Dodgson[7] as follows: -

> "'Ceala'sford' from the Old English person Cealo or Ceolla and ford. Old English Ceole 'throat', in a topographical sense, may have applied to the original site of this ford, possibly a point on the Snelson boundary about 110-813740, from which the bounds ascended Mere Clough (110-809745). However the lake at Astle park has altered the clough and the topographical interpretation cannot be proved.

It is, however, more probable that the original site was a short distance further east in a position where the two streams meet and where a mill would have been erected. During one of the recent Traction Engine Rallies, tests were carried out to establish the suitability of the land, and evidence of a road extending towards Lapwing Lane or Congleton Lane was uncovered.

Again, according to J Mc N Dodgson, Astle was 'East hill' possibly indicating a site east of the original position of Chelford.

Nothing much of any significance occurred through the Dark Ages until the Norman Conquest of 1066 and more importantly to Chelford, the bitter mid-winter of 1069-70. At that time William I was having problems with the

---

6   A History of Cheshire by Dorothy Sylvester

7   The place names of Cheshire by J Mc N Dodgson Vol. XLIV.

Cheshire people and marched his armies over the Pennines (he was also having difficulties in Yorkshire) into Cheshire, through the north-east area down into Macclesfield and then into the Cheshire basin before reaching Chester. The 'wasted' manors recorded in the Domesday Book of 1086 give an indication of the route of William's army. Stockport and Macclesfield lay in ruins. Many died and many more fled westward, leaving their fields and villages abandoned and the eastern lowlands desolate[8].

The Domesday Survey contains the following reference to Chelford:

CELEFORD -

The Earl (Hugh) Himself holds Celeford. Brun held it. There is half a hide paying Geld. There is land for 2 plough. It was and is waste.

A hide is the amount of land which can be ploughed in a year using one plough. Old English measurement was based on

1 hide, Carvcote or Ploughland	=	4 Virgates or Yardlands
1 Virgate or Yardland	=	2 Bovates or Oxgongs
1 Bovate or Oxgong	=	2 Farthingdales
1 Farthingdale	=	10 Acres
1 Acre	=	4 Rods wide X 40 rods long

An acre is the amount of land that could be ploughed by a yoke of oxen in a day.

Using these figures the size of Chelford in 1086 was 80 acres which when compared to the acreage at the 1834 conveyance of Astle Hall of 1500 acres indicates that at the time of the Norman Conquest Chelford was a very small village.

There is no reference to Astle in the Domesday Survey but Gawsworth, Goostrey, Nether Alderley, Marton, Ollerton, Peover, Siddington, Snelson and Warford, all of which were included, Peover and Siddington, are described as wastes.

It must have taken some considerable time to recover from this devastation and it wasn't until 1245-1251 that the next mention of Chelford occurs, in the Chartulary of the Abbey of St Werburgh at Chester which records the gift of land by the families of Pigot and Worth[9].

> *Robert Pigot gives to Robert de Worth, for his homage and service the whole of Chelleford, with the demesne and rents of Asthul and Wythington, paying for all services, saving the puture of the sergeants of the peace and the repairs of the heys (hedged enclosures) in Macclesfield Forest[10].*

> *Robert Pigot grants to Robert de Worth his mill of Chelleford and Wythington with all that belongs to it, paying annually for the same one barbed arrow.*

> *Robert de Worth grants to the monks of Chester the whole of Chelleford, with the mill and all that appertains to it, together with the demesnes and rents of Asthull and Wythington and the land called Long fordecroft.*

The abbot of St Werburgh in plea 31 EDW 111 (1358) claimed view of frank pledge[11] from all residents and the lands of his abbey in Chelford and Asthulle were valued after the dissolution and granted as part of the lordship of Barnshaw to the then newly-created Dean and Chapter of Chester. Subsequently it reverted to the Crown and was granted by Queen Elizabeth in 1579 to fee-farmers and then probably sold in small lots.

There appear to have been a number of disputes between the descendants of the original purchasers of the estate including a definition respecting the boundaries of Chellford and Snelleston. These commenced at the aqueduct under Chellford mill and ascending by the valley called the Mereclogh, to certain heys between the town fields, passed thence beyond the enclosure of Snelleston, continuing by the deep moss against Fanden and so following to the Lathe and the divisions of Chellford, Fandon and Old Werford[12].

---

9   St Werburgh's Chartulary Harl. MSS. 1965, F, 25

10   Names of the witnesses given in Harl. MSS. 8074F. 185b

11   Each village was divided into associations of tithings - ten men. The members of each tithing were bound to stand security for the others' good behaviour. The View of Frankpledge was the actual inspection by the authorities to make sure that it existed.

12   Harl MSS 2074

Astle was originally written Asthull. An early deed (before 1300) contains information that Robert, son of John de Asthulle, gave to Adam, his son, all his lands in Asthulle, held of the order of St John of Jerusalem by the yearly payment of 12d[13].

Astle was at this time of manorial rank but subordinate to Chelford. In a deed of 1264 Adam de Asthull (uncle of the last named Adam) granted to John, his father, 39 selions (strips of land) in Asthull and 18 selions in the fields between Asthull and the chapel of Chelleford and part of the great meadow.

A little later, Robert, son of Piers de Astelle, served in Gascony and for his services, especially at the Battle of Poitiers was granted a pardon in 1357 from the Black Prince for the death of John le Koo of Knotesford.

Though not proven, it is possible that Robert de Astelle was an archer in the Black Prince's army, as the Black Prince recruited his archers from the Macclesfield area. The Cheshire Archers had perfected the use of the longbow and were considered to be the best fighting force of the English Army. It was said that they were turbulent and lawless and raised from the lowest occupations, and that they lorded over their superiors with insolence and arrogance[14].

The Milne or Mill House estate in Astle was through the 15th and 16th century in the possession of the Henshaw family. Thereafter and up to 1749 when it was purchased by John Parker, a number of different families held the estate.

Whether Chelford saw any active conflict in the Civil War which commenced in 1643 is not known. Certainly Middlewich and Knutsford did and it is possible that the area around Chelford may have seen some minor skirmishes. Eventually the area became pro Parliamentarian. Following the restoration of Royalty in 1660, Chelford would have returned to a farming economy, prominent names in the area at that time being Furnival, Lowe, Whytell, Parker, Stanley, Baskervyle, Glegg, Smallwood, Bostock, Brook, Heald, Grosty, Booth and Wyche.

It was about this time that the persecution of witches was rife in the country and Chelford was no exception. There is evidence in the Plea Rolls at the Public Record Office, London, that on 17th October 1653 at three of the clock in the afternoon, the gallows at Boughton were used to hang three so-called witches:

---

13   The History of Cheshire by Ormerod p 712.

14   Chelford in the 19th Century by W Keith Plant.

Ellen Stubbs, wife of William Stubbs, labourer of Great Warford, her daughter, Elizabeth, spinster, of Mobberley, and Anne Stanley, wife of John Stanley, labourer, of Withington. They had been sentenced at the county sessions on October 9th after being convicted of bewitching to death Elizabeth Furnivall, wife of Ralph Furnivall, Gentleman, of Nether Alderley. She had died on 16th June 1653 after being ill for two weeks.

Seven years previously, the same three had been charged with the magical murder of Anne Lowe of Chelford but, on that occasion, the charge was not proven. Likewise, a further indictment, charging them with bewitching to death a black cow owned by Thomas Grastie of Great Warford was dismissed before coming to trial.

Following the Civil War it was calculated that the population of Chelford was 250[15], and Old Withington 295, considerably larger than the figures of 188 at the Census of 1801[16].

The Oath of Allegiance for Cheshire taken in 1723 contains the names of 58 residents of Chelford, Old Withington and Lower Withington[17].

Baptisms in the Parish Registers covering Chelford, Old Withington and Astle over the period between 1721 and 1772 list the occupations of the father and, in addition to a number of Farmers, Labourers, Husbandmen and Servants, list the following: -.

Smith	Brickmaker
Dryster	Weaver
Yeoman	Wheelwright
Ale Seller	Tanner
Joyner	Butcher
Taylor	Grocer
Shoemaker	Pumpmaker
Carpenter	Miller
Schoolmaster	Chandler
Ropemaker	

---

15   Alehouses and Alehouse Keepers of Cheshire by A J MacGregor p52

16   Chelford in the 19th Century by W Keith Plant and probably not including Old Withington. Considerable doubts concerning these figures.

17   Chelford in the 19th Century by W Keith Plant.

The range of occupations above illustrates how Chelford was at that time a self contained, self supporting village. It was only the later improvements in transportation, principally in Chelford's case, the railway, that changed the village by allowing villagers to move further afield for their needs.

The principal family in the village, the Parkers, appear to have originated in Middlewich, John Parker purchasing Fallows Hall in 1697[18]. By a series of judicious marriages and purchases the Parker family built up estates in Nether Alderley, Breightmet, Tonge, Lancaster, Bradshaw, Oldham, Harwood, Dublin and Limerick as well as Astle.

The school was endowed in 1754 and was originally sited near Astle Gate. Sometime around 1800 (probably 1788), the school was relocated in its present site having moved, according to the school Log Book of 1836, "from a low lying area some years previously". The school was rebuilt in 1892 and a new school is now being built in the centre of the village.

By the end of the 18th century the shape of the village was becoming established in the form known today. The map of 1789 shows two roads which are now only footpaths, Fulshaw Lane branching off the present Alderley Road opposite the school and a road known as Gypsy Lane branching off Knutsford Road opposite the present position of the Village Hall and extending to Peover Road.

The 1789 map also shows that Chelford Green was on the left hand side of Holmes Chapel Road as the road leaves the old centre of the village, the area now being fenced in.

The main function of the village green was as a meeting place for villagers, for dancing, singing and mocking miscreants in the stocks. It is possible that Chelford had stocks but this is as yet unproven. The village green was often the site of the water source and the village maypole and possibly an old oak tree or village cross may have existed.

The nature of the village was beginning to change and a many the occupations of the early 18th century had disappeared. However there was still, in the early 19th. century, a publican, a shoemaker, a gamekeeper, a smith, a grocer, a silk weaver, a butler (to Col Parker) , a schoolmaster in addition to a large number of farmers and labourers. The major cause of death in the early part of the 19th century was

---

18   Astle Estate Documents - John Rylands Library, University of Manchester

consumption. (For a full list covering years 1819 to 1838 see Chelford in the 19th Century by W Keith Plant.)

The first half of the 19th century contained two events that had a major effect on the village; firstly the purchasing of Astle Estate by the Dixon family and, more importantly, the construction of the railway through the village.

The Astle estate came into the possession of the Parker family in the middle of the 18th century, remaining in their possession until 1833 when it was purchased by Henry Dixon of Gledhow, York.

The Conveyance of the estate in 1834 contains a map of the village with an Apportionment list of all properties included in the conveyance[19] (see later chapter on Astle Estate).

Sometime in the early 1840's (the 1841 Census return lists a number of Railway labourers) the Manchester and Birmingham Railway began construction of a railway through Chelford some 400 metres to the north of the then centre of the village. The importance of the railway to the subsequent development of Chelford cannot be overstated. Suffice to say that if the railway had not passed through the village, Chelford would probably have remained a small insignificant village largely unknown to the general public. Instead, through the latter half of the 19th century and the whole of the 20th century it has remained an important part of the rural community of Mid Cheshire. In effect the 'centre' of the village moved to the areas around the railway station and a 'separate' village grew up to service the activities brought to the village by the railway.

The railway soon had an influence on the village as can be seen from the Whites & Co. Commercial Directory of 1860 which contained the following extract:

> "The township is intersected by the London and North Western Railway, and there is a neat station, from whence there are eleven passenger trains each way daily except on Sunday when there are only four. Mr John Wilkinson, station master. Adjoining the station is an extensive coal wharf belonging to Lord Vernon."

> "Omnibuses operate from Dixon Arms & Railway Hotel

---

19   Chelford in the 19th Century by W Keith Plant.

To Knutsford at 9.00 a.m., 2.30 p.m. and 6.00 p.m. daily (except Sunday when it leaves at 10.20 a.m.) to meet the trains at the above mentioned times to forward passengers to Knutsford.

To Macclesfield, Tuesday and Saturday, at 9.00 a.m. and return at 4.00 p.m."

Also, by 1861, a considerable amount of new property had been built in the area around the station, the 1861 Census[20] recording, in addition to the Dixon Arms, a total of seven properties in Station Road and the adjoining Knutsford Road. It is interesting to note that by 1871 this had increased to 13, to 17 in 1881 and 18 in 1891. The houses in Station Road were inhabited mainly by workers on the railway.

In the summer of 1872, there were some unusually heavy rainfalls and the lake in the Park, with its waterfall, was entirely swept away by a flood.

The Cheshire County Cricket Club ground was constructed in 1860/61 covering an area now occupied by the James Irlam Haulage Company.

Towards the end of the 19th century the prosperity of the village and its accessibility by train from the main manufacturing centres around Manchester, resulted in the building of large houses as residences for rich entrepreneurs. The 1891 Census shows that by that time Dalefields, Chelford House, Roadside (Knutsford Road), Oakleigh, Woodlands, The Grange and Mere Legh had been built.

For a few days at the end of the century Chelford hit the headlines in unfortunate circumstances. On 22nd December 1894 the 4.15p.m. express train from London Road Station Manchester, collided with a truck on the line just short of Chelford Station. As a result 14 people died[21] and seventy were injured.

And so this little prosperous, active village moved into the 20th Century. John Dixon had died in 1873 and his wife, Sophia, in 1885 succeeded by George Dixon who had married a widow, Emily Baskervyle Glegg in 1885. The influence of the Dixon family on the village was probably beginning to wane (apart maybe from the rural activities) as the village was becoming more independent.

---

20   Chelford in the 19th Century by W Keith Plant.

21   Reflections upon The Chelford Railway Disaster by Roger Roycroft.

It was in the early part of the century that Chelford Market came into existence continuing throughout the century as one of the largest cattle markets in the country.

Owing to the increasing amount of traffic in the Chelford area it was necessary in the mid 1930's to widen Alderley Road right through to Roadside Farm. Opposite Roadside Farm was a pond and prior to the widening of the road it was a common occurrence for cars to drive into it.

John Dixon, the son of George Dixon and Emily Baskervyle Glegg, was born in 1886 and married Gwendoline Spearman in 1910. Their son, John George, was born in 1911.

When John George Dixon married the family moved out of the Hall into Astle Cottage. The Hall, for a short period, became a Nature Cure Home and during the Second World War an RAOC depot. At the end of the war the Hall was in a very poor condition and Henshaws Institute for the blind considered erecting small units in Astle Park containing equipment for the blind residents to manufacture brushes. However, this venture did not materialise and the Hall continued to deteriorate until it was finally demolished.

Prior to the commencement of the Second World War the County Cricket Ground was still being used by the Cheshire Gentlemen Cricket Club[22]. Not long after the war started the ground was dug up and a cold storage depot complete with sidings erected on the site. The depot was used throughout the war to store refrigerated meat supplies which were delivered to butchers throughout the North West. After the war it was used to store margarine and sugar held against a world emergency. The site was eventually sold to a haulage company now operating a fleet of lorries.

Nothing of any major significance appears to have happened in Chelford during the Second World War. It housed evacuees mainly from Moston, Manchester and Walthamstow in London. The school Log Book contains details of the evacuees and the teachers who came with them No bombs were dropped on Chelford, the nearest being at Parkgate and a farm in Over Alderley.

After the Second World War the village roundabout was built which necessitated the demolition of the smithy and garage complete with filling station. The smithy and the garage had been very busy with a long shed that sold lamp glasses, dolly blue and clothes pegs etc.

---

22   The ground ceased to be used as the County Ground in 1883.

The electrification of the railway in 1960, followed by Dr Beeching's rationalisation and the growth of road transport, signalled the beginning of the end for Chelford as a railway goods yard. The railway used to transport large quantities of sand but when this was transferred to road transport, the railway goods area declined rapidly.

In 1965 a proposal was submitted by the Home Office to build a prison on the land to the north of the Chelford to Monks Heath road on the site used as a storage depot by the War Office during the 1939-45 War. Chelford residents joined those of Nether Alderley to fight the proposal and eventually the Home Office decided not to proceed.

There was an outbreak of foot and mouth disease in 1967/8 and for a period of 11 weeks movement around the village was restricted, social life curtailed and the cattle market closed.

It was at about this time that John George Dixon sold what remained of his land to the north east of the railway station on which, after an aborted attempt by Manchester to build an overspill estate, Seddons built an executive housing estate, completed in 1988.

To maintain tradition within the area, a number of roads on the estate were named after local fields; Barn Croft, Hitch Lowes and Wheat Moss being Chelford field names; Broom Field, Burnt Acre, Chapel Croft, Drumble Field Snelson field names and Clay Hayes and Woodfin Croft Marthall field names[23].

The night of 2nd January 1976 will be remembered by the whole village as this was the night that a mini hurricane hit the village. All roads both in and out of the village were blocked by fallen trees and many people stranded. It was some time before the village returned to normal.

John George Dixon, the last of the family to reside in Astle, died in 1976 breaking the Dixon connection with Chelford which had lasted for 142 years.

The arrival of new residents from outside Chelford has rejuvenated the village which, at the end of the century includes the following:

The Royal British Legion	St John's Fellowship
Church activities	Village Pre-School
Village School	Farmers Ball

---

[23]   Marthall & Snelson Tithe maps – Cheshire Record Office.

Women's' Institute	Sunday School
Thursday Club	Mothers & Baby Group
Guides, Brownies, Rainbows	Bell Ringers
Badminton Club	Drama Society
Bridge Club	Cattle Market
Cricket Club	Traction Engine Rally
Antique Fair	Scouts, Cubs, Beavers
Bowling Clubs	Embroiderer's Guild
RNLI	Royal British Legion

Many of the fields in Chelford contain remains of the old marl-pits. Gangs of men went around the village with their leader, dug the mud and slush out of the pits and spread it on the fields. The leader was called 'Head of the Soil or Pit', travelling with his men to receive payment for their services. The gangs had their own song:-

> "For them as grows a good turmit
> We are the boys to fey a pit
> And then yoe good marl out of it."

POPULATION OF CHELFORD 1810 TO 1991

	Male	Female	Total
1810	97	91	188
1831	95	91	186
1841	115	86	201
1851	131	129	260
1861	123	118	241
1871	142	131	273
1881	158	155	313
1891	169	172	341
1901	180	194	374
1911	195	189	384
1921	161	194	355
1931	164	177	341
1951	183	209	392
1961	210	227	437
1971	210	220	431
1981	308	224	532
1991	587	659	1246

The Population of Chelford

■Male ■Female

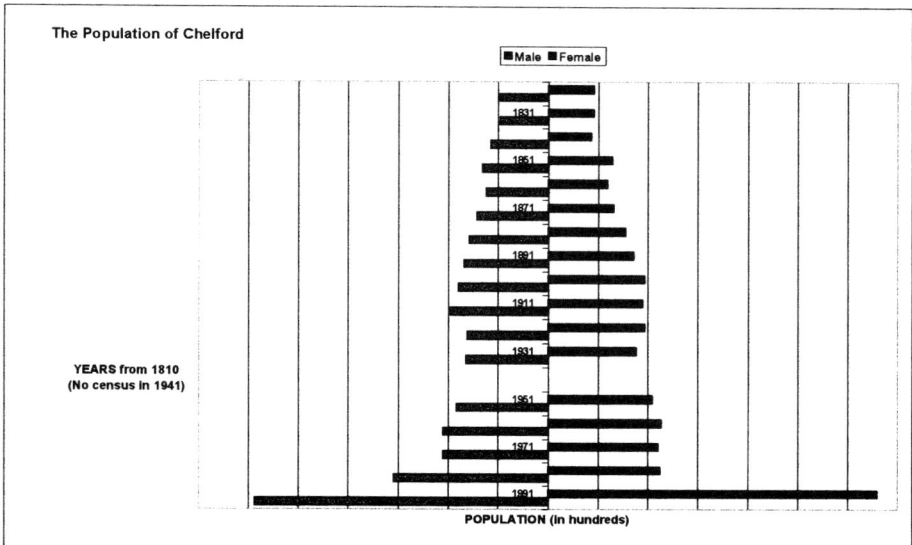

YEARS from 1810
(No census in 1941)

POPULATION (in hundreds)

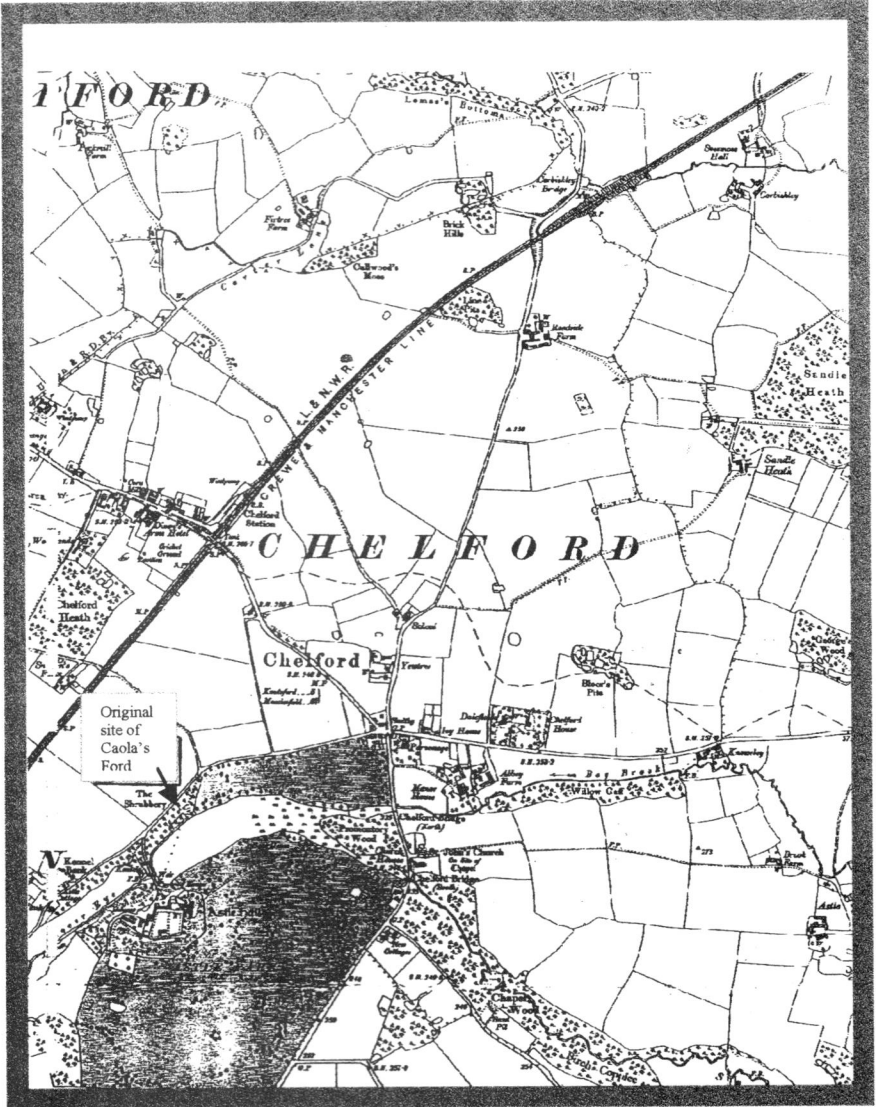

Map of Chelford showing possible location of original settlement

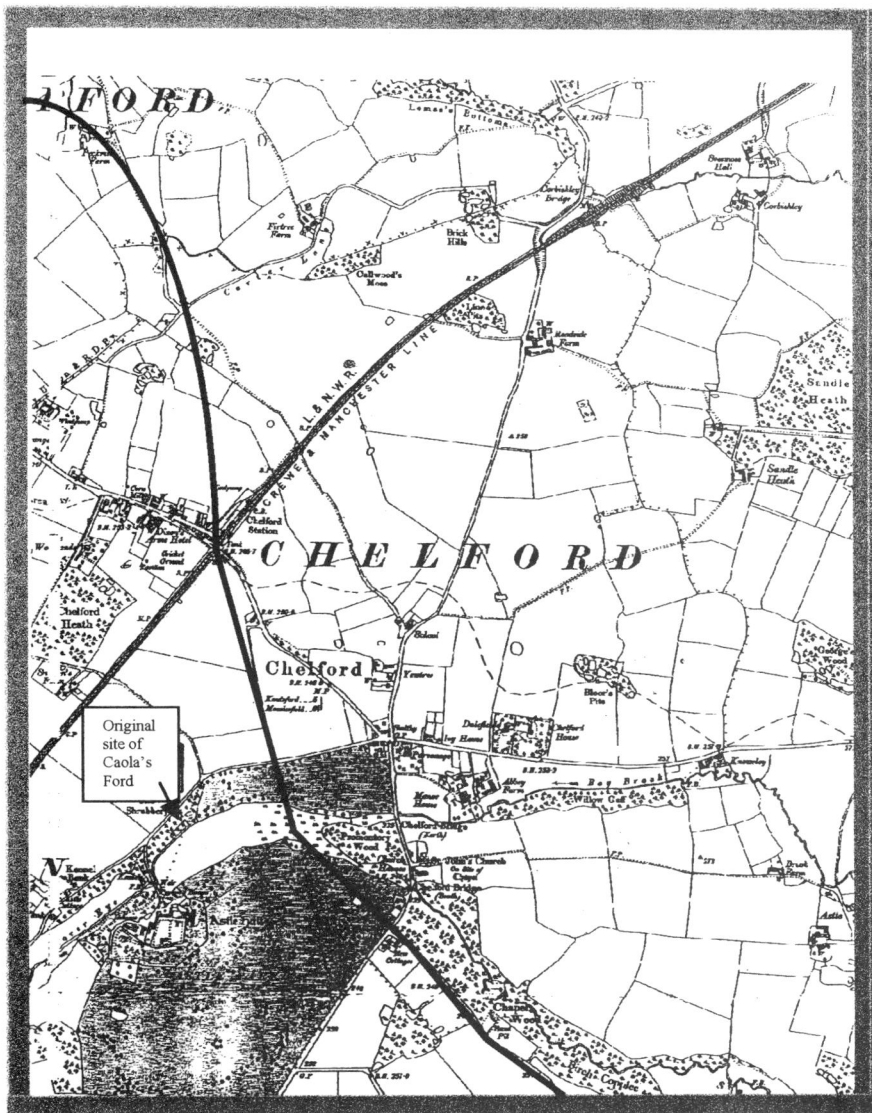

Map of Chelford showing possible route of original Packhorse Trail.

Map of Chelford 1789

1909 *Ordnance Survey Map* – *Revised 1936*

23

ST JOHN THE EVANGELIST - CHELFORD CHURCH

A chapel existed at Chelford as early as the 13th Century, probably by 1280, when Robert Worth left the Manor of Chelford to St Werburgh's Abbey on condition that the Abbot provided a fit chaplain to conduct divine service 'in the Chapel of Chelleford' on three days in the week, and to assist in the services at the altar of St Nicholas in the mother church of Prestbury on the other four days.

From this date Mass would have been celebrated in the church which was probably of 'wattle and daub' construction. A tithe barn would have existed nearby to store the tithes paid in produce. It is significant that the farm adjacent to the church is called Abbey Farm and may be the last relic of those times.

In 1365 an Inquisition post-mortem was held 'In the Chapel of Chelleford' after the death of John de Somerford[1].

No other records have been found until 1564 when it is recorded that Edward Acton was 'pryst servinge at Chelford in the parysshe of Prestburge' and had for his pains the yearly sum of £4.6s.8d[2].

From this date the know incumbents have been: -

1564   Edward Acton "pryst servinge at Chelford in the parysshe of Prestburge".

1618   "Mr. Hopwood, Clerk, Preacher of the Word of God at Chelford".

1627   "Mr. Mellor, Curate of Chelford".

1635   "David Ellison, Curate of Chelford".

1639   John Sherson.

1648   Robert Worthington. "Signed the Attestation of the Cheshire Ministers as Minister of Chelford".

1651-2 Joseph Ottiwall. "Appointed Minister of Chelford by the ManchesterClassis of Presbyterian Ministers".

1653   Ralph Worsley. "Appointed to Chelford by the (above) body".

1657   Hugh---Henshaw. Given in 1676 as "Hugh Henshaw of Henshaw, in Siddington, Clerk, and also "by free election minister of Chelford".

1678   Reginald Bancroft. "Minister of Chelford as well as of Siddington." was married at Marton Chapel on Dec. 9 1685, to Elizabeth-, daughter of Edward Thornycroft of Thornycroft, but she was buried at Chelford in May 1688.

1715-19 George Hammond.

1719   John Dean. "Nominated both by the inhabitants — who say they have a right to do so — and by William Foxelowe, Clerk, Vicar of Prestbury. Tombstone on vestry floor.

1772-95 John Parker. Buried at Chelford November 7th 1795 (not always residential). Owner of Milne House (Astle Hall), Chelford and Brightmet, Lancashire.

1780-1 Thomas Gatley, Curate of Chelford. (Dismissed due to misconduct)

1786-91 James Penny. "Officiating at Chelford", and curate of Alderley 1786-1805

1795   James Penny. Incumbent of Marton (1795-1806) and Chelford.~ His wife Elizabeth died Nov. 21 1803, aged 41, and was buried at Chelford. Her gravestone is by the north side of the tower and West End of the church". "Several of his children were baptised at Chelford".

1816   Thomas Mawdesley. Died 1839.

---

1   Cheshire Inq p.m. Record Office

2   Wages of Edward Acton. Book of Surveys, Monastery of St Werburgh – Record Office

1839	Granville John Granville.
1853	David James Paterson.
1879	Alfred Littledale Royds.
1896	Hesketh France—Hayhurst.
1902	Lionel Scudamore Stanhope.
1907	Colin Edward Beever Bell.
1914	Norman John Neil Gourlie.
1916	William Herbert Parkes. Died August 4th 1944. Buried at Chelford.
1945	John Stott Gamon.
1955	Cyril Herbert Lee.
1965	Maurice James Birks Henry.
1981	John Franklyn Ellis

The Cheshire Record Office in Chester contains a document entitled 'An account of all the money that hath been bequeathed to the Minister of Chelford'[3] the contents of which are as follows:

		£	s	d
10 January 1660	Ralph Furnivall of Millhouse in Astle Gent	50		
1663	Mr Samuel Brooks of Chelford	10		
1668	Joane Brooks of Chelford Widow	5		
1667	Randle Smallwood of Lower Withington	2	10	0
1674	William Baskervile of Old Withington	2	10	0
1683	Hugh Grasty bequeathed	4	0	0
	Mrs Elizabeth Baskervyle Widow	10	0	0
1687	Mrs Elizabeth Furnivall	2	0	0
1677	Lea Fodon of Siddington gave in her life	2	10	0
	Those gifts purchased the Land in Chelford 1677 and cost	88	10	0
1687	Mrs Elizabeth Furnivall bequeathed more	8		
1690	John Hall of Lower Withington	2	10	
1694	Hugh Hopwood of Chelford	5		
1687	Thomas Smallwood of Chelford Gent	10		
1698	Randle Baskervyle of Siddington	2	10	
about 1701	Ann Baxter of Siddington	3		
1713	Mrs Sarah Willson	10		
1712	George Bagueley	50		
1721	Mrs Dorothy Jodrel	150		

---

3   CRO p182/7/1

An account of the money given for raising Queen Anne's Bounty

Mr Parker	100		
Colonel Leigh	5	5	
Mrs Sweffinham of Summerford Booths widow	3		
Given by several other persons	12	6	9
Langham Booth Esq	5		
Raised by Timber sold out of the Chappel land	16		
Given by the inhabitants of Chelford			
Chappelry and other benefactors	101		
	242	11	9

I suppose there was some more money given for raising the Queen's Bounty, for there is six pounds and fifteen shillings lost out of Mrs Sarah Willson's legacy of ten pounds and most or all of Mr Smallwood's legacy of Ten pounds.

An account where all the money is now placed which doth belong to the Ministers of Chelford

paid in by	Mr Parrot now in the hands of John Byrn	200
	John Baskervile Esq	150
paid in by	Tho Brooke now in the hands of Mr Lowndes	21
	Mr Dean	7
paid in by	George Henshall now in the hands of	
	J Lowndes	5
	Mr Merridith	100
	Total	483

1687	Mr Thomas Smallwood left any 4 or 5 of the most substantial inhabitants in Chelford Trustees for The interest of it for the Ministers of Chelford.	10
May 1693	This money was paid into George Lowe and John Lowe, his son, Thomas Brooke and John Smallwood all of Chelford who were chosen Trustees for it, but it was lost the year following.	

1694	Hugh Hopwood left John Brooke, George Lowe, John Lowe his son, Thomas Brooke all of Chelford and George Heald of Macclesfield Trustees for	5
	Randle Baskervile left John Brooks, George Lowe and John Lowe his son, Trustees for	2 10
1699	They received it and put it out upon Interest	
	Ann Baxter left George Lowe, John Lowe, his son, John Brooks and John Smallwood Trustees for	3
in 1705	They put it out upon Interest for the benefit of the Ministers of Chelford.	

In 1720 the minister's stipend was augmented by William Stanley and Thomas Brook who gave £200. In 1762 John Parker Esq gave £200 to increase the minister's salary, then only £30.4s.9d augmented by Queens Anne's Bounty[4].

The old church, no doubt of timber and plaster, was pulled down in 1774, the document for pulling down and building the present church being dated March 25th 1774. This Georgian building was consecrated on July 23rd 1776, by Bishop Markham of Chester, under the name of "St. John the Evangelist, in Chelford". It is a plain brick building with tower and spire at the West End, which was added in 1840.

As far as can be ascertained, there is very little left belonging to the original Chapel, apart from the two painted wooden panels hanging on the north wall dated 1654 and 1721 respectively[5].

Exterior Features

An old print shows the church without the tower or chancel "as it now stands". The West End has three long windows, with the same number of small circular windows above, and another window in the gable. Above is a bell turret, which would hold one bell. Out of the top of the centre long window protrudes a long flue pipe rather like a snake. A print showing "the proposal improvements" has the

---

4   A fund established by Queen Anne in 1704 to receive and use the annates and tenths previously confiscated by Henry VIII. The revenues were used to supplement the incomes of the poorer clergy.

5   Audrey Walsh's private papers – no date.

west tower and spire, a west door with a pathway to it, and a north porch which was never built. However alterations were made 1840 which gave us the building we know today. A building of Red Flemish and English garden wall bond brick with stone dressing and a slate roof, nave, gallery and chancel. The tower has a battlemented parapet and an octagonal spire, which is covered with diamond-shaped slates and crowned by a weather vane. The nave is of four bays and the chancel, originally of two bays, was extended to four bays in 1902.

The clock in the tower was made by John Dumville of Alderley in 1770. He also made the clock in Goostrey church. Clearly the clock is older than the tower by some 70 years so that it may be that the clock used to be in the west gable of the church before the tower was built.

A fine War Memorial Calvary stands against the churchyard wall once flanked by bold Lime trees called "the twelve Apostles. The sculptor of the Calvary was Mr. G.W. Walker, who in 1925 was elected an Associate of the Royal Academy. The Calvary was given by Mr. Frank Grant as thanks offering for the safe return of his sons from the Great War. He lived at Mereleigh, Chelford, an elegant Chelford home now demolished to make way for new housing development known as Mere Court.

In the churchyard by the north chancel wall is a grave with a marble cross with the inscription: -

> *"This memorial is erected by George Dixon, of Astle. To the memory of Margaret Ellks and thirteen others who were killed in the railway accident at Chelford 22nd December 1894".*

This recalls the accident at the village station, when a train from Manchester came into collision with a goods wagon that had been thrown off the line while shunting. Seventy-nine people were injured besides the fourteen killed.

In a line with the above grave and the gable-end of the cottage built against the churchyard wall, will be found one of the earliest graves dating from 1680. There is also here, a flat circular stone which may have been the base stone or step of a sundial - it is very similar to the one at Prestbury.

A flat tombstone opposite the North door of the church has a worn Latin inscription! "Here lieth Anthony Low, Esq., late of Owlgreave (Allgreave) in the County of Derby, Doctor of Medecine who, though second to none in the skill of his art, yet shone more in virtue and love to the poor, whereby his soul was pleasing to God, who hastened to take it from the dangers of this false world, from darkness to light, from labour to rest and peace and joys eternal, in the 60th year of his age, on the 17th February, in the year of our Lord, 1729. May he rest in peace! Amen."

The Churchyard also includes the grave of Maria Elizabeth Jacson, a noted botanist and author of four books on the subject, her best known being "Florist ...." first published 1816. She lived at Somersat Hall, Uttoxeter and died on 10th October 1829 while on a visit to the Parkers of Astle Hall, probably to see the reputedly fine garden created by the Parker family.

Interior Features

The nave of the church has 18th century box pews. In 1925 some of the old wood from pews not required was used to panel the walls, and at the same time the Lady Chapel was made - using some of the old carved wood for the front of the Altar there. There is no centre aisle - a rather unusual feature - and at the West End is a gallery with vestry below. On the stairs leading to the gallery is one of the oldest pieces of woodwork in the church - a portion of late seventeenth century altar rail. "Ten rails with head used to protect windows" there. This may have been part of the altar rail of the older church. The gallery was transformed into a separate meeting room in the time of Canon Henry, and is now regularly used by the Sunday school.

The ceiling has a decorative central motif from which used to hang a wrought iron lighting unit fed by petrol gas. However with the coming of electricity in 1932 this was replaced with six individual lights.

There is an art Nouveau pulpit, altar rails, and choir stalls designed by Percy Worthington in 1903.

Prior to 1925 the walls of the nave and the walls and roof of the chancel were a mass of colour and intricate design. On each side of the chancel were beautiful paintings of Angels and Archangels and great was the distress of many parishioners when they were painted out by order of 'Parson Parkes', (as he was known to his flock).

Two fine old carved chairs, a chest on legs in the vestry, an old wooden collecting box with the date 1734 complete the old woodwork of the church. A later addition is the pair of fine oak standard candlesticks in the chancel.

An interesting memorial on the north wall is an oblong coloured wooden panel with a large shield of arms, Baskervyle impaling Davenport of Calverley with their respective crests and inscribed: -

"On ye death of Mrs Dorothy Baskervyle, who dyed ye first of
Febrii, and interred ye 3rd of Feb., 1654, at Chelford".

"This little Ile, this narrow roome, contaynes more worth shutt up in Tombe
Than can my Tongue or Pen express, to Rich, to Poore, to Fatherlesse,
Our Dorothy a Dorcas was: but now shees gone, shes dead alas ;
Let us behind then melt to teares, few lieud her life : though some her yeares
What said I ; she is gone (not yett) God's Pearles are in his cabinett,
Shees changed : not dead : no goodness dyes, like th'day starr only setts to rise."

(Dorcas:- 'a woman full of good works' – Acts 9 v36)

The famous heraldic painters and antiquarians of Chester - the four generations of Randle Holmes - were responsible for many of these painted panels which are to be found in our Cheshire churches, and sometimes portraits of the deceased were also painted. On the wooden panel a face can be seen between the quartering of the shield.

Hanging on the same wall is another gilt wooden frame with a lozenge-shaped Coat of Arms in memory of Mrs. Dorothy Jodrell who died in 1721 and "left one Hundred and Fifty Pounds. The Interest whereof to be for the better Subsistence of the Minister at this Place forever".

Two War Memorial Windows (1914 -1918) are the work of Mr. J.H. Dearle, a pupil of Burne-Jones, and are from the firm of Morris' of Merton Abbey, Surrey. One is to the memory of Geoffrey Christian Lansdale Walsh, missing at Messines June 1917, and the other to the men of the parish who were killed in the First World War who are listed on a bronze tablet below the window.

CHELFORD
SNELSON and OLD WITHINGTON

Geoffrey Christian Lansdale Walsh
Richard Boon   John William Fallon   Thomas Shore
William Bowers   Joseph Goulding   Frank Stokes
Herbert Callwood   Bertram John Harding   William Henry Tomlinson
Henry Cartwright   Joseph Edward Marsh   John Venables
Walter Cartwright   Leonard Moston   Abraham Street
Harold Crawley   John Wyatt

"Grant them, O Lord, Eternal rest
And let light Perpetual Shine Upon Them."

Curiously no evidence exists of a list of the fallen in World War II although the dates have been added to the War Memorial. However there is an inscription commemorating the Battle of Britain and a donated painting hangs on the north wall below which is written: -

In token of thanksgiving to God for His gift of valour to the members of the Royal Air Force and to all engaged in the Battle of Britain 1940, and for the victory thereby achieved this picture was presented to the church.

"Through faith they waxed valiant in Fight, and turned to Flight the armies of the aliens."

Heb XI. 34

The east window was given by the tenants and neighbours of the parish to the memory of John Dixon, of Astle 1857, and there is a small window to the memory of Sophia Dixon 1855, by the font. This font corner has panelled oak walls, a pair of fine oak standard candlesticks, and a small brass set in the panelling - all given in memory of Dr. Arthur Harold Shepard, a well-loved doctor in the parish. The Latin inscription on the flat tombstone outside the north door to the doctor Anthony Low could also be written of Dr. Shepard: - "who, though second in none in the skill of his art, yet shone more in virtue and love to the poor" (and rich), and also of his partner and successor Dr. Ernest Sandford Evans, who was Churchwarden of this church for many years.

The Lectern, given in 1887 is "cut out of solid English Oak and designed in the manner of the English woodwork of the 14th century". The design was by "G.T. Redmayne, architect of Alderley Edge and the work was well and carefully carried out by Joseph Foden, carver, Alderley Edge". "The dedication plate was chased by Mr. Wyon, Queen Medallist".

In 1903, the altar -rails were given by Mr. Reginald Arthur Tatton, of the Manor House, Chelford, and the pulpit by Sir George Dixon, of Astle. The pulpit was designed by Sir Percy Worthington, architect, of Alderley Edge, and it was carved by Mr. H. Malcolm Miller. Mr. Miller was responsible for much of the carving in Manchester Cathedral (before it was blitzed in World War II), and churches in the northwest. Mr. Miller died in 1951, and on his grave-stone in Alderley Edge Cemetery, carved by his stepbrother Sir Hubert Worthington, are the words: - "A fine Craftsman in stone, wood and bronze. He Enriched His Day and Generation With many Beautiful Things".

The Processional Cross has the inscription - "A.M.D.G. To remember Philip Wright this cross was given by his parents, relations, and friends. 1932, St John the Evangelist."

The Churchwarden's staves have the inscription "In memory of the Revd. W.H. Parkes Vicar 1916-1944 and were given in 1945, and the verger's wand has the inscription - "In memory of Clement Henry Taylor".

Some items may have come to Chelford Church by way of a farm cart - at least one likes to think so. At Sutton Old Hall, near Macclesfield (now a convent), there was a small chapel in the 17th century, which was used till about 1760, by the family of the name Belasyse who were Roman Catholics. The last Belasyse - the Earl of Falconbery - renounced Roman Catholicism, and the chapel was dismantled, but the benches and also the rich marble slab covering the altar ... with other very valuable things "were packed into a cart and taken to "Chelford chapel". What these valuable things were and what became of them remains a mystery.

The inscriptions in the graveyard and interior of the church were recorded by the Macclesfield Ferrets between 1990 and 1992[6].

When the record was made in 1992 there was a total of 621 names on the inscriptions.

Churchyard Flora

A survey of flora in the Churchyard was carried out on 9th September 1991 by Mr Ray Maycock and the list is reproduced for posterity as follows: -

List of Flowering Plants in Chelford Churchyard

American willowherb	Epilobium ciliatum	
Annual meadow-grass	Poa annua	
Autumn hawkbit	Leontodon autumnalis	
Bittersweet	Solanum dulcamara	
Black bent	Agrostis gigantea	
Box	Buxus sempervirens	P
Broad buckler-fern	Dryopteris dilatata	
Broad-leaved dock	Rumex obtusifolius	
Broom	Cytisus scoparius	
Cat's-ear	Hypochoeris radicata	
Cleavers	Galium aparine	
Common bent	Agrostis capillaris	
Common chickweed	Stellaria media	
Common couch	Elymus repens	
Common dog-violet	Viola riviniana	?
Common figwort	Scrophularia nodosa	
Common hemp-nettle	Galeopsis tetranit	
Common mouse-ear	Cerastium fontanum	
Common nettle	Urtica dioica	
Common ragwort	Senecio jacobaea	
Common sorrel	Rumex acetosa	
Common vetch	Vicia sativa	
Corn spurrey	Spergula arvensis	
Creeping bent	Agrostis stolonifera	
Creeping buttercup	Ranunculus repens	
Creeping soft-grass	Holcus mollis	
Creeping thistle	Cirsium arvense	
Cuckooflower	Cardamine pratensis	
Daisy	Bellis perennis	
Dandelion	Taraxacum officinale	
Dog's mercury	Mercurialis perennis	

---

6   A Copy in W Keith Plant's private papers.

Dove's-foot crane's-bill	Geranium molle
Elder	Sambucus nigra
Field woodrush	Luzula campestris
Foxglove	Digitalis purpurea
Germander speedwell	Veronica chamaedrys
Groundsel	Senecio vulgaris
Harebell	Campanula rotundifolia
Heath bedstraw	Galium saxatile
Heather	Calluna vulgaris
Hedge bedstraw	Galium mollugo
Hogweed	Heracleum sphondylium
Honesty	Lunaria annua
Ivy	Hedera helix
Ivy-leaved toadflax	Cymbalaria muralis
Lady fern	Athyrium perennis
Lime	Tilia vulgaris
Male-fern	Dryopteris filix-mas
Meadow buttercup	Ranunculus acris
Mouse-ear hawkweed	Hieracium pilosella d
pellitory-of-the-wall	Parietaria judaica
Pendunculate oak	Quercus lusitanica
Portugal laurel	Prunus lusitanica P
Prickly sow-thistle	Sonchus asper
Raspberry	Rubus idaeus
Red campion	Silene dioica
Reflexed stonecrop	Sedum reflexum
Rhododendron	Rhododendron ponticum ?
Ribwort plantain	Plantago lanceolata
Rosebay willowherb	Chamerion angustifolium
Sheep's sorrel	Rumex acetosella
Silver Birch	Betula pendula R
Smooth hawksbeard	Crepis capillaris
Spear thistle	Cirsium vulgare
Sticky mouse-ear	Cerastium glomeratum
Sweet vernal grass	Anthoxanthum odoratum
Sycamore	Acer pseudoplatanus
Tufted vetch	Vicia cracca
ux-eye daisy	Leucanthemum vulgare R
White clover	Trifolium repens
White stonecrop	Sedum album
Wild cherry	Prunus avium
Yarrow	Achillea millefolium
Yew	Taxus baccata
Yorkshire fog	Holcus lanatus

A – Abundant   R – Rare within site   d – Locally dom.
P – Planted   ? – Uncertain

As it now stands

Rebuilt church with proposed improvements shown below
See pages 28 and 29.

With the proposed improvements.

THE VICARAGE

Very little is known relative to the history of the Vicarage. What is known is that parts of the house date back 300 years and that it is a Grade II listed building.

According to the sales profile when the property was sold in 1979, the house was sold to the Parish as a parsonage house in 1835 previously being part of the Chelford Estate of Laurence Stanley prior to being sold to the Reverend John Parker of Chelford in 1796. There is, however, no record of this sale in the Astle Estate papers, nor is the property referred to in the Parker/Dixon conveyance in 1834.

It is described in White & Co. History, Gazetteer and Directory of Cheshire of 1860 as:

> 'The parsonage is an ancient residence mantled with ivy, situated at the cross of roads a little north of the church. It was purchased with a sum of £250 obtained from Queen Anne's bounty and £150 left by Dame Dorothy Ednell'[1].

---

1   Whether this purchase refers to the parsonage or the chapel is not clear.

1853-1879
Rev'd. David James Paterson

1879-1896
Rev'd Alfred Littledale Royds

1896-1902
Rev'd Hesketh France Hayhurst

1902-1907
Rev'd Lionel Scudamore Stanhope

1907-1914
Rev'd Colin Edward Beever Bell

1914-1916
Rev'd Norman John Neil Gourlie

1916-1945
Rev'd William Herbert Parkes

1945-1955
Rev'd John Stott Gamon

1955-1965
Rev'd Cyril Herbert Lee

1965-1981
Canon Maurice James Birks Henry

1981-1999
Rev'd John Franklyn Ellis

John Franklyn Ellis

As has been noted in the introduction, this book is dedicated to the 225th anniversary of the rebuilding of Chelford Church, to mark the end of one millennium and the beginning of another; and to John Ellis. Had the first two events not been relevant then certainly the retirement of our vicar would have been reason enough, for had John not materialised in the first place then it is doubtful if the inspiration to produce the book would ever have appeared.

In his eighteen years of ministry the villages of Chelford and Lower Withington have been constantly aware of the presence of one who cared individually for everyone who lived there regardless of their personal faith or the lack of it. In the quietest and most unassuming way he has been there in times of celebration and in times of grief. Giving personal encouragement and uplift to those who needed it and remembering those painful, private, anniversaries that the rest of the world usually forgets. But then what else would you expect from a Good Samaritan? Yet actually how many do any of us know?

In this book we reflect on the social changes that have come about during this century. Of the spread of wealth and affluence, and the decline of personal leisure time. Of the explosion in communication technology, as a result of which we often know more of what is happening on the other side of the world than of what is happening in our own local community. Truly a perfect recipe for the dissolution of social structure. For the decay of centuries old moral values and for a world where our children are taught facts but not human ideals – indeed often not taught history at all. It seems unlikely that any country actually wants to go down that path – rather it happens in the way that Alice 'just growed', by default and inattention.

Week by week these are the problems that Rev'd. John Ellis has been addressing, and leading by example. Not enough have listened, but many have, and one senses a change of attitudes beginning to emerge within the community. To survive any distance into the next millennium we are certainly going to need such a reawakening and many of us feel a deep gratitude to John personally for pointing that way. Now surely, as he retires to a well-earned rest, it is up to us to carry the flag forward and continue what he started by showing in such a practical and modest way what the teaching of Christianity is all about.

Despite quite searching inquiries it has proved difficult to discover a great deal about the background of John Ellis, other than of a life of dedicated service to his fellows. However a biography he needs and shall have. This is how it reads: -
Born in Stockport on July 25th 1934, the son of Leslie Ellis, who was the organist at St Peter's Church, in Levenshulme, Manchester.

He was educated first at St.Thomas's C of E Primary School at Heaton Chapel where he was often late due to a serious addiction to tram spotting. He attended from 1939 to 1945 and as he left the future Mrs Ellis began her schooling at the same establishment.

From 1945 to 1952 he attended Stockport Grammar School and whilst there became deeply involved with the work of the tramway museum at Crich.

There followed National Service with the Royal Army Ordinance Corps at Pirbright and Southsea from 1952 to 1955. Whilst there he was in the same unit as Henry Cooper and his brother George. This was very happy time where he was much involved with improving the reading and writing skills of his companions –though he never did get on the boxing team.

Thence to the University of Leeds from 1955 to 1958 where he gained an Honours BA in English, History, and Music. Then he went on to Lincoln Theological College from 1958 to 1960 where he first met Tony Durrans (later to become Vicar of one of our link parishes in Manchester) with whom he has since had a lifetime friendship.

The first Curacy was at St.Chad's, Ladybarn, in the Diocese of Manchester, from 1960 to 1963. This was followed a Curacy at St.George's, Stockport, in the Chester Diocese, from 1963 to 1966, and whilst there he and Anne were married in June of 1964.
In 1966 he was appointed Vicar at St.Thomas's, High Lane and from there he came to St.John's at Chelford in 1981.

John's outside interests are very few really, being always fully committed to his work in the various parishes. However he does have a passionate love of music, and amateur dramatics. He remains very committed to the Council for the Preservation of Rural England, to canals and to tramways, trains and buses.

It has never been known for John to take more than one Sunday off in any one year and the family holidays have always been within England. Many years ago he and Anne used to stay in a hotel in Blackpool run by ex Wolves footballer Dave Wagstaff who later played for Blackburn Rovers. Whilst there John kept his occupation secret – his regular weekend absences being explained as a need to visit his chain of Manchester night-clubs to check on their performance! Apparently this ruse succeeded for several years.

In 1994, to mark his 60th birthday, the villagers of Chelford and Lower Withington presented John with a new Metro car to replace his ageing A-reg model. That the collection and news of the impending presentation were kept entirely secret until the event itself spoke volumes for the popular affection and admiration that he has deserved so richly during his ministry here.

In retirement we wish John and Anne every happiness, and that they may now finally have time to spend with their family, to follow all John's transportation interests; and for Anne's knitting. In retirement we wish John and Anne every happiness, and that they may now finally have time to spend with their family, to follow all John's transportation interests; and for Anne's knitting.

To John's successor will doubtless be given the same loyalty and support that John has had from so many. We are of course all different - achieving different things in different ways - but to those who have known 'The Ellis's over the last eighteen years they will always be thought of as unique. Perhaps not irreplaceable - none of us are - but in the view of your authors, and we believe a vast number of others, a very difficult act to follow.

THE PARISH MAGAZINE

The first number of the parish magazine is dated January 1887 and it was issued at one halfpenny a month with a copy of the "Dawn of Day" as an inset. The local section of the magazine was typed, and there was a sketch of the church on the front page, showing the building from the north side with the gateway and tall lime trees – "the twelve Apostles" as they were called. There is a letter from "The parsonage" by the Rev. A. L. Royds, the vicar of Chelford at that time.

It is interesting to read of some of the changes, alterations and gifts to the church of these early years. The first number mentions a stained glass window that was placed in the church in 1886 to the memory of "Mrs Dixon" – Sophia Dixon. This was erected by the font, which she had given; though where the old font went to is not known.

In May 1887, the choir and organ were still in the west gallery, but there is no description of the organ of this date. June of this year had afternoon services at 3 p.m., but they were "badly attended" so the time was altered to 7 p.m. till September when it was 6.30 p.m. This was changed again for the winter months.

January 1888 had a new sketch of the church – the old one was fading away! The new picture showed the east and south side of the church with ivy over the walls, and some gravestones in the foreground. This copy is mostly taken up with an account of the new lectern given to the church by Mr and Mrs Seaman, of the Manor House, and it was "used for the first time on Christmas Day".

By March 1889 the sketch on the front page was once more very dim so for some months this was decorated with wild flowers. On 19th August 1890, the church was reopened after being cleaned for recolouring and installing of a new boiler – which had to be covered over.

"Texts over the eight windows were given by Colonel Dixon at a cost of £60, they are beautifully hand-painted on zinc and brighten up the wall nicely".

Brass candles were given by Mrs Arundel, and brass flower vases by Mrs Royds. The January 1896 edition has a copy of a farewell letter from the vicar – Rev. A. L. Ryods, in which he says that "in 1887 we began writing and copying the local matter and charging 6d a year for the magazine". However, it was decided to have it printed and the cost was then about 1s 6d, for the twelve months. There is also a letter from the vicar – Rev. Hesketh France-Hayhurst from Davenham Rectory, Cheshire, in the March issue, February 6th is given as the date in induction. In May 1896 all the church seats were made free, and with the June issue the front cover shows a view of the church from the south gateway. In July the choir was removed from the West Gallery to the Chancel (but not the organ) and the choirmaster was "Mr Spenseley, Trafford Road, Alderley Edge".

On 4th June 1896 Frederick Johnstone was run over and killed by a goods train. In August of that year the "Brass Altar Desk" was given to the church, and in May 1897 "cassocks and surplices were worn for the first time". Easter offerings to the church were embroidered white bookmarkers, "a White Pulpit Fall", and four almsbags.

In June 1897 there is an account of the opening of the new organ in the chancel on 21st May when "G. W. Bebbington Esq., organist of Knutsford Parish Church", gave a recital. Mr Bebbington was organist of the above church for forty-nine years till his death in March 1931. From 1865 to 1882 he was organist at Weaverham Parish Church, succeeding his father at the age of eleven. He was one of the oldest members of the Incorporated Society of Musicians and as an examiner of the Society, travelled all over Great Britain and Ireland. A fine and conscientious organist, the writer of this guide will always feel indebted to him for sound teaching.

From January 1898 onwards the Chelford Parish News was printed on a separate sheet and not on the back of the cover as before.

In June 1899 a new "Red Altar Cloth" was given to the church, and at the end of the year and for several years, the "Parochial Accounts" were printed separately from the magazine in a little booklet form.

In the January issue of the new Century – 1900 – there is a long subscription list to the Soldier's Relief Fund" – a reminder of the Boer War. At the end of this issue there is a short letter signed "A Candle" who complains of the draughts in the church, and says "he has the greatest difficulty in keeping alight".

Again in February 1900, we read of the burial of "an unknown man who was killed on the railway".

The February 1901 issue has a broad band of black for the death of Queen Victoria – a token of national mourning.

In November 1902 we read that "the new Communion Table should be in position before this magazine reached our readers", and at the same time the chancel was improved and cleaned. No record remains of the old Communion Table.

January 1903 has a note that the new altar rails, which "are a kind gift from Mr R A Tatton, of the Manor House", were not ready for Christmas, but were to "be erected during this month". The new pulpit was given at the same time by Sir George Dixon. In September of this year the church was closed for most of the month when the roof of the chancel, the ceiling of the nave, and walls were coloured and decorated by "Mr Hallward", in the style that many of our older church members will remember.

During the next few years the following gifts were given to the church: - an altar Book, Clergy Prayer Book, Altar Frontals, Book Markers, Antipenduims, a Water Cruet, Bread Box, Hymn Board, Alms Bags and alms Bason.

In June 1907 the Rev. Colin Beever Bell, only son of Canon Bell of Nether Alderley was instituted to the living of Chelford. Keenly interested in church Music Mr Bell devoted much time and trouble to the choir and bellringing. On 2nd March 1910 the present organ was dedicated by the Archdeacon of Macclesfield, the Rev. A Maitland Wood, M.A. and a recital was given by Mr Fred Burstall F.R.C.O., organist of Liverpool Cathedral. It is interesting to note that the same year, a recital was given by Mr W O West F.R.C.O., organist of St. Philip's Church, Alderley Edge, who, when he died in 1945 at the age of 86, had a record of seventy six years as church organist including fifty three at the above church.

Mr Bell died in May 1914 and there is a brass Tablet to his memory on the north wall of the chancel. During all these years the cover of the parish magazine has been the same – the church from the south gateway and "the sign" as an inset. This continued (except for a few months when the vicar, Rev. N J Gourlie had "Home words" as an inset with their cover) for some time until a change was made by Rev. W H Parkes. A new cover was designed showing Chelford and Lower Withington churches with the Chelford Calvary between and above the two sides of the 13th century seal of the Abbey of St Werburgh and arms of the Diocese of Chester. This cover was simplified in 1947 and the seal removed and later there was only a little sketch of Chelford Church at the top of the cover of the magazine.

In September 1969 the magazine changed from quarto to A5 format and for some years colour covers printed by Mowbray & Co were used. In January 1986 the present illustration of the Church as viewed from the lodge and drawn by John Biggs came into use as the front cover, initially in colour thanks to the generosity. of David Towers it reverted to monochrome in January 1991.

After many years in which the magazine was typed up by the vicar and his helpers, it moved into the desktop publishing age in February 1994. Now the vicar composes and edits and amateur computer mechanics in the parish find ways to fit the copy into the pages available. Whatever the origin of each month's Parish News the production process relies very heavily on the assembly teams. Each month they fold, collate and staple so that the band of distributors can set off on their rounds – to 700 letterboxes in the homes of the "vill of Chelleford" and Lower Withington.

Now as the new millennium is almost here, we are celebrating the 225th birthday of the rebuilding of our church in 1774. A church has almost certainly existed on the present site for nearly 1,000 years and is undoubtedly our strongest link with the past. Tremendous social changes have come about in the last century and doubtless more will follow in the next. Yet it is to be hoped that the example of those who have gone before us will not be lost, and that in the next 225 years there will be parishioners who continue to draw inspiration from the message of Chelford Church. Parishioners who will be willing to give their time to the church and, more importantly, be still willing and happy to worship there.

Events in 1999 celebrating the 225th anniversary of the rebuilding of Chelford Church.

Announced under the logo designed by Mr Alan List there have been a series of social events and indeed some are yet to come. In addition a prayer has been specially written: -

Eternal Father, as we give thanks for the faithful worship and witness of past generations, fill us with your Spirit that we may with courage, faith and imagination bring the good news of your love to the people of this parish today, in the name of Christ our King.

Saturday, March 6th

An afternoon with Rev'd Leslie Lewis – Vicar of Rainow

"An afternoon which was excellently supported when his simple talks were even funnier, more uplifting, enriching and inspiring of faith than we could have imagined.

Sunday, March 7th

The Sunday School Review

"The Review gave us a charming and memorable picture of the spirit of Sunday School work at Chelford Church. The cast of 'thousands' (somewhat depleted on the day but still mustering about 50 children and mums) gave a performance which represented yet another tribute to Christine Johnson's delightful writing and painstaking production."

April 3rd to April 5th

Easter weekend floral decoration of the church

When the church was most beautifully decorated and attracted many visitors during the whole weekend opening.

Saturday May 22nd

'225' Church Walk

When a group of enthusiasts led by Tony and Margaret Ward enjoyed a five-mile ramble with an appropriate pause for refreshment at the Parkgate Inn.

Saturday June 5th

Art, Embroidery and Ceramics Exhibition at the Village Hall

"An event which enabled us to look and delight in the expert work and hidden talents existing within the village in clay, paint brush, camera and needle."

Sunday June 20th

18th Century style service of Evening Prayer

"The church choir, augmented by members of the Grace Darling Singers sang local church music of the period, researched, supplied and conducted by Sally Drage. An instrumental band accompanied the singers and the Archdeacon of Macclesfield preached but resisted the temptation to deliver a sermon of 18th century duration."

Sunday September 19th
Dedication of the new Altar Rail Kneelers
By Canon Brian Young

Friday September 24th

Harvest Supper with Frank Topping
Who will present "Laughing in my Sleep"

Thursday September 30th

Book launch of "Chelford – A Cheshire Village"
A book produced to celebrate Chelford and its people.

At or about the Millennium

SON et LUMIERE' Presentation in Chelford Church

18th Century style service of Evening Prayer

REV. CANON HENRY RETIRES

June 1981 – A Busy Retirement
Canon and Mrs Henry in the Vicarage Garden

When Canon Maurice J B Henry, the vicar of Chelford and Lower Withington took charge of the joint parish 16 years ago he did so after an almost "roving commission" as a parson.

He was born in London, son and grandson of a clergyman, and after ordination at Wakefield Cathedral in 1938 began his work locally before moving to churches as widespread as Bredbury, Taxal, Davenham and Somerset.

Now, he and his wife Elsie, are on the move again, this time to a bungalow for their retirement at Plumley.

Canon Henry, who was Rural Dean of Knutsford for seven years, and his wife, have been most active in diocesan and parish life.

Mrs Henry started the popular Thursday Club for the over sixties and reorganised the Girl Guides after their absence for some years.

Sadly Canon Henry died 1998.

CHRISTMAS FAIR 1956

<u>Chelford Church Christmas Fair 6 December 1956</u>

(The following is an extract from County Express 6 December 1956)

Mrs Lockett (Betty Bannerman of the B.B.C.) opened Chelford Christmas fair on Saturday. The Chairman, Dr E F Evans, stressing the need to attend church, outlined the history of Chelford Church, which, he said, went back 700 years.

A vote of thanks was proposed by the Vicar (the Rev. C H Lee). Miss Julia Barber presented a bouquet to Mrs Lockett.

People bought eagerly from the well-stocked stalls and the event raised just over £300 for the funds of Chelford and Lower Withington Churches.

At the stalls were: Mrs Barber, Mrs Dunning, Mrs Sutcliffe, Miss Herbert, Miss Wyatt, Miss Cluff, Mrs Michell, Mrs Fairclough, Miss Tickle, Mrs Callwood. Mrs Hides, Mrs Barratt, Mrs Evans, Mrs Lowe, Miss Butler, Mrs Haworth, Mrs Todd, Miss Walsh, Mrs Shires, Mr & Mrs A Newton, Mr and Mrs A Massey, Mrs Hope, bellringers and choirmen, Mrs Duckworth, Mrs Leigh and mothers of the Sunday School children.

Mr R Emmens, Miss A Rowbotham, Miss J Newton, Miss P Robertson, Miss Caper, Mrs Kamm, Mrs C Worthington, Mrs Bailey, Miss Venables, Mrs Venables, Mr and Mrs Brocklehurst, Mr and Mrs Simms, Miss Jackson, Mrs Dyer, Mr and Mrs Newton, Miss Parry, Mrs Hulme, Mrs Hanmer, Mr D Mellor and Miss C Wild.

Competition winners: Mrs Stuart Johnson. Mrs Forrester, Mrs Boon and Mr N Ryder.

THE SUNDAY SCHOOL

Miss Audrey Walsh used to recount how for many years she taught the Sunday School children at the School, Alderley Road, escorting them 'in crocodile' down the road to church for Morning Service.

Mrs Elsie Henry led a very successful Sunday School which, from 14th September 1969 met in the, then, vicarage.

The next phase of the Sunday School began when the church 'Upper Room' opened in 1980, meeting there for the first time on, again, 14th September.

Mrs Henry was latterly assisted by Mrs Sue Barber and Mrs Rosemary Longworth, who continued for some time after Mrs Anne Ellis and Mrs Christine Johnston arrived in 1981. An outstanding feature of Mrs Johnston's time has been the regular series of 'Nativity' and other plays which she has written and produced. Sunday School helpers during this period have included Mrs Barbara Manwaring and Mrs Audrey Elliott.

THE FRIENDS OF THE SUNDAY SCHOOL MEETING JULY 1999

Left to right: - Shirley Wood, Sharon Strudley, Christine Johnston, Audrey Elliot, Muriel Preece and Anne Ellis.

SUNDAY SCHOOL PUPILS AND TEACHERS 1968/9

SUNDAY SCHOOL PUPILS WITH CANON HENRY c1970

53

SUNDAY SCHOOL PARTY – MID 1970'S

Members of Chelford St John's Church Sunday School at their party on Saturday

Pictured are Jacqueline Grimes, Charlotte Hallam and Emma Roycroft as they tuck into the jelly and cream.

GARDEN PARTY

Susan Bradley serving the children July 1976

Chelford Vicarage was invaded on Saturday afternoon, when stalls were set up in the hall, teas were served in the living rooms, and a cake stall appeared in the vicar's study.

The occasion was intended to be a garden party and bowls evening, in the vicarage garden, the home of the Canon and Mrs M J B Henry, but the weather forced everybody inside.

The event was attended by more than 100 people, and raised a total of £70, which will go towards church funds.

A big attraction proved to be the exhibition of dolls and dolls' clothing, organised by Miss A Walsh. The oldest doll, a wax one, was more than 100 years old, and Miss Walsh explained the histories and stories behind all the dolls.

There was also a display of brass rubbings done by Miss C Wilson, daughter of Mr and Mrs Henry, the floral decorations by Mrs A Turnock.

Mrs Stanier, Mrs J Camm, Miss A Walsh and Mrs Henry won the competitions.

The children's flower-arranging competition was won by Carole Bradley and Ralph Robertson, and the prizes were presented by Mrs Martin Bird.

During the evening some of the guest braved the elements and played bowls, and the others played whist.

The whist winners were Miss K Goff and Mrs Henry, and the bowls winners were Mrs Camm and Mr A Barber.

Mrs Waddacor presented the whist and bowls prizes.

ANON   *July 1908*

An aged owl sat on an oak,
The more he thought the less he spoke
The less he spoke, the more he heard,
I wish some folks were like this bird.

PRAM SERVICE

30 August 1984

The youngsters of Chelford had an early introduction to church recently when a pram service was held in the village.

Religion on rollers turned out to be a success and pictured are some of the children and their mums outside Chelford church.

Rev. John Ellis supervising (possibly).

CHELFORD CHURCH CHOIR 3RD AUGUST 1958

CHELFORD CHURCH CHOIR 3rd AUGUST 1958

Written on the back of the copy which is in the church is "Chelford Church Choir – August 3rd 1958 with Chairman of the 'Rural District Council', Mr Henry Burgess and his wife. (Civic service held on July 13th)."

Names on photograph in position they appear.

George Floy — Geoff Street — John Peel Jackson

Leigh Eyers — John Lawrence — Councillor H Burgess — Rev'd Cyril H Lee — Sidney Cleaver (organist) — Harry Callwood — Ernest Pimlot

Mrs G Forrester

Audrey Rowbottom — Pamela Eyers — Joan Baskerville — Susan Lee — Mrs T Newton — Joyce Newton

Mrs E Taylor (Verger) — Michael Street — Allan Gaye — Richard Forrester — Ronnie Dakin — Mrs Burgess

Chelford Church Team 1971

Chelford Church Team including P Baskerville, M Baskerville, A Egerton, K Egerton, D Norbury, N Kerrigan, T Davenport, N Baskerville, P Hall and R Brown.

CHELFORD CHURCH GARDEN PARTY- IVY HOUSE c1975

Left to right: - Nurse Freda Kerrigan, Barbara Camm, Josie Parfitt, Jennifer Holt, James McLeod, Unknown, Rev Henry (behind) Karen Newton, Patricia McLeod, Bessie Henshall.

61

CHELFORD BELLS

The present church of St John the Evangelist was consecrated on 23rd July 1776 to replace a former church, which by that time was in a very poor state of repair. The tower and spire were added in 1840 with a single bell until the present ring of bells was added in 1885.

However, Chelford bells go considerably further back than that, there being in existence an old bell dating from the 16th century. In 1958 Mr J W Clarke, author of 'Church Bells of Cheshire', visited the church and took moulds of the inscription on the bell, subsequently submitting the following report:

'The inscription is perfectly clear when it is realised that some of the letters have been put down sideways. The two animals, which appear to be dogs, are intended for pigs associated with St Antony.

The inscription on your bell reads: -

"(pig) 1568 (pig) + ANTONY ORA DEO AR".

The initials AR are probably those of the donor. The date is most certainly 1568 and I should say that the bell is a recasting by an itinerant founder of the pre-reformation Sanctus bell[1]. The re-casting was very probably done in the churchyard. In reproducing the inscription he did not even know when the letters were the right way up. Having finished the work he would fill in the hole in the churchyard, pack up his tools, collect his money and take to the road again."

In later years the bell was, for a considerable time (more than a century) at Withington Hall and only returned in 1953.

It is believed to be one of the oldest, if not the oldest, dated bell in Cheshire.

---

[1] Omerods 'Cheshire' records the fact that Chelford Chapel had a bell in 1548 and the re-casting of 1568 could have been taken from the earlier Sanctus bell. There is also a body of opinion that dates the bell as 1508, not 1568.

The present ring of bells came about as a result of a meeting held in the village school on 23 January 1885, followed by a further meeting on 20 February of that year when all aspects, including costs, were discussed. An appeal was launched to raise the £350 to install a ring of six bells and by 17th June 1885 the money had been raised. As a result an order was placed with Messrs Massey and Son of Alderley for the lowering of the belfry floor. A further order for the casting of the bells was immediately placed with Messrs. Mears and Stainbank.

To raise the necessary funds a committee was formed comprising John Dale, Thomas Wilson, Samuel Bucktrout, Samuel Read, James Callwood and Henry Jackson.

The new peal consisted of six bells and the bells were dedicated on Wednesday 17 June 1885, the first peal being rung by ringers from Gawsworth and Alderley. It must have been a 'big day' in the village. The school logbook recorded the following:

> 'The Church Bells were dedicated today: the children had a half-holiday in consequence.'

The Macclesfield Courier and Herald including in their description of the event:

> 'In such a place (Chelford) and on such an occasion we were not surprised to see in every avenue young men and maidens, old men and children in their best bib and tucker wending their way to the church in obedience to the call of their sixth bell as it tolled the invitation to all far and near.'

The ringers were taught by Colin Edward Beever Bell (son of the Rector of Alderley) who was later ordained, and served as Vicar of Chelford from 1907 until his death in May 1914.

One of the main supporters of the project had been Major Dixon of Astle Hall and it was an appropriate coincidence that the first wedding for which the bells were rung was that of Major Dixon and Mrs Baskervyle Glegg of Withington on Saturday 4 July 1885.

In 1922 it was found that the bells were in need of repair, the sum required to restore them being £144. A series of fund raising events took place to raise the necessary capital and the bells were re-hung with new gudgeons and ball bearings.

The bells were rung on a regular basis up to the commencement of the Second World War, when a ban was placed on the ringing of church bells. Bells were only to be rung should Britain be invaded. Certain precautions were taken should there be an air raid - an extract stating: -

> 'Buckets of water and sand have been placed in the Church, belfry and the roof, and extra taps are being fitted in the belfry and vestry to which a fire hose may be connected'.

The Home Office ban on ringing was removed in June 1943 but it was some time before the sound of bells returned to the village. In fact it was well into 1945 before Chelford's own team rang the bells. The Parish Magazine for November 1945 recorded:

> Once again our own ringers, thanks to the enthusiasm of Mr C H Taylor are ringing the Church Bells. We are grateful to the ringers, who are, Mr C H Taylor, Mr J P Jackson, Mr H Callwood, Mr E Pimlott, Mr J Dakin and Mr R Barratt.

1957 saw the death of two of Chelford's most loyal ringers, William Callwood, who was buried on 1st May aged 83 years and Clement H Taylor, who was buried on 14th September aged 80 years. The latter was the last of the original band of ringers at Chelford having been a ringer for 70 years.

By 1958, sex equality had arrived and two ladies had joined the band, Miss Joyce Newton and Miss Audrey Rowbottom.

Chelford Church has always been fortunate in having over the years many long-serving ringers and only four tower captains. The first tower captain was J W Taylor and he was succeeded by his son, Clem Taylor, in 1920, Clem remaining in the post until Ernest Pimlott took over in 1948. Ernest was the captain up to his death in 1981 when he was followed by Derek Bradshaw.

Ernest Pimlott probably did more than anyone else to further the advancement of bell ringing in Chelford and, in his memory, the ringers of the 1980's presented to the church a book that they had prepared giving details of all 86 peals rung on the bells up to that date. Altogether Ernest rang a total of 143 peals, 60 of which were at Chelford.

By 1987 it was apparent that the bells were in need of renovation and re-hanging and an appeal was launched in May 1987 to raise the sum of £15,000 to cover the work. The capital required was raised in 7 months and the work carried out by Messrs Eayre & Smith Limited assisted by volunteers, including Chelford's own bell ringers under the leadership of Mr Derek Bradshaw. The first peal on the re-hung bells took place on 24th January 1988 and was rung by six of the volunteers who had been involved in the work in memory of Tom Newton (34 years Churchwarden) who had recently died. The bells were re-dedicated by Rev'd Richard Gillings, later Archdeacon of Macclesfield, on Sunday 17th April 1988 during a Thanksgiving Service.

Author's note   *Most of the information contained above has been extracted from the peal record book compiled by Prunella Bradshaw and thanks are due to her for her permission to use these records in this publication.*

Chelford has a further connection with bells - its handbells.

Handbell ringing began in the early part of the 1960's when the WI formed a team of ringers, the prime mover and conductor being Miss Audrey Walsh. Originally the team rang by numbers but when Prunella Bradshaw became the conductor they started ringing from a music score.

As the team became more experienced the sphere of activity spread beyond the confines of Chelford district including participation in handbell rallies throughout the county.

The Chelford Handbell team was formed in 1971, ringing the handbells belonging to the W.I. The team consisted of , the Pimlott family (Ernest, Edna and their two daughters, Christine and Judith), and Freda and Jean Turnock. They were joined later by Brenda Burgess and Joan Sutcliffe. The first performance was given at Alderley Edge Chapel Guild. In 1975 Brian Hornby and Sue Couling joined the team and in 1982 the team consisted of P. Bradshaw (who took over as conductor when Ernest Pimlott died in 1981), Sue Couling, Joanna Davies, Anne Ellis, David Ellis, Stephen Ellis, Brian Hornby with Edna Pimlott as secretary.

The original set of 12 handbells was purchased for £40 in 1960 and sold in 1980 for £350 when Ernest Pimlott bought his own set of 32 bells.

In March 1997 the 12 handbells belonging to Chelford Church were returned and the Church bought the 32 bells belonging to the Pimlott family. The bells are now being used by the pupils of Chelford School perpetuating the village tradition of handbell ringing.

Author's note: - We are grateful to Mrs Pimlott for information enabling us to prepare the above article on Handbells.

CHELFORD BELLRINGERS c 1950

Top row – left to right: Arthur Street, John Lawrence, Harry Callwood, J P Jackson, Arthur Campbell and Ian Davidson.

Bottom row – left to right: Arnold Worth, Bob Barratt, The Rev'd. J S Gamon and Ernest Pimlott.

THE PIMLOTT FAMILY OF HANDBELL RINGERS

Edna and Ernest with their daughters, Christine and Judith

VICAR WITH BELLRINGERS 1975

Standing: -E Pimlott (Captain), P J Moody, Rev. Henry, G Barber, A Street
Sitting: - C A Pimlott, W Street, E A Moody, C A Street, J A Pimlott

ST JOHN THE EVANGELIST CHELFORD VICAR AND RINGERS CHRISTMAS 1925

Left to right: J W Taylor, W Callwood, S Hyder, J Moores, T Baskerville, Front: Rev. W H Parkes (Vicar), C H Taylor (Captain).

Local band who ring a peal to celebrate
the Centenary of the Bells,
left to right:-
Derek Bradshaw, Alastair Bradshaw,
Graham Bradshaw, George Barber,
Stephen Okill, David Ellis,
Also Bosley (7 m/y)— June 21st 1985.

Local band who rang a peal to celebrate the Centenary of Bells 21st June 1985
Left to right: - Derek Bradshaw, Alastair Bradshaw, Graham Bradshaw, George Barker, Stephen Okill, David Ellis.

70

CHELFORD HANDBELL RINGERS

The Chelford team of handbell ringers who took part in the 7th North west federation Rally - late 1970's

71

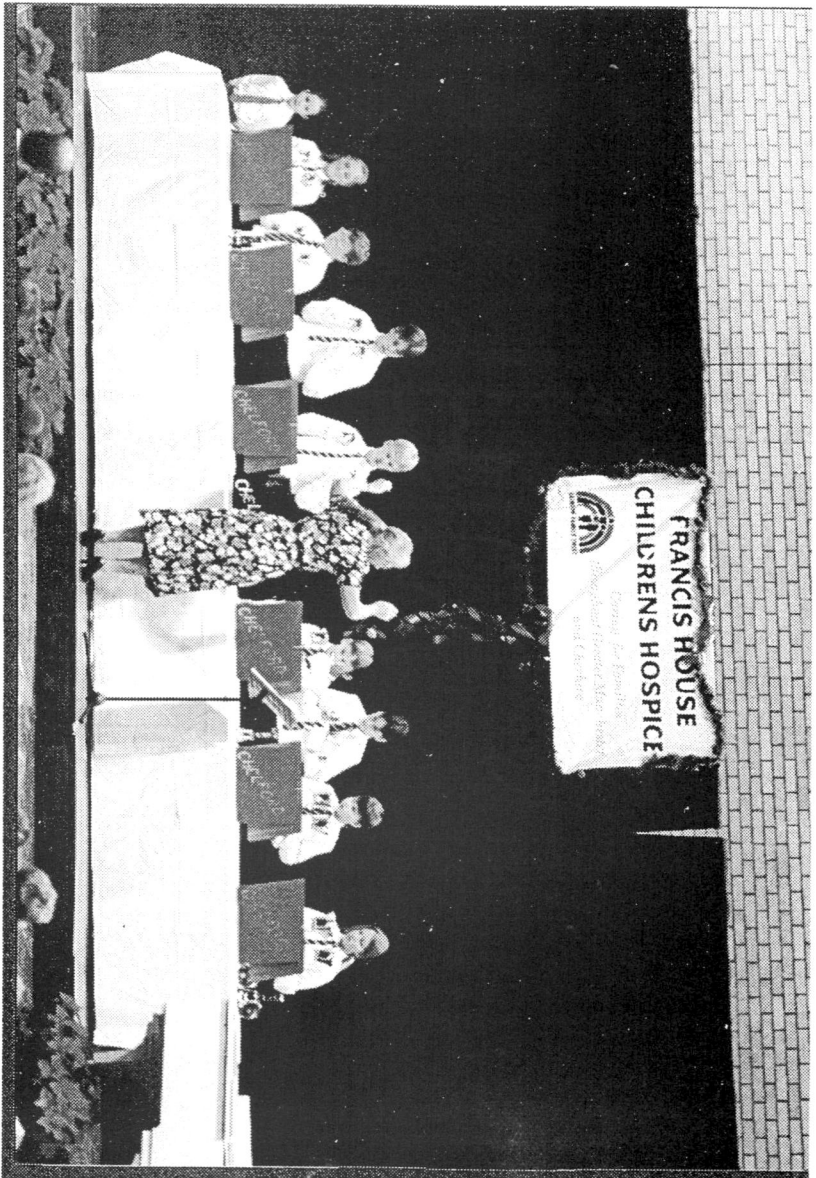

CHELFORD HAND BELL RINGERS – PRUNELLA BRADSHAW CONDUCTING

72

ASTLE ESTATE

The Astle Estate dates back, to the reign of Richard I or King John (end of 12th century). Originally written Asthulle it gave its name to a local family Hesthull or Asthull, the family being mentioned in early deeds enabling a pedigree to be established[1].

The Milne or Mill House estate in Astle was in the 15th century in the possession of the Henshaw family, Thomas Henshaw being listed in Cheshire Recognisance Rolls[2] between 1409 and 1426. In 1445 a list of gentry in Macclesfield Hundred includes Thomas Henshaw 'of Milnhouse' and the name occurs throughout the 15th and 16th centuries. However, the family had left Milne House by the beginning of the 17th century when it was in the possession of Anthony Furnivall, a descendant of a yeoman family of that name which had settled at Betchton. Ralph Furnivall, son of Anthony, married Elizabeth, daughter of John Fallows of Fallows Hall, c 1640. In 1653 Ellen Stubbs, her daughter Elizabeth, and Ann Stanley (possibly also a daughter of Ellen Stubbs) were hanged at Boughton for bewitching to death Mrs Furnivall, wife of Ralph Furnivall and daughter of Mr John Fallows, of Fallows Hall. Ralph Furnivall had two daughters, Elizabeth, who never married, and Anne, who married Philip Leycester. In 1676 he parted with Milne House to Elizabeth Furnivall, his sister-in-law[3]. In her will, dated 5th January 1685-6 she bequeathed Milne House to Joseph Lowe, the third son of George Lowe of Chelford, and his heirs for ever.

George Lowe lived at Milne House until c1720 when it appears to have been sold to Christopher Whytell of Barmyncham, Yorkshire. He duly lived there, leaving the house in his will of 22nd February 1732 to his eldest son Christopher who, at that time, was 9 years of age. It was eventually purchased in 1749 by John Parker who erected Astle Hall on the site of the old house.

The Parker family appears to have come from Middlewich. The first member of the family to reside in Chelford being John Parker who was buried at Alderley in 1711. He purchased Fallows Hall, Nether Alderley in 1697[4] and in his will proved at Chester 28th August 1711 he is described as 'John Parker of Astle Esq.'. His wife was, Sarah, daughter of James Grundy of Bolton-le-Moors, Lancs and together they had three sons and one daughter. The eldest son, John Parker, Esq., succeeded to the Astle estates and others at Breightmet, Lancs, probably through his wife, Alice, daughter of Thomas Smith of Breightmet who he married in 1723. He was living at Bath in 1765

---

1   Harl MSS 2099, f260-1

2   Cheshire Record Office.

3   The Furnivall family still held land in Chelford in 1834 when the Dixon family purchased the estate - Chelford in the 19th Century by W Keith Plant.

4   Box No. 1 Bundle No. 1 Astle Estate Documents, John Rylands University of Manchester Library.

and died in 1768 being succeeded by his only son, the Rev. John Parker of Astle and Breightmet who was incumbent of Chelford from 1772 to 1795[5].

The Rev. John Parker married Jane, daughter and heiress of Robert Gartside of Manchester (merchant) and they had one son, Thomas, and five daughters.

Thomas succeeded his father in 1795 and in the same year married Dorothy, daughter of Thomas Cholmondeley Esq., of Vale Royal[6]. Thomas and Dorothy had no issue and the estate was purchased in 1833/4 by Henry Dixon Esq., the eldest son of Lydia Parker (the third daughter of Rev. John Parker and Jane Gartside) who had married John Dixon of Gledhow, Yorkshire. Thomas Parker died in 1840 and was buried at Chelford. During the 18th and the early part of the 19th century the Parkers purchased small estates in the Chelford area and inherited through marriage a number of other estates in Lancashire and Ireland. By this time they must have been a very prosperous family.

John Dixon of Gledhow and Chapel Allerton near Leeds, who married Lydia Parker in 1784, was descended from an old Yorkshire family which was living at Heaton Royds in 1564 and was subsequently active in the Civil War. John Dixon, who was a Colonel of the 1st West Yorkshire Militia died on 18th April 1825 leaving Henry Dixon his son and heir. Henry parted with some of his Yorkshire estates and purchased the Astle and Chelford estates from his uncle, Colonel Thomas Parker in 1833 and seated himself there. On his death, without issue, 3 August 1838, his brother, John Dixon, who married Sophia, daughter of T W Tatton of Wythenshawe in 1840, succeeded him. John Dixon was High Sheriff of Cheshire in 1843.

The sale of the Astle Estate to the Dixons, and more particularly the conveyancing of the sale, including an Apportionment Map, gives a complete picture of the estate as it was in 1834[7].

John and Sophia Dixon (nee Tatton) had a total of eleven children, seven boys and four girls. The eldest, George, was born in 1842, succeeding to the title at the age of 31 when his father died in 1873. He married Mrs Emily Catherine Baskervyle Glegg (widow of John Baskervyle Glegg of Withington Hall) on 4th July 1885. George had been educated at Eton and at the age of 17 entered the Army, serving with his regiment, the Kings Own Borderers for 13 years. His interest in military matters did not cease when he left the Army, as he joined the 5th Cheshire Rifle Volunteers.

---

5   It is doubtful if he carried out many Church duties during his period of office. In 1780/1 a Mr Thomas Gatley is mentioned as Curate of Chelford and from 1786 to 1791 Mr James Penny, Curate at Alderley officiated at Chelford.

6   The settlement drawn up for this marriage contains many details relative to the Astle Estate including a list of Tenants and Farmers (John Rylands Library, University of Manchester/Chelford in the 19th Century by W Keith Plant).

7   Chelford in the 19th Century by W Keith Plant.

George and Emily had two children, John (the heir to the estate) born in 1886 and Sophia Evelyn, born in 1887, who, together with three children of Emily's previous marriage, lived at the Hall.

The coming of age of John in 1907 was reported in great detail in The Macclesfield Courier and Herald of Saturday 15th June with the following description of the event:

> 'On Thursday last Mr John Dixon, only son and heir of Colonel George Dixon, of Astle Park, Chelford (the highly esteemed Chairman of Cheshire County Council), reached his twenty-first birthday, and the happy occasion was commemorated by the estate tenantry and others in a most joyous and fitting manner. Colonel Dixon is such a prominent and devoted worker in the county concerns of Cheshire, such a kind-hearted and generous neighbour, and such a considerate and estimable landlord, that an event so interesting as the coming of age of his son was bound to attract a good deal of attention, and notwithstanding that the weather was unpleasantly wet, the celebrations on Thursday, characterised as they were with the greatest possible harmony and good feeling amongst all concerned, will mark the day as a red-letter one in the annals of the Astle Estate. Relatives, farm tenantry, cottagers and neighbours all assembled to do honour to the young heir, and to wish him all good fortune that life can bring, and a career as creditable to himself and as serviceable to the community as is that of his respected father.
>
> The climatic conditions were undoubtedly damp, but the dampness did not in any degree mar the enthusiasm of those who took part in the pleasant celebrations. The Park itself presented a festive appearance, a profusion of flags and bunting testifying the unusual nature of the occasion. At the entrance to the gardens willing hands had erected a triumphal arch of evergreens, bunting, and flags with a motto which summarised the feelings of everybody in the words, "Long life and happiness". A large marquee had been erected in front of the hall in which the tenantry, cottagers, and children were to be entertained during the day, and over the entrance to this appeared another motto, "Health and happiness".

John married Gwendoline Spearman on 24th December 1910, their eldest son, John George Dixon, being born in 1911. When George Dixon died in 1924 John took over the estate.

The Hall had been remodelled from the 'old' house retaining its old low proportions and slightly projecting wings but with a smooth new face, sash windows and tripartite 'Wyatt' Windows at the ends. For a time after the rebuilding the older timber-framed fabric of the house remained at the back of the hall.

In 1926 the Hall was bought by Mr R S Provis and converted into a nature cure home. The Daily Despatch, Tuesday 1st June 1926, contained a detailed report (see later).

Gradually through the middle period of the 20th century the estate was sold off and nothing now remains of the original Astle Estate.

PARKER & DIXON OF ASTLE

John Parker jnr. Astle = Jane Gartside
b 1728
d Nov 1795

Thomas Parker = Dorothy Cholmodsley
b 10 Apr 1766
d 1 Aug 1840
No issue

Lydia Parker = John Dixon
b 10 Dec 1763 b 27 June 1753
d 18 Feb 1844 d 18 Apr 1825

Jane
Alice
Ann
Mary

Henry Dixon = Emma Matilda
b 19 Nov 1794 Sacheverol Wilmot
d 3 Aug 1838

John Dixon = Sophia Tatton
b 13 Feb 1799
d 10 Mar 1873

Francis
George
Charles

Lydia
Mary
Jane
Anne
Emma
Annabell

George Dixon = Emily Catherine
b 23 May 1842 Baskervyle Glegg
d 14 Apr 1924 (Widow)

John Wyheham
Charles Egerton
Henry Grey

Frederick Parker
William Arthur Tatton
Edward Wilbraham

Anna Lavinia
Sophia Lydia
Jessie Maria
Eleanor Georgina

John Dixon = Gwendoline Spearman
b 1886   b 1887
d 7 Aug 1976   d 1974

Sophia Evelyn

Mary B Glegg
Emily B Glegg
John B Glegg
} stepchildren

John George Dixon
b 1911
d
(lived & died in Switzerland)

Beryl

Nigel

Jonathan

For more information see Chelford in the 19th Century by W Keith Plant

77

VALUABLE CHESHIRE ESTATES

SPECIFICATIONS

Of the

CAPITAL MANSION HOUSE,

CALLED

ASTLE HALL,

WITH

PARK, MANOR, ADVOWSON, INNS, DEMESNES, and very valuable FARMS,

Containing together upwards of

Two Thousand Six Hundred Acres

OF

FREEHOLD LAND,

Situate in the very best part of the justly favourite

COUNTY PALATINE OF CHESTER

Being in the several Townships of

ASTLE, SNELSON, CHELFORD, ALDERLEY, PEOVER, AND LOWER WITHINGTON,

About Five Miles from Knutsford and Holme's Chapel; and seven from Macclesfield and Congleton. THE MANSION HOUSE is replete with every accommodation, well suited as a Residence for a Nobleman, or any large Family, delightfully seated in a PARK of about ONE HUNDRED AND SEVENTY ACRES.

Ornamented with

A BEAUTIFUL LAKE,

Covering nearly Twenty Acres,

An the ESTATE comprises sundry most excellent Dairy Farms, with capital Farm Houses and Outbuildings well stocked with Game, being bounded on every side by the strictly preserved Manors of Sir Henry M Mainwaring and Sir John Thomas Stanley, Baronets, and John B. Clegg, Wilbraham Egerton and Davies, Davenport, Esquires.

The Road and Neighbourhood are of superior desriptions and

THE CHESHIRE HOUNDS

HUNT THE COVERTS

Which will be Sold by Auction

By MESSRS. DRIVER

AT THE GEORGE INN, AT KNUTSFORD,

On Wednesday, the 9th day of October, 1833,

At One o'Clock for the hour of TWO precisely,

IN FIFTY-THREE LOTS

(Unless an acceptable offer should be previously made by Private Contract, of which due notice will be given.

Printed Specification with Plans annexed, and Tickets for viewing the Mansion House and Grounds may be had on application at the offices of Messrs, Cririe, Slater and Heelis, Princes Street, Manchester; Mr Roscoe, Solicitor, Knutsford; Messrs. Clarke and Fynmore, Solicitors, Craven Street, Strand; and of Messrs. DRIVER, Surveyors and Land Agents, No. 8, Richmond Terrace, Parliament Street, London.   may also be had at the Auction Mart, London; and the Farms and Lands will be shewn upon application to Edward Jackson, the Bailiff, aAstle Farm.

Sale Specification – Astle Hall 1833

SPECIFICATIONS.

LOT 1.

ASTLE-HALL PARK & DEMESNE

In Astle, Snelson and Chelford Townships.

A MOST CAPITAL MANSION-HOUSE,

VERY SUBSTANTIALLY CONSTRUCTED.

e principal part—comprising all the best Family Apartments, being a modern Erection, and senting a regular Front of One Hundred and Twenty-two feet, most delightfully seated in a remarkably well timbered Park, containing about 160 Acres of rich Grass Land, embellished with, and including a most beautiful Lake, covering nearly 20 Acres; and contiguous is a very valuable DAIRY FARM with a Cottage Ornée, Dairy House, and a convenient Poultry Establishment, neatly fitted up, forming an agreeable resort, being distant across the Park about one quarter of a mile from the Hall.

The PARK, abuts upon the Turnpike Road leading from Knutsford to Macclesfield, and on the opposite side is situate Chelford Chapel, in which are sufficient Pews and Accommodation for the Family and Servants, and contiguous is
A VERY EXCELLENT FARM in hand, called ASTLE FARM,
and surrounding which are sundry other very capital Farms, in the occupation of most responsible Tenants, including the well-accustomed INN, called *The Archers.*

Sundry neat DWELLING HOUSES, SMITHY & SHOP, forming in the whole a most valuable Domain.

The modern part of the House comprises,
On the principal Entrance Floor, a SUITE OF VERY EXCELLENT APARTMENTS, elegantly fitted up, with beautiful Mahogany Doors, consisting of a Breakfast Room, 21 ft. by 16 ft. 6 in.; large Library with two Fire-places, 40 ft. by 23 ft.; Drawing Room 31 ft. by 21 ft.; and a noble Dining Room 34 ft. 6 in. by 19 ft. 6 in., with large bow, and an Ante-room communicating therewith. A spacious back Hall with Water-closet at the end, and a handsome oak Staircase with mahogany Rail, leading to a spacious long Gallery on the principal Chamber Floor, communicating with seven large airy Bed Rooms, two Dressing Rooms, and a Water Closet.

The other portion of the House comprises, a Gentleman's Room, Housekeeper's Room, and large light Closet, Butler's Pantry, with interior Sleeping and Plate Room, a Steward's Room, large Kitchen, Larder, Scullery, spacious Servants Hall, with Knife & Boot Room adjoining, and four Men Servants Sleeping Apartments over. A very light and convenient secondary Staircase, besides a back Staircase leading to the First Floor, on which are a large Bed Room with a Ladies Boudoir, on one side, and a Dressing Room at the other. Two other Bed Rooms, House Keeper's Sleeping Room, Housemaid's Closet, and large Bedroom for Lady's Maid, and besides are two other Bed Rooms, and two Garrets.

Sale Specification – Astle Hall Park and Demesne

Under a considerable part of the House are very excellent Ale and Wine Cellars, with groined arches.

There is a Brewhouse, Washing House and good Laundry, with a Feather Room over, a paved Yard, also a capital well enclosed Drying Ground, and large Coal Yard.

A spacious Court Yard with substantial Buildings on three sides thereof, comprising Coach Houses, or standing for four Carriages, and Corn Granaries over; on one side is a Stable for six Horses, another for five Horses, with Saddle Room adjoining, and an open Stable for four Horses, with Lofts over all. At the other end is a Box Stable, two other four-stall Stables and a Harness Room, with Loft over,

AT THE REAR OF THESE
Is a Slaughter House, Cow House, Waggon Lodge, and an excellent Barn with two Bays.

Capital Piggery, Ice House, and Hay Barn.

AN EXCELLENT KITCHEN GARDEN
enclosed with lofty brick walls well clothed with choice Fruit Trees in full-bearing.

Gardeners' and Tool Houses, besides another Kitchen Garden, with a Pinery, Grapery, and an ELEGANT NEWLY ERECTED GREENHOUSE IN THE PLEASURE GROUNDS, which are particularly tastefully disposed, and highly decorated with a beautiful Flower Garden.

PARTICULARS OF THE PREMISES IN HAND.

No. on Plan.	Description.	Cultivation.	A.	R.	P.	
1	Astle Hall, Outbuildings, Yard, Kitchen Garden and Pleasure Ground		7	1	32	In Astle
2	The Park		111	3	13	
14	Ditto _____ late Irvine		1	0	14	
15	Ditto _____ ditto		1	2	0	
17	Part of Fish Pond Wood		1	2	28	
23	Wood		1	3	28	In Snelson
24	Road		0	0	30	
25	Part of Meadow		0	2	6	
26	Part of Lake		1	1	13	
27	Remainder of Ditto		16	1	13	
28	Remainder of Meadow		17	0	19	In Chelford
29	Wood		2	3	6	
30	Lodge		0	0	19	A neat thatched building
	EXTENT OF THE PARK		163	3	21	
18	Dog Kennel Field		3	2	25	
19	Orchard		0	0	37	
20	Wood		1	0	6	In Snelson
21	Ditto		0	0	29	
22	Ditto		0	1	15	
			169	1	13	
	THE DAIRY FARM.					
3	Dairy House and Buildings		1	0	36	Besides the Dairy House and Cottage Orneé are the Poultry Houses, Shippons, Barn, Piggeries, Bake-house, and Boiling House
4	Wood		10	2	15	
5	Wood Field		4	1	18	
6	Lime Field		6	1	27	
7	Gorsy Croft		6	1	22	
8	Great Wood Meadow		4	1	7	
9	Little ditto		1	3	28	
10	Walk Mill Field		4	0	31	
11	Rough Hays		5	0	0	
12	Wood		1	2	12	
13	Further and Middle Meadow		5	1	30	
16	Part of Fish Pond Wood		1	1	8	
			50	2	34	In Astle
	Carried forward		220	0	7	

NATURE CURES IN LOVELY HOME

HISTORIC MANSION'S NEW USE

FASTING REMEDY

Following his addresses to the Manchester Rotary Club some weeks ago, in which he described his own cure from pernicious anaemia 'by fasting,' Mr. R. S. Provis has bought Astle Hall, Chelford, Cheshire, and has retired from his business as an auctioneer in the city to run the hall as a nature cure home, the first established in the North.

Astle Hall is an historic mansion, and, when the seat of the late Sir George Dixon, was one of the show places of Cheshire. It has been restored by Mr Provis to its original splendour, and has a magnificent lake with waterfall, a water garden with lilies and fountain, a large number of glass houses (in which are growing peaches, nectarines, and grapes), four acres of vegetable gardens, and in all $12^2/_2$ acres of gardens, the whole being set in some of the finest wooded country in the North of England.

Mr. R. S. PROVIS.

Interviewed at the hall by a *Daily Dispatch* representative yesterday, Mr Provis showed the enthusiasm of youth in his new enterprise. "I can tell you," he said, "that a fortnight here will make you feel fitter than you have ever felt. We have a most competent staff, and hope to open in July with at least 30 patients – we have that number waiting for us to open, and we shall be able to accommodate about 50 when the equipment is completed.

DESPERATE CASES

"There are treatment rooms for all classes of sickness, and we take anyone suffering from any disease that is not contagious or mental. The treatment includes osteopathy and chiropractic massage, electric blanket, sun ray, and ultra-violet ray. In the grounds are chalets each fitted with hot and cold water and electric light. In these the patients will have pure air for every minute of the day.

"We shall not overlook the recreational side of life," Mr Provis added, "for we have three grass tennis courts, clock golf, and equipment for concerts indoors, as well as a wireless receiving set at each bed patient" side.

"It is likely that we shall get only those patients who have been given up by their doctors," said Mr Provis, "but our resident osteopath will diagnose on all ordinary cases, and very serious cases will be required to pass their own doctor."

Turning to his own cure, which he is ever ready to detail, Mr Provis said there was only one word to describe it; it was "wonderful." In the hands of doctors for a long, long time, he was without health or strength, and on admission to a health home such as he has now set up at Astle hall, he could not walk two yards. Within one day of fasting he walked 100 yards, and within twelve days, walked five miles and climbed 27 steps, two at a time, "without knowing I had a heart."

FASTING FOR STRENGTH

Since his cure he has been examined by an insurance doctor, who gave him a certificate by which it appeared that his organs and activity were those of a man of 32, though his age was 58. All human diseases are curable by natural methods, Mr Provis maintains.

The pain of disease was a friendly warning of danger from the body, and on experiencing it "we should immediately adopt the rational method, and instead of giving the body more work to do by taking food and drugs we should rest it and leave the body to work out its own salvation, which it will most certainly do. When it has got rid of the intruder, disease, it will tell you when it is ready for further food." Scientific fasting thus became a source of strength, not weakness, as is commonly understood.

Mr Provis mentioned that since the publication of the story of his cure he has received over 200 letters, some of them coming from Australia and India, asking for advice.

"I am not on a money-making stunt," Mr Provis concluded, "but the home has got to pay for itself."

In reply to a question by the *Daily Dispatch* representative, he said the charges would be from eight guineas a week, according to the room occupied.

ASTLE HALL
NATURE CURE HOME LTD

Where to regain your strength

Astle Hall, Chelford, is an old English Mansion which was at one time one of the foremost show-places of Cheshire. It has now been restored to its former magnificence and provided with all the equipment necessary for curing human ills and disorders by natural methods.

No better site could have been found. The Hall is surrounded by a splendid park of 160 acres, with an expansive outer-circle of spacious pasture lands. The park is intersected by a trout stream, which is broken by a waterfall with a drop of 18 feet. It also comprises extensive greenhouses and gardens, which supply the Hall with a profusion of the finest fruits and vegetables all the year round, and its varied scenery is enhanced by a lake, the playground of wild fowl, the swan and the contemplative heron. Indeed this sequestered beauty spot of Cheshire is admirably fitted by Nature for the promotion of that tranquillity of mind and body which is the attribute of good health.

Astle Park and Lake

Games may be pursued at pleasure – tennis in the grounds (3 grass courts), coarse fishing in the lake, and golf within easy reach. Everything combines to make Astle Hall ideal for the work of healing and for recreation.

The Treatment

The aim of Astle Hall Nature Cure Home is to promote human health and happiness. Few people are really fit, although the normal condition of man is good health, and all our natural forces are in league against disease. Indeed the curative powers of Nature are remarkable. She can expel disease and repair tissue, but in order to pursue her constructive work she must be given a chance to assert herself. Astle Hall Nature Cure Home is equipped to exploit these natural forces inherent in everyone in whom there is a trace of vitality left, and the natural drugless methods of healing are practiced here by none but qualified experts.

Our system applies to every case of dis-ease and physical disorder, especially where no vital organ has been impaired by the ravages of the surgeon's knife, but for the welfare of those undergoing treatment we are compelled to refuse all contagious and mental cases.

Initially, Astle Hall is not a Nursing Home. Its atmosphere is one of brightness and cheerfulness, its vision of life as of something to be enjoyed. It is our business to restore your health, get you well and teach you how to keep well. A stay with us is a wise economy and the most profitable holiday you could spend. The large accommodation in the Hall is supplemented by 11 outdoor chalets adjacent to the Hall, and as these chalets are sheltered from the north and east winds, and are replete with electric light and hot and cold water, they are ideal for the less serious cases.

Each case on entry undergoes an expert examination, and according to the diagnosis any of the following methods of treatment may be prescribed –

SCIENTIFIC FASTING   ELECTRIC BLANKETS
OSTEOPATHY   CHIROPRACTIK
ULTRA VIOLET RAYS   SUNLIGHT (natural and artificial)
MASSAGE
HOT AND COLD SITZ BATHS

Staff

The fully qualified Staff
Is under the direct superintendence
of the resident osteopath
R. LESLIE WADE
D.O., D.C..

Astle Park Lily Pond and gardens

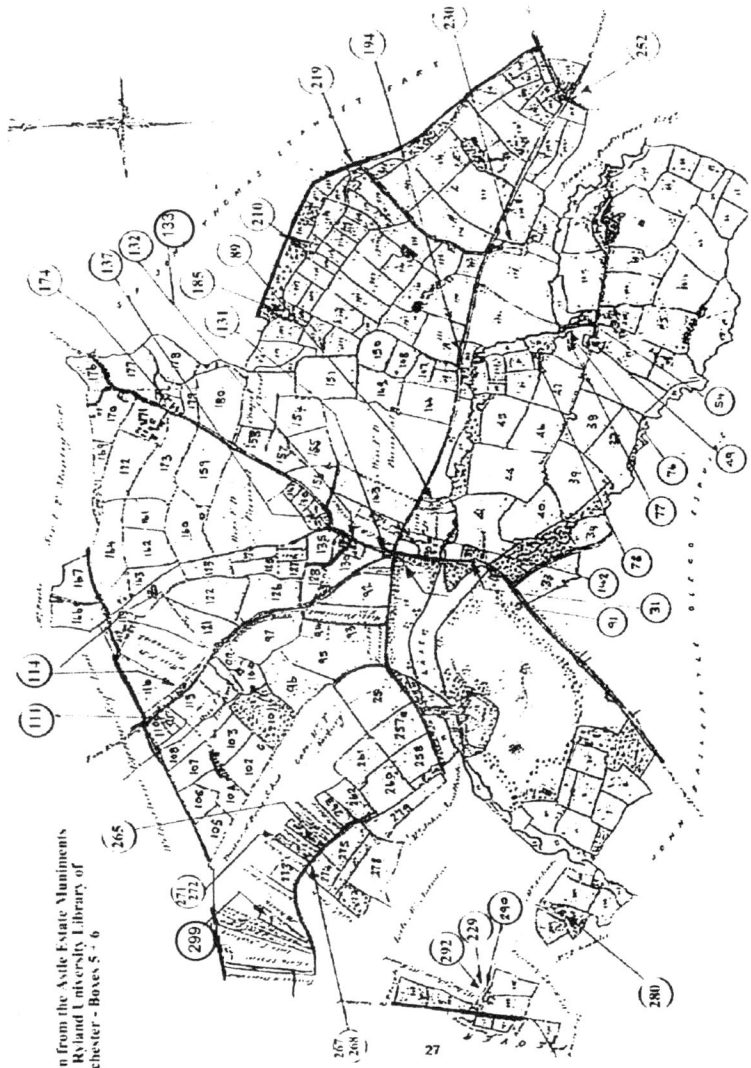

Taken from the Astle Estate Muniments
John Ryland University Library of
Manchester - Boxes 5 + 6

Area marked in circles indicates places of residence

PARKER/DIXON ESTATE CHELFORD 1834
For identification see Chelford in 19th Century by W K

85

ASTLE HALL,

ASTLE HALL c 1850

TURNPIKE ROADS

The Highways Act of 1555 (which remained in force for 280 years, i.e. up to 1835) stipulated that local parishes were responsible for the upkeep of roads within their boundaries. The Act specified that persons holding land, arable or pasture, with an annual value of £50 of more had to supply two men, with horses or oxen, a cart and tools for repairing highways, to work four[1] consecutive days each year. Landless cottagers had to work this statute labour themselves or find substitutes.

Unfortunately, despite this act, the standard of roads did not improve to any extent due mainly to the lack of control. With the increased amount of traffic, gradually through the 18th century, turnpike trusts were formed and by the end of the 18th century it was generally accepted that these trusts had improved the quality of the roads.

Turnpikes continued to be created until the railway age and by the middle of the 19th century between 10 and 20% of all roads were turnpikes. However, from 1850 'disturnpiking' was actively pursued and before the end of the century the last tollgate disappeared.

The trustees were mainly local landowning gentry who appointed officials to control and operate the trust. Travellers paid tolls according to a scale of charges listed on a tollboard at a tollhouse. No tolls were paid by pedestrians, clergymen, soldiers on the march, voters at elections, traffic going to and from church or to funerals, mail-coaches, traffic associated with farming operations and livestock moving between farm and pasture.

The presence of milestones is usually regarded as evidence of turnpike roads.

As far as Chelford is concerned there appear to be two tolls connected with the village, one on the road to Holmes Chapel and the other on the Knutsford Road opposite the site now occupied by the Village Hall. The toll bar jutted out into the road and the tolls were collected through a window. In its later years the toll collector had an iron rod operated from within the cottage which saved him from having to go out in bad weather or at night. Across the road from the cottage was a well with steps down to it. No records appear to have survived for the Knutsford Road toll but records exist for the Twemlow and Withington tolls on the Chelford to Holmes Chapel Road.

---

[1]   Increased to 6 days in 1563

There is a possibility, but not yet proven, that Merehills Cottage on the Knutsford side of the village was also a toll house. (See chapter relating to Merehills.)

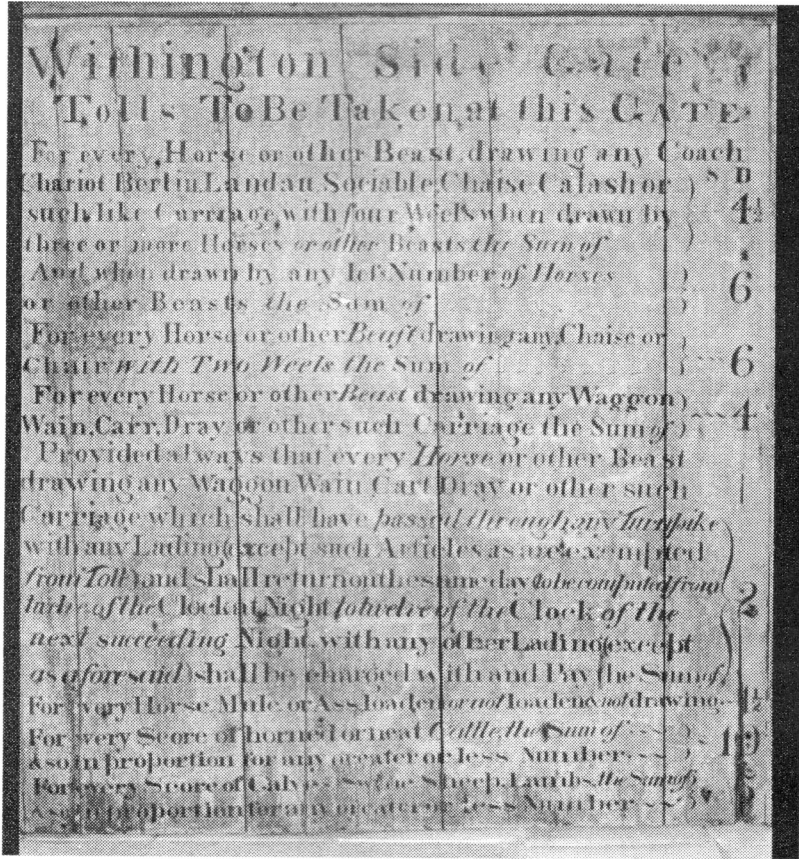

WITHINGTON SIDE GATE
TOLLS TO BE TAKEN AT THIS GATE

	S	D
For every Horse or other Beast drawing any Coach Chariot Berlin Landau Sociable Chaise Calash or such like Carriage with four Weels when drawn by three or more horses *or other* Beasts *the sum of*		4 ½
And when drawn by any less number of Horses or other Beasts *the sum of*		6
For every Horse or other *Beast* drawing any Chaise or Chair *with Two weels the sum of*		6

For every Horse or other *Beast* drawing any Waggon Wain, Carr,
Dray or other such Carriage the sum *of*   *4*
Provided always that every *Horse* or other Beast drawing any
Waggon Wain Cart Dray or other such Carriage which shall have
passed through any Turnpike with any Lading (except such Articles
as are exempted *from Toll)* and shall return on the same day (*to be
commuted from such of the* Clock at Night *to twelve of the*   *2*
 Clock *of the next succeeding* Night with any other lading
(*except as aforesaid*) shall be charged with and Pay the Sum *of*
For every Horse Mule or Ass loaded *or* not loaded not drawing   *1½*
For *every* Score of Horned or neat *Cattle the sum of*
A soin proportion for any *greater* or less Number   *10*
For every Score of Calves Swine Sheep Lamb *the Sum of*
A such proportion for any greater or less Number   *9*

An example of operating costs can be shown in the turnpike records held at the
C.R.O. Chester for the year 1866[2].

*General Statement of Income and Expenditure of the Turnpike Road from Holmes Chapel
to Chelford between the first day of January and the 31st day of December 1866.*

1866		£	s	d	1866		£	s	d
	Last years balance	1	-	-	Paid Clerks Salary £1.1.-				
	Withington tolls	30	"	"	advertizing meeting postages				
	Twemlow tolls	45	"	"	as per account		2	9	6
					Paid at meeting			5	-
					" Leigh Dividend		47	9	-
					" Hilditch Dividend		3	13	-
					" Glegg. Dividend		21	18	-
					Balance due to the trust			5	6
		£76 -		-			£76 -		-

1866   Dec 25th Examined fallowed

John Dixon
Chairman

The total debt is now reduced to 983 12 10

2   Ref: QDT3/15 Cheshire Record Office.

THE VILLAGE SCHOOL
The first 150 years

For the vast majority of villages the history of the village school is not a long one (though that of Chelford is longer than most as will be shown later) and many schools were built during the Victorian period. In 1820 only one in four children in England were receiving any kind of education and most of the adult population could not read or write. Parents considered book-learning to be a complete waste of time as children were more use to them working on the farms or in some small cottage industry to supplement the family's income.

Charity schools, supported by donations from the local gentry or more well-to-do villagers, supplied the main form of education. In many cases, (as in Chelford) private individuals provided building plots for schools, and the income to support the charity schools usually came from interest on endowments and voluntary donations. In some instances each child contributed 'school pence' towards the teachers salary. However it was frequently a condition laid down by the original benefactor that a certain number of pupils from poor families had to be taught free of cost.

The 'school pence' persisted until schooling became free in 1891.

In addition to the charity schools there were privately run dame schools set up by respectable women who charged a few pence for basic lessons such as reading and writing. These schools were nearly always held in the residence of the teacher and one such school may have been held at Oakleigh, Knutsford Road, the 1874 Commercial Directory referring to a Miss Miriam Hiles and a ladies boarding school. The 1871 census records a Mary Hill as head of the house, a widow aged 53, her daughter Miriam, unmarried aged 23, a schoolmistress and a stepson James Hill, (a railway clerk)[1] unmarried aged 36. The family were still resident at Oakleigh in 1881 but by 1891 the family had moved. Whether Oakleigh was a boarding or a day school is not known. It is possible that, since James was a railway clerk, the family moved to Chelford from Bury (both Miriam and James were born in Bury) to work on the railway and Miriam set herself up as a schoolteacher.

Until the end of the 19th century education was not compulsory and children were not forced to go to school except by their own parents.

During harvest time children were required by their parents to help with the harvest. A number of schools issued warnings but to little avail as the needs of the

---

1   Chelford in the 19th Century by W. K. Plant

village did not extend to the education of its children. The school Log Books show how difficult it was for the teachers to maintain any sort of continuity. The Log Books and the Managers Meeting Minutes of Chelford School for the second half of the 19th Century show considerable problems relative to the running of the school and at one stage it was doubtful if the school would survive.

The Chelford School Log Books and the Managers Meeting Minutes give a picture of what it was like in the school. It appears that the school floor was only cleaned twice a year and the sanitary arrangements left a lot to be desired. The building would have been cold in winter (even if there had been any form of heating). The seats were hard, loose wooden planks on iron supports, usually with no back support.

If the children were lucky the charity schools may have provided free uniform but in most schools, Chelford included, pupils wore everyday clothes and cast-offs from older children in the family. It was only at the end of the 19th century and the earlier part of the 20th century that school uniform came into common use.

Chelford School Pupils c 1900
Elijah Page – left hand end of second row from back

91

The school Log Books contain details of the 'crimes' committed by the pupils. Punishment was usually by caning with a birch rod kept in water to maintain its suppleness. If the 'crime' was less severe then punishment could be by detention or humiliation in the form of having to wear a dunce's cap or a placard hung around the neck.

From 1891 when attendance at school became compulsory, conditions improved (Chelford school was rebuilt in 1893) and in 1906 a nationwide school meals service was introduced to improve, it was said at the time, the health of the nation's children. In fact prior to this Act, (1875,) Medical Officers of Health had been appointed and district nurses used to visit schools to check for infectious diseases and nits and lice in children's hair.

It was about the turn of the century that many of the present schoolyard games originated, hopscotch, skipping, singing and rhyming, tag, conkers, etc., all hardly changed today.

As far as Chelford is concerned, the earliest documented evidence of the school is the original Deed of Endowment, a copy of which is contained in the Parish Registers[2].

The deed is itself a lengthy document, the following extracts covering the main areas of interest.

5 April 1754

John Parker having built a School and School House at Astle conveys them to Trustees and then appointed to their successors for ever to be elected by the survivors as vacancies occur; by the name Deed of Endowment for the maintenance of the said School as provided by the said John Parker and others, amounting to £250 to be laid out in land. The deed directs the Master for the time being to teach children to read and such other instructions as the Trustees shall direct "and gives him possession of the House," "so long as he shall conform to the Rules therein contained and to such other Rules and orders as shall hereafter be made in pursuance of this Deed". It then directs $^2/_5$ parts of the clear profits to be paid to the School Master for teaching to read English 13 poor children from the townships - Chelford, Astle, Lower Withington, or to the tenants of Mr Parker or his heirs in Nether Alderley, these children now to be appointed by the Trustees the other $^2/_5$ parts of the clear profits to the said Master for teaching to read English 13 poor children from the township of Chelford and Astle - now to be appointed by the Trustees and the remaining $^1/_5$ of the profits to provide books for the School and School repairs and incidental expenses - lastly – no Master is to retain possession of the premises except by permission of the Trustees and the Trustees having the power to make from time to time Rules and Regulations "for the School Master and scholars, which are to equally binding as if they had been contained in the Deed above mentioned".

The Deed of Endowment is dated 1754 and therefore Chelford has had a school since that date. However, there is evidence[3] in the Parish Registers that a school master was resident in Chelford in 1732 with the marriage of Nathaniel Fallowes, schoolmaster, and Esther Booth, both of Chelford, being recorded. Whether Nathaniel Fallowes was a schoolmaster in Chelford or elsewhere and only resident in Chelford is not known. Certainly, as shown by the deed of Endowment, Samuel Kennerley was the schoolmaster in 1754.

Using the P.R., the Census Returns, the Managers' Minutes, School Log Book and Commercial Directories it is possible to establish a list of masters and dates as follows:

1754	-	?	Samuel Kennerley
1769		1778	John Pennington
1788		1828	Not Known
1828		?	James Harvey
1832	-	1839	William Holland
1839	-	1860	Peter Whalley
1860	-	1865	Isaac H Helling
1865	-	1866	Henry Smith
1866	-	1870	John Bruce Reed
1870	-	1874	Mr Hallows
1874	-	1875	Mr Burcham (Temporary appointment)
1875	-	1876	Albert Edward Moody
1876-		1876	I Young
1876	-	1878	J Lucas
1878	-	1914	Elijah Page
1914	-	1927	J Warren Naylor
1927	-	1927	Annie Upson (Temporary)
1927	-	1932	May Grace Hilda Mollart
1932	-	1950	Lilian Cash
1950	-	1973	Dorothy Eliz. Herbert
1973	-	1993	David George Bailey
1993	-		Ruth Taylor

---

[3]   Cheshire County Record Office

Documentary evidence suggests that the original school was on the site of Astle Lodge (called Astle Gate on the Deed of Endowment and subsequently used as the house of the Astle Estate gamekeeper). It is believed that the school was moved to its present site sometime around 1788, and the following information is contained in the Managers' Minutes of 1836.

> "The School House and School were many years since removed from a low damp situation near Astle Gate to their present airy and healthy situation at Chelford - at Col. Parker's expense.

The surviving School Log Books and Managers'/Trustees' Minutes commence in 1839 and by referring to these records it is possible to piece together a picture of how the school developed.

In 1839 the schoolmaster, William Holland, resigned, leaving at Christmas and being replaced by Peter Whalley who remained at the school until 1860.

During Peter Whalley's period of employment, nothing of major importance appears to have taken place. When he died on 11 November 1860, Peter Whalley's widow received the sum of £9, this being a half year's salary due at Christmas.

A Mr Isaac Helling was appointed Master in 1860 remaining at Chelford, until 1865, despite offering his resignation after 15 months.

The next decade proved to be a turbulent period for the school. In March 1865 Mr Helling was cautioned by the Trustees when a complaint was received from a mother of one of the free scholars. Mr Helling was accused of having "beaten her boy on the head with his fists". Several witnesses were examined but the case was not fully proved. He was informed that if similar charges were brought against him he would be dismissed. In April 1865 further complaints were made against the schoolmaster for inefficiency and mis-management of the school, which resulted in several children being removed and sent to other schools. Mr Helling was requested to resign at the next half year (24 June next) as he was no longer considered fit to hold his position at the school. As Mr Helling refused to resign the Trustees had to dismiss him forthwith.

A new Schoolmaster, Mr Henry Smith, formerly master of Addlethorpe National School, Lincolnshire, commenced in July 1865.

Mr Smith resigned his position in September 1866 and was replaced by Mr John Bruce Reed, the latter remaining until he resigned in 1870.

The 1869 Log Book contains the following: -

Joseph G Challinor had been rough in the playground and was reproved. John Mee was absent due to injury by a fall. Pupils Barber, Plant, Potter and Twemlow were commended for careful and exact writing. Twemlow left to go with his parents to Manchester, he sent a pleasing letter before he left. Young Slater was punished by his father by flogging for truancy from school but was not re-admitted. This did not cure him but because he had lost his mother, allowance was needful.

Summary of H. M. Inspectors Report on the School for year ending 31 March 1869.

"The results of this examination are but moderately satisfactory. There is a general want of order and method in the conduct of the School, which must seriously interfere with its efficiency, and until this defect be remedied, little or no progress can be secured. The elementary subjects should receive closer attention, especially the writing. Religious Knowledge fair - Sewing fair."

My Lords have allowed an unreduced Grant with considerable hesitation. Unless better results are shown next year, especially in Arithmetic and the ninth supplementary Rule is strictly observed, the Grant will be reduced under Article 52^d.

The 1870 Log Book contains a summary of the Inspectors' Report stating that 'Mr Hallows deserves great credit for having worked up the school to its present state of efficiency'. However the Trustees' and Managers' Minute Book makes no reference to a Mr Hallows.

Over the next five years the academic performance of the school appears to have improved despite a period in 1871 when the school was closed due to an outbreak of scarlet fever which had broken out in Lower Withington. At least two pupils died of the disease during the epidemic.

By 1874 the average attendance was 46 and there were 63 pupils on the books. The 1874 Log Book contains the following interesting account of an old custom said to take place in this area of the country.

In June 1874 the school had routine work except for Wednesday 6th when the annual Withington Club Walk was held. On 23rd June the children carried out an old custom, practised here and in parts of Lancashire, of locking up the school and taking population of the school in order to compel the breaking up for midsummer. Upon the promise of a pardon the children gave up the population and the breaking up took place the next day.

Albert Edward Moody was appointed as schoolmaster on 27th March 1875 taking over a school that, according to the Inspectors' report for the year ending 31st March 1875, was not totally satisfactory. It said that the school was suffering from the disturbance created by a change of teacher. Examination results were not satisfactory and special attention to writing, spelling and arithmetic was needed. School Master A E Moody, Sewing Mistress, Mrs Moody.

The 1876 report was no better and one tenth was deducted from the grant for faults of instruction. As a result, following a Managers' Meeting in April 1876, Albert Edward Moody was given 3 months notice.

The School Log Book and the Managers' Minutes do not give a clear picture of what followed. The following entry in the Log Book dated August bears no name but it is possible that a Mr I Young was the writer.

"I this day enter my protest against the way in which this school is carried on. The house and school are in a most shameful condition and the water closets for most parts unroofed. The way in which the stipend is raised is so complicated that some teachers, on the arrival at Chelford, have immediately left again declaring that they have been deceived.

I should surely advise any teacher who may come here (for I pity the man) to adopt this course as a protracted stay will only entangle him in greater expense. As my pocket has been hurt in coming here and as I thoroughly believe that no good will be done under the present arrangements, I have made this protest out of duty to those who may succeed me in this most disgusting situation."

There then follows a rebuttal.

22nd September - I Young, Ex-pupil teacher (Art 60), has been in charge of the school since 10 July his entry is as false as it is impertinent. On 26th Mr I Lucas this day takes possession of the school premises. Mrs Lucas to act as Sewing Mistress - D J Paterson

Certainly, sometime around this period Joseph Lucas was appointed Master, a record in the Log Book under his name stating: -

I have found the scholars in a very backward state and few in number, very much is required to bring them to an efficient state having all reduced to the lowest extremity, the apparatus, poor.

The Log Book and Minute Book entries appear to differ in that the Log book states Mr I Lucas took possession of the school with Mrs Lucas acting as Sewing Mistress on 26 September 1876. The Minute Book states that Mr J Lucas was appointed as Schoolmaster at the meeting held on 8 November 1876. The Log book also says on 6 October 1876, Mr Joseph Lucas was appointed Master of the school commencing 2 October.

Joseph Lucas didn't last long either, as on the 18th January 1878 he was given 3 months notice and the Rev. Paterson was authorised to look for a new master.

At the Managers' meeting on 20th March 1878 the testimonials of Elijah Page were presented and on 31st March 1878, even though he was not a certified Master, he was taken on at a salary not to exceed £52 per annum with Mrs Page allowed £6 per annum as Assistant Mistress.

The appointment of Elijah Page turned out to be a stroke of luck. He, more than anybody, built up the school and his name is still respected within the village.

The number of pupils continued to grow and by January 1885 the school numbered 43 boys and 39 girls. It was said that the increase in attendance was probably due to the practice of prize giving for good attendance.

In October of 1885 Mrs Page became ill and she died on 26 January 1886. It was recorded that she was satisfactory in her manner and had taken the infants' class and taught the girls sewing.

Early in 1887 a free gift of a playground was given for the use of the school by Sir George Dixon.

Between 1886 and 1890 the school was closed on a number of occasions due to epidemics of whooping cough and scarlet fever.

The Managers' meeting of 29th August 1891 decided that education should be free to all scholars in the school and to ask certain parents of scholars to become subscribers to the school.

At the meeting held on 7th July 1892 it was decided that the accommodation of the School was insufficient and the construction of a new classroom approved.

It is not clear from the Log Book and the Managers' Minutes whether the new school was built in 1891 or 1892 or whether it was necessary to build a new classroom after the school was rebuilt. The 1891 Log Book contains the following: -

The new school was not yet finished by the end of September but the children attended as well as could be expected under the present circumstances. By October 7th because of difficulties for the children working created by the colder weather it was feared that a holiday would have to be given and by 14th the children were sent home until the new school was finished.

According to the records, the children returned to the 'New School' on 24th October.

The dimensions of the school were stated to be: -

School room	Length 40 ft	Breadth 24 ft	Height 16.5 ft
Classroom	Length 20 ft	Breadth 16 ft	Height 16.5 ft

The debt on the rebuilding of the school was cleared by 1895 and money was allocated for the building of a new pettie and for enlarging the playground.

At the end of 1895 the number of children on the school books had risen to 106 (55 boys and 51 girls) with an average attendance of 85.2%.

Miss Page, who had been assistant teacher for two years at a salary of £6 per year, retired to get married and Miss Hewitt was appointed.

Towards the end of the century the school was used for evening classes to meet the need of the working classes for further education.

The 1898 Log Book contained the following: -

Because the school had been closed for over a month because of an epidemic of measles, it had been excused the annual examination. Miss Hewitt was regularly late arriving at school which resulted in other people having to stand in for her class until she arrived. In November Fred Bloor, F Blackhurst, W Haigh, T Fryer, J Bagnall and P Slater were punished for throwing snow after being told to stop by the Master.

and in 1899, the following: -

Miss Hewit arrived at 9.30 on 11 January - late again. The Governing Body of the Chester Diocesan Association had granted £20 Grant Aid in order to increase the staff for the current year. In March Mrs Ward washed the school for the first time this year. On 24th March Miss Hewitt was late again and Kate Meikle had to teach the infants in her absence. In August Miss Edwards, a student, taught for a week while she was on holiday from Warrington College. In November a concert was held one evening in the schoolroom, the proceed to be for the relief of sick and of the present war. The proceeds from the children's entertainment was £5.10s.0d which was paid to the vicar.

Miss Hewitt used to travel to School from Davenham every week by bicycle. During the week she lodged in the village.

At the turn of the century it would appear that in addition to Elijah Page, lessons were taught by Miss Hewitt and Miss Bishop, both receiving a salary of £37.10s.9d per year. Miss Bishop resigned in December 1901 and Miss Yvonne Elizabeth Cheetham was appointed as Assistant Teacher in the school.

The Education Act of 1902 came into force on 1 July and, to meet the Act, four Foundation Managers (Col. Dixon, Rev. Stanhope, Mr M A Tatton and Mr J D Haigh) were appointed.

To celebrate the opening of the new school a separate publication is being prepared containing full details of the school through the first half of the 20th century. The following is a summary of events over this period.

Entering the 20th century, we see the introduction of the new Education Act in 1902 and in 1903 notice had to be given to the Education Authorities when the school was to be closed for a day or half a day when needed. In 1904 Chelford School joined the Church School Association. In May 1904 it was resolved that 4 weeks summer holiday be taken consecutively commencing after mid-July.

During the first half of the century the school was regularly closed due to epidemics of measles, german measles, chickenpox and scarlet fever. There were also regular school visits by the village doctor, Dr Shepard, and the school nurse.

CHELFORD SCHOOL JULY 1955 – MISS HERBERT AT THE PIANO

The number of pupils at the school was very high in those early days and in 1906 there were 104 children on the register. The school hours varied from winter to summer – 8.30 a.m. to 3.30 p.m. in winter and 9 a.m. to 4 p.m. in summer. The flagpole (since disappeared) was used to depict significant events such as the death of HM the King in 1910 when the school was closed for three days. The number of pupils increased dramatically in 1941 when 31 evacuees were admitted to the school from the Manchester Education Authority and 24 from Walthomstow, London.

Major events in the life of the village were celebrated by the school and its children. Col. Dixon of Astle Hall gave the children and teachers of the school and Sunday school regular treats at the Hall, with games and racing for prizes. They were also invited to tea at the Hall to celebrate the Coming of Age of John Dixon. Empire Day on 22nd May 1925 was celebrated by half-day holiday from school and the children and teachers were again invited to afternoon tea and sport at Astle Hall by Lady Dixon. A trip to Blackpool was organised in July 1931 in which 55 pupils attended and the children's fares were were paid for by funds raised by the Annual Rose Day Festival held earlier in the month. The rest of the proceeds from the Rose Day went to pay for the installation of electric lighting in the school.

Like all schools, Chelford School has had its 'peaks' and 'troughs' but it has survived very well through the two World Wars of the 20th century and the dramatically changing world. A new era is beginning with the relocation of the school from Alderley Road to Oak Road in September 1999. To continue the tradition, Chelford Parish Council are presenting the school with a new flagpole and flags.

CHELFORD PRIMARY SCHOOL – VICTORY PARTY
6TH OCTOBER 1945

Back row: - Alan Dakin, Kenneth Jackson, Kenneth Moss, Brian Bush, John Baskerville, Geoff Burgess, Elizabeth Newton, Nancy Dale, Doris Walton.
Middle row: - Phillis Barber, Marjorie Lowe, Peter Newton, Kenneth Hamilton, Donald Burgess, Clive Moulton, Brian Mottram, Gwyneth Bromley, Hilda Burgess, Audrey Bailley, Margaret Newton, Donald Lowe, ? ...?, Jill Newton.
Front row: - Wilfred Dykes, Alan Moulton, Barbara Gibbon, John Oliver, John Sproston, John Barber, Alan Baskerville, Kenneth Bromley, Audrey Rowbotham, Lincoln Dakin, Joan Baskerville, Joyce Newton, Hilda Normansell, Rita Snelson, Sheila Lowe, Paul Carrington.

Chelford School Victory Day Celebration tea.

The School Log Book for 1873 contains a list of songs sung regularly in school by the children.

The words and music of two of these songs have been found in the 1861 issue of The Glasgow Infant School Magazine as follows: -

THE LITTLE BIRD.

To be sung slowly.

Oh do not frighten or destroy   The lit - tle bird with golden wing, That carols forth the notes of joy,   To cheer us   in the time of spring, To cheer us   in the   time of spring.

See how she nestles on the bough,
And nourishes her tender young;
Mark how her warm affections flow,
And listen to her gentle song.

'Tis cruel to distrurb her nest,
Or pilfer to supply a cage;
We, who with liberty are blest,
Should never in such acts engage.

THE COCKATOO.

There is a bird of plumage rare, Which oft in gild - ed cage we view; Pro-cur'd with cost, preserv'd with care, We mean the gaudy cock-a - too. He is a bird of price and fame, And talks as parrots of - ten do; For if we ask him what's his name, He'll say 'Tis pret-ty cock-a - to Cock - a - too, cock-a - too, pret - ty, pret - t cock - a - too, His answer is to all you say, Just pret - ty, pret - ty cock - a - too.

103

The following is a list of songs (including the two shown above) at the school in 1873.

The school song	*From Turners school songs*
Address to spring	*Mullah's*
To farmyard	*Mullah's*
The Ploughboy	*Mullah's*
Be kind to each other	*Hunters*
Good Order	*Training school song book*
The Daisy	*" " "*
The frost looked forth	*" " "*
Lateness for school	*" " "*
Song to my mother	*" " "*
The Cockatee	*" " "*
Love at Home	*"family friend" 1870*
Little Bird	*Children's friend 1872*

CHELFORD SCHOOL CHILDREN 1999

MISS HERBERT RETIRES

Miss Herbert receives her gift from Canon M J B Henry

Between them is Miss E Woodcock and, on the right, the assistant mistress, Mrs N Hargreaves.

After 23 years as headmistress at Chelford C. of E. Controlled School, Miss Dorothy E Herbert retired on 31 August 1973.

On Friday, at a presentation ceremony at the school, Miss Herbert was given a Minton bowl and cheque on behalf of parents, friends and staff. Canon M J B Henry, Vicar of Chelford, made the presentation.

Miss Herbert, of The School House, Chelford, had taught for 40 years and always in Cheshire. Before moving to Chelford, she taught at Woods Lane Secondary School, Cheadle Hulme. On her retirement however, she will move to Hampton-in-Arden, Warwickshire.

Her successor will be Mr D G Bailey, who lives in Macclesfield and at present teaches at Prestbury.

CHELFORD SHOP AND POST OFFICE

According to Josie and Dennis Parfitt who owned the shop and Post Office from 1961 to 1976, the building was constructed in the middle of the 17th century using jet black oak timber beams normally associated with the building of sailing ships. In fact the beams are curved as in the prow of a ship and as Middlewich was at that time a boat building centre, it is possible that the beams came from that area. Whether the building was constructed as a shop or was just a cottage is not known.

The earliest record of a shop in Chelford occurs in the Parish Register for 1739 when the baptism of Mary, daughter of Samuel and Sarah Tomson, (subsequently spelt Thompson) Grocer, is recorded on 10 April. Subsequently their son William was baptised on 21 January 1740.

Samuel died on 1st October 1765 aged 73 years and Sarah died on 29th February 1772 aged 68 years.

The next reference to a grocer in Chelford is the baptism of Joseph, son of John and Anne Jackson, on 29th April 1753. At some time between 1740 and 1753 the Jacksons must have taken over the shop. The marriage of a John Jackson to Ann Deakin, both of Chelford, is recorded in the Register on 22nd May 1752 and on the fairly safe assumption that this couple is the same family, they must have taken over the shop between mid 1752 and early 1753.

There are no further references in the Registers to either a shopkeeper or grocer until 19th November 1815 when the baptism of Mary, daughter of William and Hannah Turner, Grocer, is recorded. A daughter had previously been baptised on 16th January 1814 when, William was described as a Gamekeeper. Whether William 'doubled' up as a grocer and a gamekeeper is not known.

In 1822 the first reference to a shopkeeper occurs with the baptism of John, son of William and Ann Gilbert, on 22nd September.

By 1827 the Gilberts had moved to be proprietors of the Archers Inn and in 1830 there is the first reference to William and Hannah Dale, a Grocer, when their son, Job was baptised on 7th March.

The Parish Register of 1834 contains a reference to the baptism of Isabella, daughter of William and Hannah Dale, when William's profession is stated as Grocer and Shopkeeper.

On the 1834 Conveyance, when the Dixons acquired the Astle Estate, the property on the site of the existing Post Office is described as 'a shop, warehouse, outbuilding, gardens and lands with a total area of 6 acres.

The 1841 Census lists William Dale, aged 35 (recorded down to the nearest five) as a shopkeeper, his family comprising of his wife, Hannah, aged 30, Job aged 11 and his daughter, Isabella aged 7.

William Dale died on 11th August 1842 aged 37 years and his wife, Hannah, took over the shop. The 1851 Census contains the following information:

Chelford Shop	Hannah Dale	Head	Widow	44	Provision shopkeeper farming 3 acres	born Manchester
	Isabella Dale	Dau.	UM	17		born Chelford
	Harry Davies	Servant UM		20	General Servant	born Astle

Hannah died on 23rd February 1861 aged 54 years having given up the shop some years previously, probably, based on information from the Parish Registers, some time between March 1852 and April 1854. James Jackson Gledhill, the next resident, was listed as a Coachman on the occasion of his son, Thomas Heald Gledhill's, baptism on 7th March 1852 and a Shopkeeper when his son James, was baptised on 30th April 1854.

Within the next two years the shop had become the Post Office, the register entry of the baptism on 20th April 1856 of Maria, daughter of James Jackson Gledhill and Mary Ann Gledhill describing James Jackson as a Postmaster.

Therefore a Post Office must have been established on its present site between April 1854 and April 1856, one of the oldest, if not the oldest Post Office in the NorthWest still on its original site.

Whites Commercial Directory of 1860 contains the following information:

'Post Office at James Jackson Gledhill. Letters arrive from Congleton at 7.00 a.m. and are despatched at 6.15 p.m.'

The 1861 Census describes James J Gledhill as a Postmaster and Shopkeeper and in the 1871 Census, as a Shopkeeper and Coachmaker. By 1871 a servant had been added to the household, no doubt reflecting the increased importance of the Post Office to the village.

The expanding activity of the Post Office is also reflected in the 1871 Commercial Directory, which contains the following description: -

James Jackson Gledhill, Grocer, CoachBuilder and Postmaster.

Post Office – James Jackson Gledhill, Postmaster. Letters from Crewe delivered at 7.00 a.m. and 2.15 p.m.: despatched at 11.20 a.m. and 8.30 p.m. on weekdays and on Sundays, delivered at 7.00 a.m. and despatched at 8.30 p.m. only.

According to the 1881 Census, James Jackson Gledhill's eldest son, Thomas H Gledhill, had taken over as Postmaster, being listed as a Brewer in addition to Postmaster and Shopkeeper.

Sometime between 1881 and 1891 the Post Office was taken over by John David Haigh, the husband of James Jackson Gledhill's daughter, Maria. By 1891 the shop employed a Shop Assistant and Telegraph Clerk in addition to a General Servant.

CHELFORD POST OFFICE c 1910

In the course of the 20th century the shop has been owned by a number of people including, in the early part of the century, the Hague family followed by

| ? | to | 1946 | Mr and Mrs Carter |
| 1946 | to | 1951 | Mr and Mrs Hides |

1951	to	1961	Ivy and James Robertson
1961	to	1976	Josie and Dennis Parfitt
1976	to	1978	? and Stanley Stretton
1978	to	1982	Maureen and Jack Hancock
1982	to	1988	Peggy and Peter Jung
1988	to		Ruth and Bernard Annikin

When the Parfitts took over in 1959 one of the first things that they did was to enlarge the shop to its present size. The original entrance through the porch was bricked up and a snooker table given to the local scouts so that the shop could be enlarged.

The Annikin family arrived on the 23rd February 1988. On the 24th July of that year a driver approaching from Macclesfield lost control of his car which mounted the kerb and entered the shop. Even though it was pension morning there was no option but to close the shop as the building was declared unsafe. The shop remained closed for 10 days.

For safety reasons the Post Office section was moved to the far end of the shop and in June 1994 a complete refit saw the removal of the old shelving and cubby holes of the original telephone exchange.

Post Office business continues to expand, partly as a result of the closure of the Post Office at Over Peover and the reduction of hours at Lower Withington, making the Chelford shop the main Post Office serving a large rural area.

The story of this ancient shop would not be complete without its ghost. Dennis and Josie Parfitt have confirmed that on a number of occasions, with the shop empty they experienced the smell of thick twist as though somebody had just lit a pipe. It was always in the same place, in an area through the present door where the telephone exchange and letter collection used to be. Maybe one of the local rural postmen coming to collect his deliveries.

Josie Parfitt, Jenny Lowe and Susan Chadwick – c 1965

Amy E Jones, Rose Bank, Chelford
                                    July 1908

To think kindly of each other is good,
To speak kindly of each other is better,
To act kindly one towards another is best of all.

MAIL COACH
by Mrs L Findlow of Macclesfield

This is a picture of my Grandfather, Joseph Robinson, who was the driver of the Royal Mail Coach, which ran between Macclesfield and Chelford from 1870 – 1900. Royal Mail was taken from Park Green Post Office to Chelford Railway Station to connect with the midnight train to Crewe. The main line did not run through Macclesfield in those days. For 30 years he did this journey, 7 nights a week.

John David Haigh and Maria (nee Gledhill) together with children at front of Post Office c 1895. John David Haigh was resident Postmaster from 1882 to c1916.

CHELFORD PARISH HALL

The Reverend Colin E B Bell, Vicar of Chelford, wrote in the Parish Magazine – August 1907 – "We do need a Parish Room for which ramifications in connection with parish work can grow, a room for the transaction of parochial business, and where Bible Classes, Choir Practices, Mother's Meetings, Bellringers and other Guild meetings may be held; where the Library can be carried on and all social gatherings take place, fitted too with a gymnasium and other recreation for the young men in the evening. This is sorely needed."

The parish moved quickly for in the November Magazine we read, "A Meeting was held in the Schoolroom on Monday, 30th September, Colonel Dixon presiding. A Committee was elected consisting of the Rev. C E B Bell, Messrs A H Dixon, F M S Grant, JD Haigh, G Moss, H J Reiss, Dr. A H Shepard, Messrs J Snelson, R A Tatton, J L Walsh, G S Welsh, T Wilson Jnr., which met on the following Saturday when it was resolved that plans and estimates should be secured from two firms.

An appeal leaflet was issued at the beginning of 1908. "Subscriptions are now invited for the erection of a Parish Room in Chelford. It is intended that there shall be one large room for Gymnasium, Meetings, Entertainments, Dances etc., and smaller ones for Reading and other purposes. Col. Dixon has very generously given land for the site. £750 will be required, but if more is forthcoming it can well be used."

By June 1908 it was reported that satisfactory progress had been made and the plans of Messrs Massey & Sons of Alderley Edge had been selected with the ground already staked out and work on the foundations about to begin.

A List of first subscriptions was published

A H Dixon Esq. £100, R A Tatton Esq. £100, F M S Grant Esq. £100, Col Dixon, £50 plus the land, E Broadhurst Esq. £50, Lord Egerton, £25, H J Reiss Esq. £25, G S Weelsh, £10, Dr Shepard, £5, J Moxon Esq. £5, Lady Elphinstone, £2, Mr Tipping, £2-2-0, Mr S Clarke, 10s, Chelford Working Guild (sewing), over £100 "in instalments".

The hall was officially opened on 30th July 1908. The land was donated by Colonel George Dixon but the pressure to have the hall built seems to have come from the then vicar of Chelford, the Reverend Colin Bell. He, with Colonel George Dixon and Frank Morrison Seafield Grant of Mere Leigh, Chelford, were the original trustees of the hall which is a self-supporting registered charity.

OFFICIAL OPENING OF VILLAGE HALL

Master Gresswell, Mrs Gresswell, Mr W Gledhill, Mr E Barber, Mr R Bradley, Mr T Wilson, Mr J Moss, Mr Haigh, Mrs Royds, Col. Dixon J.P: (Centre), Mrs Bell, Mrs Dixon, Major Alan Sykes, Mr Patten, Rev. Colin Bell.

114

By October 1908 the following rules applied:-

❑ The Club will be open between the hours of 6 pm and 9.30 pm (Sundays excepted).
❑ No newspapers, books, or other publications, shall be removed from the Reading Room.
❑ No beer or spirituous liquors allowed to be sold.

A Souvenir and Quotation Book was produced by the committee and sold at the Great Opening Bazaar in order to raise further funds. The cover was printed in gold on black and a surviving copy is reproduced here. The total count of contributors was 128 and some of their offerings are scattered within this book. It is hoped to reproduce the complete book at a later date.

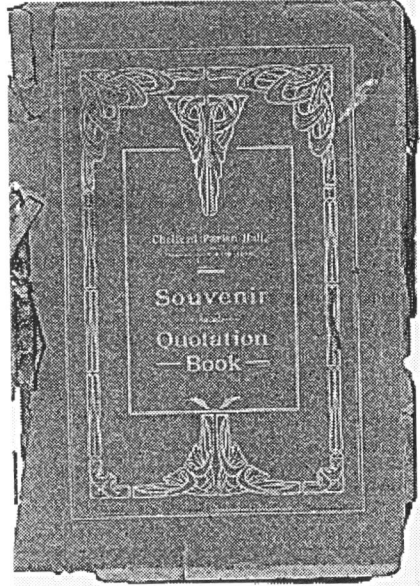

It appears from the records which still exist that the hall was first used primarily as a billiard club (the first account book refers to "Chelford Parish Club") and a reading room. In keeping with the moral tone of the time, the original trust deed stated that "no malt spirit or intoxicating liquors shall be sold or consumed on the premises". It was not until 1974 that the Charity Commissioners approved a scheme removing that restriction although one of the trustees at that time observed that it "was not always observed"! Dances were also held regularly for which the pianist (who appears to have been the sole musician) was paid five shillings (25p) for his evening's work.

The original building (which is still in place under the present cladding) was timber sparred and remained as originally built until the 1950's when the stage extension was erected and central heating installed (inside toilets were added in 1945). Electricity was connected to the hall in 1931 but, prior to that, lighting had been provided by acetylene produced on site from calcium carbide. The hall was heated by coal until the improvements of the 1950's when oil central heating was installed. At that time, the land for what is now the car park was transferred to the trustees.

In 1989 serious structural problems arose which would clearly cost a great deal to rectify and certainly more than the sum of £15,000, which was then held. The cost of renovating and extending the hall (to include surfacing and draining the car park) totalled £150,000 funded by generous personal and corporate donations and a wide variety of fund raising functions, principally Car Boot Sales. The result of much hard work is a well-used hall, which should not need any major expenditure for many years.

An appeal booklet was produced in 1989 which carried the following letter from Rev'd John Ellis:

"The green hut is a lifeline for the village. Everything relies on it – from the under-fives to the over-sixties, from the badminton to the bingo, organisations like the W.I., Chelford Players and numerous other groups and individuals for their social and fund-raising events. Over the years many thousands of pounds must have been earned for various causes through the use of its facilities.

The Village Hall has another function – to unite the whole community. It is perhaps the only thing we all in Chelford have in common. It belongs to us all. During its 80 year history it has been a focal point for the village. Within its walls have taken place events of serious importance, of celebration, and lots of fun. It has served us well.

Now it needs the village, with the help of wider support, to unite in serving it. To guarantee its future for the service of generations to come. In my experience there is no surer way to unite a body of people than working together to meet a challenge. The amount of money needed is not phenomenal by today's values. We can do it – and we can find great enjoyment and satisfaction in the process.

The group of local worthies who proudly stood to be photographed outside the hall after the opening ceremony on 30th July 1908 might be grateful to know that their work has endured so long and achieved so much. Now it's *our turn to build for the present and the future – an improved and extended Village Hall to serve the Chelford of the next 80 years and more."*

The Souvenir and Quotation Book produced for the opening of the original hall contained a contribution submitted by W J Farrington and entitled 'A Psalm of (Chelford) Life'.

A Psalm of (Chelford) Life

Tell us not, in doleful numbers,
"Chelford's Hall is but a dream",
Say no more that Chelford slumbers,
We're less stolid than we seem.

Generous friends have come to aid us,
Friends to plan, to give, to act;
Of their kindness none can raid us,
Now our Parish Hall's a fact.

Other places might remind us,
We were not yet "Up to Date";
This reproach we leave behind us,
We have wiped it off our slate!

Much instruction and enjoyment,
We may from our Hall derive;
Much relief from our employment,
So may mind and body thrive.

Thanks to all kind-hearted donors,
May their gifts long valued be;
May theirs be rewards and honours
Now and in posterity.

Let us welcome all around us,
Unto this our Opening Fete;
Let all people that surround us
Know our Hall is "Up-to-Date".

Mr Farrington, if he were still alive, would surely have been gratified to learn that his hopes for the future of the hall were realised and that "generous friends" have continued to aid the hall in time of need.

117

ARAB-LIKE
VILLAGERS

DELVING INTO WELLS
FOR WATER, OR-

SIX-MILE TREK

From Our Special Correspondent
CHELFORD, Friday.

There are 350 inhabitants in the Cheshire village of Chelford – but no water supply! They get water like Arabs in an Oriental dessert, from wells dug deep into the ground, or by horse and cart from district miles away.

If a farm labourer in Chelford is not lucky enough to find a well-spring on his small plot of land, or if he cannot afford to send a milk-float, six miles to Alderley Edge for a supply, he has to go thirsty unless it rains!

Aeroplane drops over Chelford; high speed cars glide through its narrow lanes; newspapers are delivered here every day. But Moses at the dessert rock had a better supply of pure water.

Out of the Bare Rock

The seven or eight large houses in Chelford districts have taken a hint from Moses and fashioned their own gushers out of the bare rock.

They have spent scores of pounds on equipping themselves with supplies of well-water, and now that it is suggested that Chelford should be put on the Stockport Corporation pipe-supply they are not so keen.

It would mean an increase in the rates, and they say "why bother?" For they already have a satisfactory source of water.

And so have the rest of the inhabitants – when it rains.

Farm labourers form mainly the rest of the inhabitants, add they cannot afford even the £3 minimum levy which has been suggested by the Ministry of Health.

"The well water obtained hereabouts is definitely not healthy," said one of Chelford's two doctors, to a *Manchester Evening News* representative. "But I don't want my name mentioning as having said that, I prefer to keep out of the whole business."

In Buckets from Ponds

The village's water champion is Mr. L. Walsh, who has drawn the attention of the Minister of Health to the fact that cottagers had to get their water from ponds, carried in buckets across fields, or by milk-float from districts six miles away.

Some had even been reduced to begging water from farmers after it had been used to cool milk.

Mr. Walsh is a realist.

The Macclesfield Rural District Council are trying to get their schemes passed to give Chelford its much-needed water supply. They want to get the job done, and talk about who shall pay for it afterwards.

The Ministry of Health have approved their plan-on paper. But before they sanction its commencement they demand that all Chelford shall be canvassed to say how much they are willing to pay for the privilege of having healthy water.

"We have been held up for more that a year by that canvas," said a Rural District Council official to-day.

Twelve Months' Wait

"We have already prepared and submitted a scheme to the Ministry of Health. The scheme is to supply water to Chelford and the neighbouring village of Snelson from the Stockport Corporation.

"It was in response to a suggestion from the Cheshire County Council that we first drafted the scheme twelve months ago. But the matter now is entirely in the hands of the Ministry of Health.

"The inhabitants of Chelford and Snelson, numbering 541 precisely, will have to find £6,800 between them. The County Council will make a grant of assistance, as will the rural district and the Ministry of Health.

"Big houses do not want to contribute anything. They have their own supplies, they say. And the small houses cannot afford to contribute.

"I think we ought to be getting on with the job, instead of trying to persuade money out of these cottagers on the grounds of moral liability!"

M Wood, Knutsford Road, Wilmslow   July 1908

O, wad some pow'r the giftie ie us,
To see oursel's as others see us!

Emily Hague, Fallows Hall, Chelford July 1908

Be unto others kind and true,
As you would have others be to you.

Billy Grundy   July 1908

None takes his way alone;
All that we send into the lives of others,
Comes there is a destiny which makes us brothers,
back into our own.

119

THE MANOR HOUSE

The house which is situated on the left-hand side of Macclesfield Road immediately prior to the Chelford roundabout is a mixture of Tudor, Stuart, Georgian and Victorian styles. The forecourt is largely seventeenth century, the south side principally Georgian and that which is seen from the road to Holmes Chapel is mostly nineteenth century.

Its origins are not entirely clear – it is certainly one of the oldest residences in Chelford. The timber-framed barn to the north of the house erected in close proximity to the field which adjoins the church and old glebe house suggests that it probably served as the parish tithe barn. The size of this barn and solidity of construction indicates a 16th century date.

Of the house itself it is known that in 1671 John and Mary Brooke lived there, an inscription carved over the west doorway reading:

> John)   Brooke   ECCL 2.11
> Mary) 1671

However, this may be misleading as the beam appears to be late Tudor and may have been part of the modifications to enlarge the size of the original Tudor house. It is only after entering through the old doorway that a stone passage is encountered and the walling of the ancient Tudor house is seen. The whole of the eastern wall of the long passage is of timber framing of the late fifteenth century placed on plinths of local stone, the panels between the main uprights being filled with original wattle and daub. The rough-hewn timbers are extremely hard and probably formed the outer west end of the original Tudor house.

The north east wall of a first floor passageway contains a number of windows, a pane of the smaller window bearing the following inscription scratched by some sharp implement.

Date and signatures written with a diamond on one of the landing windows.

120

The house was for many years the home of the Brookes family of which there were several branches. On the death of Robert Salisbury Brookes Esq. in 1814, this branch of the family became extinct in the male line and it appears that soon after this date the house was divided into a number of different residences.

The Land Tax Returns for the period are not clear. There is a farm and land owned by R J Brooke and occupied by John Broadhurst in 1785 and Edward Broadhurst in 1795. The same property is occupied by a John Walker in 1815 and owned by the Executors to the late R J Brooke. Whether this property included the Manor House is not clear for the Mellor family who are known to have resided in the house at a later date are also listed in the Land Tax Returns[1].

From the mid 19th century records it is obvious that a number of families resided in the house, certainly two and possibly three. The 1832 Register of Electors, the 1841 and 1851 Census returns and the list of Parliamentary Electors for 1845/6 list George and Hannah Beech as occupiers of Manor House Farm. Additionally, the Land Tax returns of 1825 list George Beech, as occupier of a farm owned by Miss Furnival. There is however no reference to a George Beech in earlier Land Tax returns.

The 1851 Census lists both a Manor House Farm and a Manor House. George and Hannah Beech lived in the farm and Charles Nichols, a coal engineer, and his wife, Hannah, lived in the Manor House.

In the 1860 Commercial Directories, Charles Nichols was listed as a bridgemaster and surveyor in the county of Chester and Thomas Beech (obviously the son of George) as a farmer at the Manor House. The 1861 Census lists the same Thomas Beech as a farmer of 100 acres at Manor House Farm.

Unfortunately the 1871 Census does not offer any clarification. The enumerator listed the property in the Macclesfield Road area recording William Bloor and family (a farmer of 56 acres), Thomas Bradford and family (a farmer of 125 acres), Charles Nichols (County Bridgemaster) and Henry Seaman together with Duncan Campbell, joint occupiers.

By 1874 the Commercial Directory lists Samuel Read as a farmer at Manor House Farm, Charles Nichols resident at Dale Fields and a Wm Mc Connell Esq. as resident at the Manor.

---

1   Chelford in the 19th Century by W Keith Plant

The position is clarified somewhat by the 1881 Census which records Samuel Baskerville and family as resident at Abbey Farm, Samuel Read and family resident at Manor Farm and Henry G Seaman (a Bank Cashier) together with James S Daly (a Barrister at Law) as joint owners of the Manor House.

Photographs of Charles and Hannah Nichols in the possession of John Gledhill provide written confirmation that they lived at Dalefield House.

From the 1891 Census it is quite clear that the residents of the Manor House were Henry Seaman, a Bank Manager, and his wife, Jessie. Frederick P Dixon, (Henry Seaman's brother-in-law) and his wife Olive Dixon were also recorded as being in the house. Frederick Dixon was the son of John Dixon of Astle Hall. The family had a cook, a parlour maid, a kitchen maid and a housemaid.

Manor Farm at this time (1891) was still occupied by Samuel Baskerville and his family.

From the 1891 Census, it was apparent that this area of the village was heavily populated. In addition to the house and farm, there were two families living in Manor House Yard, Mr Gray,(a coachman) his wife and five children, Mr Evans, (a gardener), his wife and three children and Richard Devine, a servant from Ireland living in Manor Farm Building.

There is one other reference to this area of the village. In the 1834 Conveyance where William Mellor is shown as resident in a farm in the area of the Manor House. He is recorded in the 1861 Census but not in the 1871 Census. At the time of the 1834 Conveyance, William Mellor was farming over 145 acres in an area on either side of Knutsford Road from the Village Green to the boundary with Marthall.

A William Mellor appears in the 1825 Land Tax Assessments, the sum assessed as £3.9s.0d. He is also listed in the 1815 assessments. However in the records for 1795, the farm assessed at £3.9s.0d is in the occupation of James Mellor. It is obvious from the assessment records that in 1785 a George Corner occupied the farm.

The Parish Records show that a James Mellor died in 1815 aged 30 and it is probable that James and William were in fact brothers with William taking over the farm when James died.

The proprietor of the land between 1785 and 95 was a William Lowe who owned land throughout the village.

William Mellor was married twice, firstly to Hannah and according to the Registers had four children, Joseph baptised 1809, Robert baptised 1810 and twins, Hannah and Elizabeth, baptised June 1812. Hannah died on the 2nd February 1812 age 32, presumably whilst giving birth to the twins. William then married Mary and a total of ten further children were born, George 1816, William 1817, Isaac 1819, Mary 1821, Thomas 1823, James 1825 (died 1843), John 1827 (died one month after being born), John 1828 (died 1836), Anne 1831 and Jane 1836. A large family even by the standards of the time.

In addition to this large number of children, according to their gravestone, two sons, Samuel in 1803 and William in 1804. were born to William and Hannah.

The 1851 Census records William Mellor as farming 120 acres with the reduction of 25 acres since 1834 probably constituting the area around the railway station purchased by the railway company.

The 1860 Commercial Directory lists Thomas Mellor as a farmer who must have taken over the farm from his father in the 1850's.

By 1871 the Mellor family had disappeared from the census returns.

Throughout the 19th century the house would have presented an entirely different picture to that of today. It is known that around 1870 the courtyard to the house was divided into sections to serve the needs of a farmer tenant and an odd assembly of lean-to buildings placed against the old structure completely hid much of the ancient timber framing. An assortment of rain tubs collected water from the roofs and a giant pump occupied the centre space of the present lawn to the north of the house. From old photographs of the time it can be seen that much of the house had the appearance of having been drenched in whitewash. To complete the picture of a rural farmhouse, hens are seen to have free range over the forecourt, whilst wooden milking pails are observed drying on the cobbled walks[2].

It was at about this time that the house was divided into three, the main portion being occupied by Henry Seaman and James Daly in 1881.

In 1895 Richard Tatton acquired the house, adding another wing to the north and west.

Some time after the Tattons left, Lady Victoria Murray leased the house and made extensive structural and decorative improvements.

---

2   Cheshire Life August 1952

According to a list of Chelford residents' in 1924 a Geoffrey Key lived at the Manor House.

In 1927 Mr Bertram Everall Shiers purchased the freehold of the property from the Astle Estate.

M Haig, Chelford   *July 1908*

A little bit of patience often makes the sunshine come,
And a little bit of love makes a very happy home,
A little bit of hope makes a rainy day look gay,
And a little bit of charity makes glad a weary way

Fague, Chelford   *July 1908*

Owd Time – He's a troublesome codger-
Keeps nudgin' us on to decay,
An' whispers, "Yo'ur nobbutt a lodger,
Get ready for gooin' away".

MANOR HOUSE

125

MERE COURT

Mereleigh, as the property was formerly known, was built around 1862. There is no reference to it in the 1861 Census returns and, as the original conveyance of 1862 shows that the property was sold by John Dixon to J. H. White, it is therefore probable that this was the year when the house was built.

The property was probably called Mereleigh because the word Mere means 'boundary' and Mereleigh lay on the boundary of the ecclesiastical parishes of Chelford and Marthall.

According to the 1871 Census, James H Murray and his wife, Blanche were living in the property, and on the night of the Census, (5 April 1871) James's sister-in-law, Evelyn S Stanley and five servants were present. James was recorded as aged 30, a cotton spinner, born in Manchester and his wife aged 27, born Brighton, Sussex.

By 1874, the Commercial Directories list a Frank Glover as resident and in the 1881 Census a Johnson P Smith, his wife, Isabella, a step daughter, a daughter and two sons. Also resident at the time of the Census was a school governess and three servants[1]. Johnson P Smith was recorded as a Home Trade Merchant aged 47, born in Worsley, Lancs.

A different family was resident in 1891, with an Edward W Bother, a 37 year old Barrister at Law and his family together with five servants (including a coachman) being recorded in the census of that year.

In 1895 Mereleigh was bought by J W Glover (perhaps a relative of the Frank Glover who lived there in 1874) and sold once again in 1907, this time to Frank Grant who lived there until 1921.

Between 1921 and 1928 Mereleigh had a further three owners before being bought by Philip Boddington of brewery fame. Philip Boddington lived with his family at Mereleigh until he died in 1953. It was he who changed the name to Merecourt.

Since the original building of the house it had grown from a modest house to a relatively large manor house with extensive gardens and paddocks.

---

[1]   Chelford in the 19th Century by W Keith Plant

On Mr Boddington's death, Merecourt was bought by Macclesfield District Council who intended to use it as the main Council Offices. However, following objections from local residents, this idea was abandoned and the property put on the market once again.

It was in 1970 that the Production Group Company purchased the property, moving its staff from their offices in Styal to Merecourt in 1972. It was used in this capacity until the mid 1990's when it was sold for housing development.

S Snelson, Old Withington, Chelford
July 1908

Good Nature and Good Sense must ever join,
To err is human, to forgive Divine.

E Snelson, Old Withington, Chelford
July 1908

I'll not willingly offend,
Nor be easily offended,
What's bad, I'll try to end,
And endure what can't be mended.

DALEFIELDS AND CHELFORD HOUSE
Macclesfield Road

The earliest specific reference to Dalefields is in the 1874 Commercial Directory, which lists Charles Nichols, County Surveyor, as resident in Dale Field House.

However it is probable that the house is considerably older. The 1871 Census contains the following record for a house and its occupants on Macclesfield Road.

Charles Nichols	Head	Married	68 yrs	County Bridgmaster	born Stafford
Hannah Nichols	Wife	Married	65 yrs		born Pott Shrigley
Sarah Barns	Servant	UM	20 yrs	General Servant	born Bootle Lancs
Hannah Millar	Servant	UM	14 yrs	General Servant	born Chelford

Furthermore, 10 years earlier in the 1861 Census, the family is again listed but with different servants.

Hannah Jones	Servant	UM	16 yrs	House Servant	born Woolstanton Staffs
Silas Brooks	Servant	UM	20 yrs	Labourer	born Shrigley
John Brooks	Visitor	UM	16 yrs		born Shrigley

The 1860 Commercial Directories list Charles Nichols as a bridgemaster and surveyor for the County of Chester.

The 1851 Census lists the Nichols family as resident in the Manor House but this may have been a mistake by the enumerator or the family may subsequently have moved from the Manor House to Dalefields.

128

The full record for 1851 is as follows: -

Charles Nichols	Head	Married	48 yrs	Coal Engineer	born Stafford, Staffs
Hannah Nichols	Wife	Married	45 yrs		born Shrigley
Nancy Brook	Servant	UM	21 yrs	Cook	born Shrigley
Hannah Brook	Servant	UM	17 yrs	Housemaid	born Shrigley
Sarah Brook	Visitor	UM	73 yrs	General Servant	born Shrigley
James Hunt	Servant	UM	20 yrs	Groom & Guarding	born Adlington

There is no reference to the family in the 1841 Census.

Charles Nichols

Hannah Nichols

Charles Nichols died in 1876 and his wife, Hannah, in 1879. By 1881 the house was occupied by Richard L Crankshaw, a 26 year old India Merchant born in Manchester, his wife, Emily, aged 23 born in Chadderton, John Raworth, a 33 year old butler, Ellen Cusworth, a cook, and Annie Morris a 19 year old housemaid.

Richard Crankshaw was still resident at Dalefields in 1891 but by 1892, the Commercial Directory of that year lists Francis J Headlam as resident.

In the 20th Century the property was occupied by: -

The Brodie-Hoare family until c 1919 before moving to the Grange.

The Duckworth family who were manufacturers of concentrates and additives for soft drinks. Their factory was in Macclesfield and they exported worldwide.

Mr and Mrs John Scott 1978-1981. Mr Scott was a perfume manufacturer.

Ian and Christine Johnston with Christine's parents, George Read (deceased) and Hilda Read, 1981 to date.

The property today consists of a house and cottage set in about one hectare of land. The property was clearly once part of the land of Chelford House as there is continuity of planting in the southern part of the plot, the northern part of the plot being a walled kitchen garden. The main wing of Dalefields was built in 1903, but the small north wing was probably built much earlier, perhaps as cottages for the staff at Chelford House. Judging from the style of the brickwork, Dalefields Cottage originated as stabling/coach house/cottage to Dalefields.

A small addition was made to the north wing in 1929. A garage block was built in 1939 and demolished in 1978. An extension was added to the cottage in the 1970's. The main wing of the house built in 1903 remains structurally unaltered, although there have been decorative changes. The house still has the original roof drainage-fed water reservoir (not used), a cellar and a stable for ponies.

The first reference to Chelford House is in the 1874 Commercial Directory, which lists Samuel Hignett Smith Esq., A.K.C., a surgeon as resident[1].

---

1   Samuel Hignett Smith subsequently moved to Moss Grove – Now Ivy House (Chelford in the 19th century W Keith Plant.)

The 1881 Census returns include the following details relative to Chelford House.

William Munglaw	Head	Married	55 yrs	Iron Founder	born Coseley Staffs
Catherine Munglaw	Wife	Married	50 yrs		born Birmingham
Catherine Ann Munglaw	Grd. Dau.		5 yrs	Scholar	born Manchester
Hannah Burgess	Servant	UM	31 yrs	Cook	born Brinnington
Alice Fletcher	Servant	UM	18 yrs	Housemaid	born Manchester

Both the 1891 Census and the 1892 Commercial Directory refer to George Stafford Welsh, aged 31, Cotton Merchant from Manchester as resident at Chelford House. On the night of the Census they had two visitors from Cumberland, possibly the brother and sister of George's wife, Elizabeth.

MEREHILLS – CHELFORD

Or more commonly known by the older generation of Chelford residents as *"Jessie Slater's Sweet Shop"*.

MEREHILLS

The signpost on the left-hand side of the picture says 'To Peover' and the advertisement on the right hand side of the picture says 'J Broadhurst and Sons, House and Church Decorators'.

Merehills cottage was situated where Dixon Drive now joins Knutsford Road directly opposite Pepper Street, the road to Peover. Carter Lane ran alongside the cottage. Though officially within the parish of Marthall, it was considered by all the villagers as part of Chelford. Many residents can still remember the shop and particularly Jessie Slater. According to Alan Barber, whose father ran the Insurance Company with whom the shop was insured, the thatched roof of the cottage used to catch fire regularly from sparks created by passing steam wagons. Audrey Walsh remembered calling at the shop for sweets when she was a little girl on her way home from Astle Hall after playing with the Dixon girls.

The cottage was demolished in April 1962 when the main road was straightened. Mrs Jessie Coombes (nee Slater) left the shop and for the remainder of her life lived in one of the council houses in the village.

In an interview with Miss Audrey Walsh in October 1962, Mrs Coombes recalled some of her memories of living in the cottage.

"It was originally the Merehills Toll Bar and my grandmother used to collect the tolls through the little window that was to the right of the front door – on the Chelford side[1].

I remember walking to Macclesfield, (14 miles there and back), as a child of five. My mother had promised to buy me a little umbrella to take to Sunday School. As it would not rain on the way back I put the umbrella in the water tub in the back yard to see how it would stand up to getting wet. The result was a whipping and being sent to bed.

I clearly remember the railway accident in 1894 when fourteen people were killed. One poor woman – Margaret Elks – had both her legs cut off and as no relatives came forward, she was buried in Chelford churchyard where a gravestone was erected in her memory by the squire, Sir George Dixon. Many of the coffins were made in the shed behind the cottage and the pitch for them was boiled on the kitchen fire.

I had a great affection for the old pump in Pepper Street. Every day an old woman called Mrs Steel would come from her cottage near Snelson Common to get her water from the pump. She always said the water from that pump made the best cup of tea for miles around. She was always knitting and as she came to and fro with a covered water pail she always had long steel knitting needles under her arms – knitting as she walked – with her red shawl flowing behind her."

The Slater's connection with the cottage goes back to 1848/9.

---

[1]   No evidence has come to light to confirm that Merehills was a toll cottage though it is possible it operated as such prior to demise of tolls at the end of the 19th century.

133

The Tithe Map taken on 25th August 1847 shows Merehills as Ref. No. 368, the Apportionment list accompanying the map containing the following information[2].

Landowner	Occupiers	Description	Measure A R P	Rent £ s d
Egerton Wilbraham Esq.	Hurst John	Cottage & Garden - 3 -	- 1 4

By 1851 the occupiers had changed, the Census of that year recording the following[3].

John Clark	Head	Married	32	Prov Dealer	bn	Chorley, Cheshire
Mgt Clark	Wife	"	29		b	Mottram
Mary Clark	Dau.		2		bn	Marthall

Therefore the Clark's must have moved in 1848/9, possibly when they married.

White's Commercial Directory of 1860 lists John Clark – Shopkeeper.

The next reference to Merehills was in the 1861 Census[4] when in addition to Mary, four other children were living with their parents namely, Levi ?, aged 8, Ellen aged 6, Olivia aged 5 and Betsy aged 1.

By 1871 Mary had married, the 1871 Census [5] listing her as Mary Jepson, Daughter and a Servant. Betsy was recorded but there was no reference to Levi ?, Ellen or Olivia. There was also an addition to the family, John aged 9 born at Marthall.

According to the 1878 Kelly's Commercial Directory, John Clark was a Shopkeeper at Merehills.

By the time of the 1881 Census[6], the situation had changed, the record of the family taken by the enumerator of the Census being as follows:

Marthall - Shopkeeper

---

2   Cheshire Record Office.

3   Cheshire Record Office ref.: MF 2/19   2163   ff 286

4   Cheshire Record Office ref.: MF 234/10   2593   ff 93-101.

5   Cheshire Record Office ref.: MF 24/18   3687   ff 87-95.

6   Cheshire Record Office ref.: MF 146/10   3510   ff 98-106.

Mgt Clarke	Head	Married	60	Grocer & Provision	Bn	Mottram
John Oliver Clark	Son	UM	19	Wheelwright Apprentice	Bn	Marthall
Ellen Slater	Dau.	Married	26	Labourers wife	Bn	Marthall
William Slater	Son in Law	Married	28	Farm Labourer	Bn	Lower Withington
Annie Slater	G. Dau.		1		Bn	Lower Withington
Alfred Clarke	G. Son		9	Scholar	Bn	Macclesfield

The name of Slater enters the family when William Slater married Ellen Clarke. John Clarke may have died sometime between 1878 and 1881 as Margaret. is listed as head of the family, though not as a widow. Possibly John Clarke was not resident at the cottage on the night of the Census.

The last available Census was in 1891 and this records little change:

> John Oliver was not recorded.
> William. Slater is recorded as a Gardener.
> Ellen Slater had become a Laundress.

There was an additional daughter of William and Ellen Slater, namely Miriam aged 4.

There was also a visitor recorded, a Jane Roberts, a widow aged 70.

Kelly's Commercial Directory of 1892 lists both

> Mgt Clarke   a Shopkeeper   Merehills
> John Clarke   a Wheelwright   Merehills.

However, by 1906 Margaret had disappeared from the records and the only person referred to at Merehills is John Clarke, Wheelwright.

Four years later, Kelly's Commercial Directory lists William Slater, Shopkeeper, who probably took over the shop when John (Oliver) Clarke became a farmer.

So certainly by 1910 the Slater name was connected with the shop and for the next 24 years (i.e. up to 1934) William Slater is recorded in various directories as a shopkeeper in Marthall. By this time William Slater would have been 81 years old. His daughter, Jessie, succeeded him, married and remained at the shop until it was demolished in 1962.

S C Everard, Remenham, Hindhead   July 1908

Oh, a trouble's a ton
Or a trouble's an ounce,
Or a trouble is just what you make it;
And it isn't the fact that you're hurt that counts,
But only – how did you take it?

May Wilson, Sunny Bank, Chelford   July 1908

Be natural, if you wish others to remember you
with pleasure, forget yourself, and be just what
God has made you.

A Chelford Mouse   July 1908

Let not little things distress you,
Let not little cares oppress you;
Tomorrow must not cross your way,
Until tomorrow is today

ROADSIDE FARM

The 1834 Conveyance drawn up when the Dixon's bought the Astle Estate lists Roadside Farm as Item 174 occupied by Widow Kennerley, the size of the farm being 161 A 1R 22P, the largest farm on the estate[1]. Mary Kennerley is also listed in the 1840 map showing the land to be compulsorily purchased for the construction of the Manchester and Birmingham Railway through the village[2].

Thus it has been established that the Kennerley family were residents at Roadside Farm in the early 1830's. Going further back, the 1825 Land Tax Returns[3] list a Joseph Kennerley as the occupier of a farm paying tax of £4 15s 8d, the same

---

1   The apportionment states 'A messuage, tenement and farm with the outbuildings and garden and lands thereto belonging now or late in the occupation of Widow Kennerley.

2   The amount of land covered by this purchase was:-

	a	r	p
Mary Kennerley	6	0	0
George Beech	0	2	24
William Mellor	5	3	38
Samuel Norbury	2	0	38

3   Chelford in the 19th Century by W Keith Plant

Joseph Kennerley being listed in the 1832 Register of Electors as Occupier of Farm as tenant at a rent of £50 and upwards per annum.

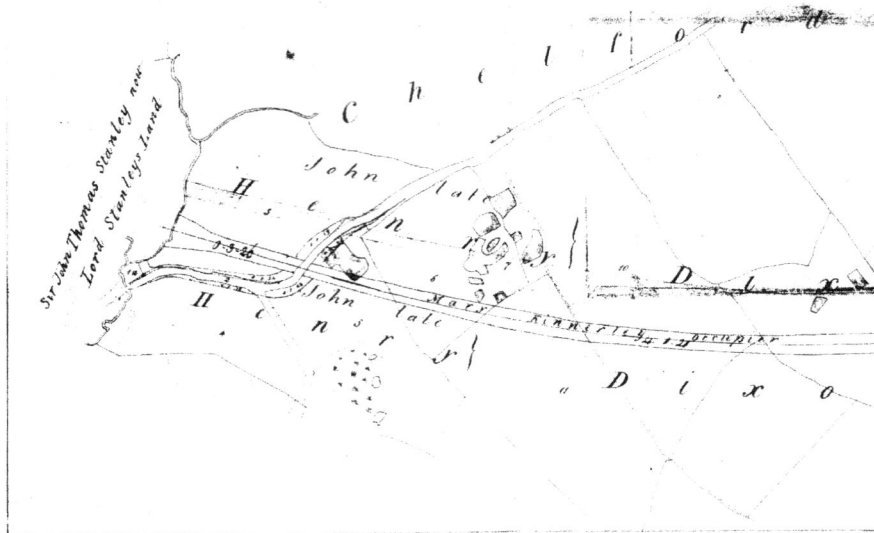

Land to be purchased for construction of railway 1840

The 1825 Land Tax Returns show that the farm was owned by Thomas Parker Esq and Joseph Kennerley was the occupier.

Under an Act in 1780 assessment for the Land Tax became a necessary qualification for voting at county elections. Duplicates of the annual assessments for each township were deposited with the Clerk of the Peace. This practice continued until 1832 when Land Tax ceased to be an electoral qualification and an annual register of electors was required to be made.

By looking back through the earlier Land Tax Returns and assuming the sum assessed to be the same, ie £4 15s 8d, it is possible to establish that in 1815 the occupier was a Wm Broadhurst, and the owner, T Parker. In 1795 the occupier was John Brentnall and in 1785, Wm Brentnal, in both cases the owner being William Swettenham. It therefore looks as though the Parker family purchased the farm from Wm Swettenham some time around the turn of the century.

It is possible to establish from the Parish Registers that a John Brentnall son of William and Elizabeth Brentnall (farmer) of Chelford was baptised on 31 May 1753 followed by William who was baptised on 15 May 1755, Jasper, baptised 5th

May 1757, Samuel, baptised 27 Jan 1760, Thomas, baptised 17 Jan 1762 and a further son (name unknown) in 1764.

The earlier records refer to farmers in Chelford and it is apparent that Roadside Farm was a farm, at least from the early 1700's if not earlier.

Returning now to the mid 19th century we find that the 1841 census refers to Mary Kennerley aged 60 and George Kennerley aged 15. However by 1851 the census shows that George had married and taken over the farm, as he is listed as a farmer at Kennerleys Lane, farming 160 acres.

The full 1851 record taken by the Village Schoolmaster, Peter Whalley, on 5th April is as follows[4]:

Kennerleys Lane

George Kennerley	Head	Married	29	Farmer of 160 acres employing 5 labourers	born Chelford
Harriet "	Wife	Married	32		born Chelford
William "	Son		7	Scholar	born Chelford
John "	Son		5	Scholar	born Chelford
Mary Ann "	Daughter		2		born Chelford
Susannah "	Daughter		8 months		born Chelford
William Mellor	Nephew		15	Agricultural Lab	born Alderley
John Whitney	Servant	UM	27	Agricultural Lab	born Alderley
John Shaw	Servant	UM	17	Agricultural Lab	born Alderley
Eliz Forest	Servant	UM	18	House Servant	born Snelson
Sarah Massey	Servant	U	12	House Servant	born Old Withington

This is the only reference to Kennerleys Lane in any of the census returns and it is possible that the census enumerator called the section of the road near the farm (or the path leading up to the farm), Kennerleys Lane after the then residents. There was at this time another family of Kennerleys resident at Archers Inn, namely Joseph and family. Joseph was 33 at the time and had born in Alderley. Were George and Joseph brothers, the sons of Joseph and Mary Kennerley?

Over the next twenty years there is some confusion relative to Roadside Farm.

> The 1860 Commercial Directory does not specifically refer to Roadside Farm, nor does the 1861 Census. There are however two possibilities: -
>
> Edward Moss aged 37, Farmer of 175 acres employing 4 men or

---

4   Chelford in the 19th Century by W Keith Plant

Thomas Norbury aged 39, Farmer of 140 acres employing 3 men and one boy.

There could of course be a third possibility, and that is that the farm was recorded as outside the village of Chelford.

However, based on the grouping of residences in the census, the first possibility (ie Edward Moss) is the more likely.

However, by 1871 we are more certain, as the first record taken for the census by the enumerator (who must have started his visitations at Roadside) refers to a farm of 154 acres in Chorley Road, farmed by Thomas Norbury plus 4 men and two general servants. Together with his wife and three children there were 11 people at Roadside Farm on the night of the census.

Corn Binding – Team from Roadside Farm with Mrs Lena Newton (Tom's Wife)

By 1881, Roadside had changed hands again and according to the 1881 census it was now occupied by James Callwood and his family (wife, five sons and four daughters) plus six servants, giving a total of seventeen on the night of the census. If they all lived in, it makes you wonder where they all slept. The family moved from Alderley (where James was born) in 1877/8 to set up house in Chelford.

The 1891 census refers to two houses on the site, Roadside Farm and Roadside Farm Outhouse. A total of 15 were resident on the night of the census on 13th April.

In 1902 the farmer was James Callwood

Arthur Newton took the tenancy in 1920. He had four sons, Tom, Percy, William, and Arthur, and two daughters, Nellie and Alice. All four sons farmed locally. Nellie moved to Manchester after her marriage and they had a milk round. Alice (Venables) farmed at Holly Tree Farm in Withington.

Tom Newton took the tenancy in 1934 and in 1969 it passed to Raymond Bailey (he and Margaret [*Tom Newton's daughter*] married in 1966). In 1969 after Raymond died Margaret continued farming and married Jo Norbury in 1981.

The tenancy was given up in 1998, the land being set to neighbouring farms whilst the house, (having been rewired and having central heating installed) is to be privately let.

ROADSIDE HOUSE

Built at the road side about 1880 the house was originally designed to be a butcher's shop, which explains a lot about its design, but it was never actually used for that purpose. The first known inhabitant was Mr R.A. Tatton who appears in the 1891 census and in Kelly's Directory for 1892. He was a Civil Engineer and the brother of Thomas Egerton Tatton, of Wythenshawe Hall, Cheshire, and was shown as having both a Cook and a Parlourmaid, In the 1896 Directory he was listed as living at the Manor House whilst a Miss Lyon occupied Roadside House.

In 1910 Lady Dalrymple-Horn-Elphinstone was the occupier and a headstone to her dog, Fruagh, remains in the garden. At that time the name given was 'Rode Syde' and this persisted through the occupancy of Mr Godfrey Grant Astell in 1914 until Dr Evans bought the property in 1934 from a Mr Thomas Scott. A 'temporary' surgery was built in the garden in 1936 – and lasted until 1983. The house itself was the scene of most of the CAD's rehearsals under the forceful direction of Mrs Evans and it is related that 'Bowling for Pig' often took place when garden parties were held in the summer months. After Dr Evans retired in 1963 he was followed by Dr Roycroft and his family who live there still.

ROADSIDE HOUSE, Knutsford Road

THE WALSH FAMILY

In small villages some families have a truly profound effect. That certainly was true with the family begun by the marriage of Frances Crompton to John Walsh in the early 1880's.

Frances Elizabeth Crompton, to give her full name, was born in 1866 at Butley, near Prestbury. However the family roots were in Bolton with the inventor Samuel Crompton. Not that Frances was gifted on an engineering sense, indeed far from it. Yet gifted she certainly was, both as a writer and as an artist. The cover illustrations for this book are from her brush and a splendid collection of her watercolours is safely kept at the Cheshire Record Office.

She recorded life meticulously, sketching wherever she travelled and making copious notes on her journeys and of the world about her. In the event though it was not travel diaries that made her famous – fascinating though they are, but the writing of children's stories. The first to be published was entitled 'Friday's Child' and the Manchester Guardian commented "...we hope for more from the same pen". That wish was granted and a total of 29 stories were published between 1888 and 1903 demonstrating her great understanding of children, of art, of music and of the countryside. Frances died in 1952 after a lifetime of village involvement, just two years after the death of her husband, John. Her epitaph could have come from 'Castle Building', in which she had written of her addiction to storytelling: *'For after all.…what is one but a beginner at the very end'*.

John Leopold Walsh was, and remained, a bank manager. A man of solid reputation, firm and dependable around whom the rest of the family revolved, but it would seem rather aloof from his children as was often the case in those times. And children there were in some profusion. The names of several features elsewhere in this reminiscence, but to enumerate they were: -

Arthur St. George Walsh, born in 1893,. He survived the horrors of the First World War and gave his life to teaching at the Chester Kings School. When he eventually retired he continued his association with the school by running the 'Old

Boys' department with unfailing vigour well into his 90's. Arthur's love was learning and his clothes were always as his mother described in her Gardening Dairy (below). With a knapsack on his back he walked the two miles to the station to commute weekly to Chester where he lived 'in digs' whilst researching all the affairs of Kings School, only to return by the same route at the weekend to be with his sisters. He died in 1992, still busily working for his beloved school.

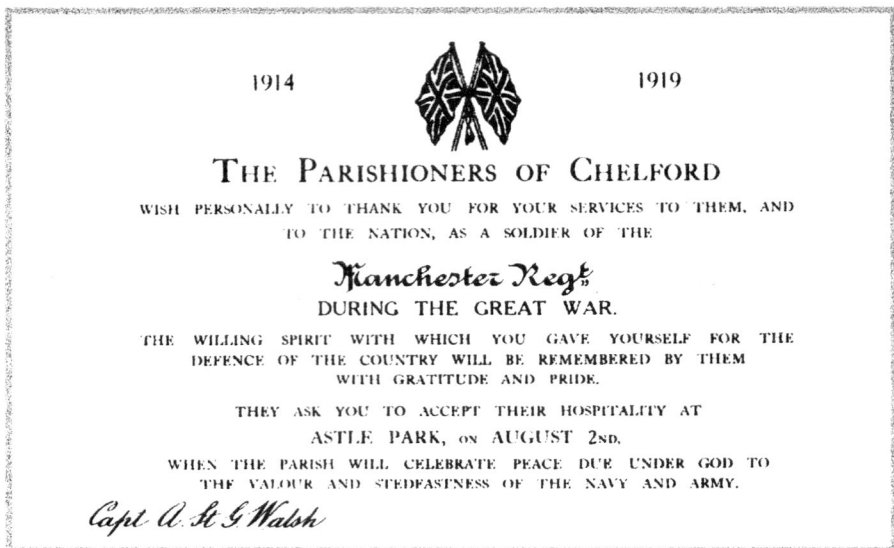

1914   1919

THE PARISHIONERS OF CHELFORD

WISH PERSONALLY TO THANK YOU FOR YOUR SERVICES TO THEM, AND TO THE NATION, AS A SOLDIER OF THE

Manchester Regt

DURING THE GREAT WAR.

THE WILLING SPIRIT WITH WHICH YOU GAVE YOURSELF FOR THE DEFENCE OF THE COUNTRY WILL BE REMEMBERED BY THEM WITH GRATITUDE AND PRIDE.

THEY ASK YOU TO ACCEPT THEIR HOSPITALITY AT ASTLE PARK, ON AUGUST 2ND,

WHEN THE PARISH WILL CELEBRATE PEACE DUE UNDER GOD TO THE VALOUR AND STEDFASTNESS OF THE NAVY AND ARMY.

Capt A. St G Walsh

Roger Crompton Walsh, born in 1898, was profoundly deaf from childhood. He too served in the army in the First World War despite his disability. Subsequently he became a poultry smallholder but his main love was with Scouting. He ran the Chelford Troop from its formation in 1934, managing single handed during the Second World War, and was known to generations of scouts simply as 'Skip'. A quiet, gentle, man with an abiding passion for the mountains and the countryside he ran the family garden, tended his faithful briar pipe and cycled prodigiously until his death in 1974.

John Quentin Walsh was born in 1904. After university he entered the church and held his last ministry at Wybunbury, dying at the age of 84

Geoffrey Christian Lansdsdale Walsh was born in1897 and posted missing, as were so many, at Messines on June 22nd 1917. In his memory a stained glass window was placed in Chelford Church. In The Gardening Diary, 1915-1924 Frances Walsh described the difficult years of the First World War. Two sons,

144

Arthur and Geoffrey, were 'at the front'. Both returned home, briefly, in December 1916 on which she wrote... *"Geoffrey looks very well indeed, and though still only a cadet, is dressed as an officer, and presents a most spick and span appearance after Arthur's worn clothes"*

There were three girls: -
Eleanor Elizabeth Walsh was born in 1866 but died just before her first birthday.

Audrey Cecil Walsh was born in 1899. She was a dedicated worker in the community in very many organisations, not least in the Women's Institute. However her greatest achievements were in historical research, notably on Cheshire Churches. An avid reader and annotator of books and articles she was also a great collector, and the home that she shared with her sister was a veritable treasure house of books, furniture and ornaments – much of which was left to national and county archives. Audrey lectured in her neat and precise way, to audiences across the county. She was a home bird, looking after her parents, her brothers, and her sister with great diligence and a quiet but impish sense of fun until she too needed the care of others. Death finally robbed us of her charms in 1998

Gwenifer Walsh , referred to in the family as 'the kid' was born in 1906. Music was her love and her forte and though she shared many village activities with her sister it was with her fellow musicians that she was at her happiest. Many young people in the village and from afar went to her for music lessons on the piano. Yet the violin was the instrument she preferred and many were the string quartets that assembled at the house and played on into the night. At her funeral in 1999 the service was unique in the moving performance given by the string quartet of which she had so long been a part. It summed up the elegance, charm and erudition of her life in a truly magical way.

With the passing of Gwenifer the family was gone. A family who lived for each other and for their friends, who adapted to enjoying the telephone and sound radio. No need was ever felt for the glow of a television screen in their lives – which was thought odd by many. Yet if you consider the hours wasted by most families 'just watching' each evening, instead of 'doing' there is a compelling explanation of why village institutions are prone to wither away.

It was a great privilege to have known the Walsh family, and a tragedy that none of the children married and that we should be left with no one to continue their lineage. But we have their legacy, a record of devotion to others, of study, discovery and research. Of helping by deed and example, and of asking very little from life in return. As a family they were special, but not unique; merely painted here as an example of the kind of family that lived in the village for most of this century. In human terms they were enduring and dependable and we are the poorer without them. For who is to follow in the footsteps of such families? And will there be enough of them?

Thanks are due to the Cheshire Record Office for permission to use information of Frances Crompton contained in Issue 11 autumn 1997 of the Archives and Local Studies Newsletter.

The picture of the church on the front cover is taken from a watercolour by Frances Crompton; her collection of stories, paintings and sketches now stored in the archives of the Cheshire Record Office[1]. It is well worth visiting the record office to see the collection, many of the paintings and sketches being of local interest.

---

1   Cheshire Record Office CRO ref: D5454/7 Colour Book – Box No. 4

GLEDHILL FAMILY OF CHELFORD

The Gledhill name has been connected with Chelford since the late 1840's, Thomas Gledhill was probably the first licensee of the Dixon Arms. He is listed in the 1851 Census with his family and described as a Coach Proprietor and Inn Keeper farming 17 acres. At that time six servants, plus one niece, acting as a servant, were recorded. Prior to the Dixon Arms, Thomas was a Victualler and Inn Keeper at the 'Wheat Sheaf', Macclesfield. Thomas died in 1857.

Thomas's eldest son, James Jackson Gledhill, was recorded as Postmaster and Shopkeeper in Chelford in 1861 and 1871. The latter census describing Thomas and Maria (the two eldest children of James Jackson Gledhill and Mary Ann Heald) as Coachman and Shopkeeper respectively.

Considerable information is known concerning James Jackson Gledhill and Mary Ann Heald's children.

Joseph never married and lived at Knowsley Farm which was worked by his brother Walter. He had a cycle repair shop in what was left of the Gledhill Coach Works alongside the Post Office.

Thomas Heald Gledhill was recorded as Postmaster and Shopkeeper in 1881 but, by 1891 had moved to the Dixon Arms where he was living with his wife, Sarah, and seven daughters.

James was an artist and art master at Manchester Grammar School and later, Headmaster of Dewsbury College of Art.

Arthur left the village, moving to Neasden where he had a tailoring business.

The last remaining brother to reach manhood (two other brothers died young) was Walter who in 1891 lived in Station Road and was described in the census as a Coachbuilders Manager. He eventually took over the Coach Building Business begun by his father, James Jackson Gledhill, presumably when his father died in 1890. The business was sited at the back of the Post Office and, judging from a photograph of Walter and his workers taken c 1910, must have been of a reasonable size.

JAMES J. GLEDHILL,

COACH

Builder,

POST OFFICE, CHELFORD.

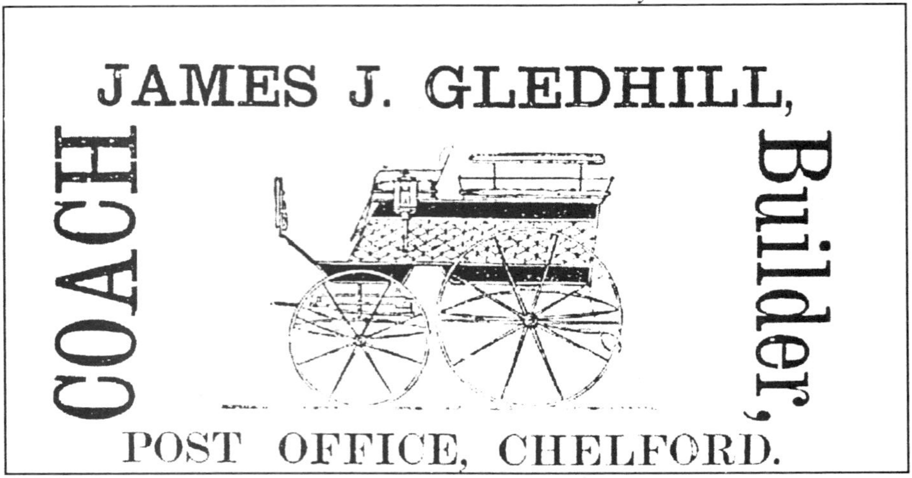

For many years the Gledhill sign was displayed on the side of the Post Office building.

Walter appears to have been a prominent member of the village, being involved in events at Astle Hall as a representative of the Dixons' tenants. He is mentioned in many of the Hall records.

The only daughter of James Jackson Gledhill to reach adulthood was Maria, born in 1856, who married John David Haigh in 1880 and acquired the Post Office in 1882 when her brother, Thomas Heald Jackson, moved to the Dixon Arms. It has been said that John David Haigh was very well respected and public-spirited. He was involved in running the local football team and was the superintendent of the Sunday School. Sometime during the 1914-18 war the business was sold and the family moved to Cheadle Hulme where Maria died in 1922 followed by her husband in 1929.

Two of Walter Gledhill's grandsons still live in the village, John who is tenant at Knowsley Farm and Frank who farms at Astle farm.

It would appear that the Gledhills originally came from Yorkshire, Thomas being born in Leeds and his wife, Elizabeth Jackson, being born in Halifax. They moved to the Macclesfield area in 1825.

Walter Gledhill and workers c 1910

A typical coachbuilders workshop end 19th century

GLEDHILL FAMILY OF CHELFORD

THOMAS GLEDHILL
b 4 Feb 1803 Leeds, Yorkshire
m 4 Jan 1827 = Elizabeth Jackson
(b 1804 d 1851)

1851 Census + Coach Proprietor + Inn Keeper (Dixon Arms
Farming 17 acres

James Jackson φ
b Macclesfield 16 Jun 1827
m = Mary A Heald 1850
(b Ringway 1826 d 1906)
d 11 Feb 1890

John
b. Macclesfield

Mary
b. Macclesfield 1833

d 22 Mar 1857

Thomas
b. Macclesfield 1836

Elizabeth
b. Macclesfield 1839

Maria
b. Macclesfield 1844

φ Shopkeeper + Coachmaker (Post Office)
in 1861 + 71
Coachmaker, Alderley Road in 1881

Thomas H
b 21 Jan 1852
Snelson
m Sarah A Knowles
(Postmaster +
Shopkeeper 1881)
(Dixon Arms 1891)
d 22 May 1918

James
b 28 Mar 1854
Chelford
m Eliz. Barber

Maria
b 1856
Chelford
m John David Haigh
24 Aug 1880
(b 1854 d 1929)
d 28 Dec 1922

John
b 1859
Chelford
d 5 Mar 1859

Arthur
b 1861
Chelford
d 19 Mar 1927

Robert
b 1862
Chelford
d 2 Jan 1865

Joseph
b 1865
Chelford
(lived in Carter Lane
with mother in 1891) d 28 Dec 1932

Mary Ann
b Jan 1868
Chelford
m Sarah
(lived in Station Rd.
d 24 Sept 1932

Walter
b 12 Aug 1856
Chelford
m Sarah
(lived at Knowsley Farm
on death) d 5 Apr 1951

Daughter
d 24 Sept 1870

Mary (Ethel)
b 1878
Chelford
m Thos Wilson (Sunny Bank Farm)
Apr 1903

Annie
b 1879
Chelford

Jessie
b 1882
Chelford

Nelle
b 1884
Chelford

Nora
b 1886
Chelford

Lilly
b 1998
Chelford

Edith
b 1990
Chelford

Gertrude
b 1901

Maria
b 1890
(Station Rd)

Bertha
b 1882
(Station Rd)

Frank
b 1894
(Station Rd)

d 29 Dec 1961

John
(Knowsley farm)
m Rita Snelson

Amy

Dora

Frank
(Astle farm)
m Christine Mary

Walter Worthington
b 1897

Cicely

d 23 Jun 1889

d 21 Dec 1987

Helen Shirley

Ian James m Judith Lee

Amy Eliz
Rebecca Louise
Harvey Lee

CORONATION FESTIVITIES AT CHELFORD

Extract from the Wilmslow & Alderley Advertiser Friday 8 August 1902

On Tuesday Coronation festivities were held at Chelford, when the whole of the programme arranged for the 28th June was carried out. Col. Dixon, J.P., very kindly allowed the use of his beautiful gardens and grounds for the occasion, and the inhabitants spent a very pleasant time.

Excellent arrangements had been made by a local committee, which was representative, and a capital programme was gone through. The afternoons proceeding embraced free teas for the residents of Chelford, Snelson and Old Withington. The repast, which was of a very substantial character, was served up in a spacious marquee in the park.

At two o'clock the school children assembled at the village school and a procession having been formed they marched to Astle Park, the Macclesfield Volunteer Band leading the way. Amongst those who accompanied the children was the Vicar, the Rev. L. S. Stanhope. During the afternoon sports took place in the park. The events arranged for the afternoon including handicaps for the boys, 220 yards for men over 17, 120 yards for men over 30 and under 40, 100 yards for men over 40, a wheelbarrow race, egg and spoon race for ladies, and a cycle sprint. These were watched with much interest. At 4.30, tea was provided for the children, and shortly after five o'clock the adults sat down in the marquee to enjoy the "cheering cup," and the usual solid comforts. Punch and Judy appeared at intervals during the afternoon and evening, and the show here greatly amused the company. About seven o'clock Coronation mugs were distributed, and later in the evening there was dancing, the evening's proceedings closing with a display of fireworks near the large lake. It should be stated that immediately after tea the school children sang the Coronation song, "Hail! King of many nations." The Volunteer Band played popular selections during the afternoon and evening, and their performances formed one of the most enjoyable features of the rejoicing. Amongst those present were Col. Dixon, J.P., Mrs Dixon, the Misses Glegg and Mr B Glegg, J.P. The following were the members of the Coronation Committee: - Colonel Dixon (Chairman), Rev. L. S. Stanhope, Messrs W. H. Cooke, Thomas H. Gledhill, Joseph Gledhill, J. D. Haigh, Saml. Bucktrout, Alfred Bloor, James Baskerville, George Moss, Sydney Baskerville, Wm. Barber, T Wilson, Jun., and F. Hardwick (secretary and treasurer). The members of the Sports Committee were the Vicar and Messrs J. Gledhills, S. Baskerville, F. Hardwick and G. Moss.

The following are the results of the sports: - Event 1, Jock Mieckle, 1 Harold Gleave 2: event 2, Edward Rowland 1, F Evens 2; event 3, Jones Bell 1, Geo. Steel 2; event 4, R Saul 1, Charles Fryer 2; event 6, R Saul and F Archer 1, H Tomlinson and Fryer 2; event 7, Miss Bloor 1, Miss Grant 2; event 8, Alfred Clarke 1, J Antrobus

THE VILLAGE DOCTOR

There have always been health carers in every village and town to whom people went for help. The first literature on General Practice in Britain was written about 250 years ago when the healers were a collection of non-professional people such as the Lady of the Manor, the parish clerk, the parish priest, the grocers and spicers and of course, the itinerant quacks. Doubtless Chelford was no exception.

The first documented medical practitioner in the village was Dr Henry Ballachey who lived at Moss Grove opposite the Vicarage (later known as the Ivy House). Not only was he interested in the physical well being of the villagers but he also took an active interest in Chelford and the surrounding villages by standing for election to the newly formed District Council. The election took place on 15th December 1894 as a result of the Local Government Act of 1894 with William Hall as the presiding officer and Elijah Page poll clerk. Dr Ballachey was elected by 49 votes to 32.

On 22nd December 1894, just one week after his election to office, a railway disaster occurred in Chelford and subsequently, the following letter was published in The Times: -

> *Sir,*
>
> *As one of the passengers in the train wreck in Chelford on Saturday 22nd December, I wish to bear testimony to the manner in which the local doctor, whose name I unfortunately do not know (Dr H H Ballachey), attended to the sufferers.*
>
> *I see that the names of several medical men are mentioned in the press as having rendered valuable service to the wounded, but I see no mention of the man who was on the spot one and a half hours before they arrived, and who, by his absence of fussiness, and by his quiet and tender attention to the victims, that day greatly alleviated the horrors of the situation.*
>
> *In consequence of my travelling in one of the back three carriages, which suffered no damage, I was uninjured, and was able to assist my fellow passengers who were not so fortunate, and I had many opportunities of seeing the splendid way in which the local doctor worked under many disadvantages.*
>
> *Yours faithfully*
>
> *Wilson Dunning (of Rochdale)*

31st December 1891

It was obvious that the whole village must have felt extremely proud of their doctor. Little did Dr Ballachey realise that the pledge he made to the electors of Chelford and Snelson, recorded in the Macclesfield Courier, would test him to the limits just 7 days later.

Ladies and Gentlemen,

> *I beg to thank those of you who placed me at the head of the poll and thus elected me your representative on the District Council. I trust I shall carry out the duties assigned to me to your complete satisfaction.*

Dr Shepard

In 1903 Dr Arthur Shepard succeeded Dr Ballachey, holding surgeries in his own home 'Moss Grove' which he renamed 'The Ivy House'. The property was well known before the doctors' arrival, as a local hostelry, 'The Robin Hood', known parochially as 'The Archers'. Other medical men had lodged there in the late nineteenth century but they practised at local hospitals nearer Manchester. Dr Shepard was assisted in his practice by his wife and had no employed staff other than those engaged on household duties. Patient records as such were not kept in those days. His only record was a ledger giving details of the date the patient was visited or consulted at his house, the patient's name and the reason for the consultation and the medication from which could be determined the fee charged – which might or might not be eventually paid. The Parish Register shows that the infant death rate dropped dramatically soon after Dr Shepard arrived, an improvement that was not generally seen in medical statistics at that time.

Dr Shepard married Muriel Sandford Evans, sister of Dr Ben Evans who was later to join him in the practice. He regularly visited his patients with his horse and trap until he graduated to a bicycle and then a car. Dr Milner later became his assistant and married Sir Edwin Stockton's daughter from Jodrell Hall.

With the coming of the Insurance Act of 1911 doctors were able to dispense not only medicines but also money. Certification of the inability of patients to work due to illness meant that they could at least afford to eat and resist, to some extent, the steady slide into debt and pauperism that had been the fate of so many before them. Suddenly 'the certificate' became the most important document and patients quite understandably found it far more significant than any written record of their symptoms.

SKETCH OF IVY HOUSE

Dr Ben Evans joined the practice in 1929. He had been seriously wounded in the 1914-18 war and spent nearly two years in hospital, which made him decide to enter the medical profession. He qualified at St Thomas's Hospital in London and consented to come and assist his brother-in-law for a short spell - which lasted until the 31st December 1962.

154

Dr Evans was very keen on amateur dramatics which led to his meeting his wife Dorothy. A lady called Daphne Peel was arranging a pantomime at the neighbouring village of Peover. Dorothy had arrived at Eaton Hall, Congleton to look after her ageing cousin, Crawford Antrobus. Daphne asked Dorothy to be 'Principal Boy' and Dr Evans was the 'Comic King'. They were married on 7th July 1932 and lived at Roadside House. The surgery was still in Dr Shepard's home, Ivy House, and the dining room was the waiting room. A similar arrangement was made at Roadside House but in 1936 Dr Evans had a surgery, dispensary and waiting room built opposite his front door at Roadside House. The surgery was always known as the 'Green Hut'.

DR BEN EVANS

Dr Evans was 'on call' seven days a week and 24 hours a day. Arrangements were made for the Alderley Practice to cover from 2pm to midnight every Wednesday to allow him a little free time. Although Mrs Evans was not medically qualified, she helped her husband with dispensing and accidents. In those days the Post Office was also the telephone exchange so if Dr and Mrs Evans were going out to dinner they gave the Post Mistress, Mary Carter, their telephone number and she would redirect the call if necessary. They had a housekeeper named Maggie Tickle living in who helped look after their two sons, John and Edmund, kept all the patients in order and, when the Evans' went on holiday, was housekeeper for the locum.

In 1939, at the commencement of the World War II, Dr Evans had to have an assistant. The first was Dr Elizabeth Thompson – a clever Scot with two boys much the same age as the Evans boys – and there were also refugees staying in the house. Petrol rationing caused a few 'difficulties' for their evening excursions but there was usually some patient in the proximity who ought to have a visit!

When Dr Thompson had to leave as her husband was posted to Birmingham, Dr Peggy Anderson took over as Dr Evans assistant. She stayed with the practice during the war years. Dr Anderson originated from Padgate near Warrington and was one of four children. During this time she lived at the local hostelry 'The Dixon Arms' and as she was unmarried at that time, the staff at the hostelry kindly provided a telephone answering service for her when she was out on visits. She later married the Rev Lankey, the vicar of Padgate and left the practice at the end of 1954. Her husband later became the vicar of Wincle and Dr Anderson often returned to act as locum when required.

In 1942, Sir William Beveridge, a retired civil servant, produced his report on the Welfare State, in which the National Health Service was to be an important part. His ideas were accepted by all as a vision for a bright future, in a world 'fit for heroes'! On the 5th July 1948 the National Health Service was born. It was no revolution, rather an evolutionary transition over a century, through sick clubs, the National Health Insurance Scheme of Lloyd George and traditional family practice developed over centuries. Dr Ben Evans would have experienced no changes in relation to his patients, premises and staff, or his work on that historic day. The major difference would have been relief that no longer did he have to charge fees and try to collect them and that he received a regular income. With every citizen having free access to the National Health Service, the General Practitioners' workload became intense with many medically trivial requests and no supportive backup or organisational help available to them.

In 1955 Dr Stanley Pratt joined the practice, in which her remained until his retirement in 1985. The surgery continued to be run from the 'Green Hut' which comprised of a small waiting room, tiny dispensary and a consulting room. The open surgeries were held at regular times and patients just attended and moved from seat to seat around the little waiting room until it was their turn to see the doctor. There were 13 chairs round the room with an electric fire at one end. With the practice covering a rural community, inclement weather brought the patients out in droves as they were unable to get into the fields to work. That's when they would find time to fetch the elderly members of the family down to the surgery for their check-up.

There was insufficient work for two full time partners, so Dr Pratt continued his work as anaesthetist at Pendlebury Hospital on a Monday and Withington Hospital on a Tuesday afternoon. The District Nurse was Nurse Hughes who was eventually succeeded by Nurse Kerrigan who, after her retirement, continued to help at the surgery as a receptionist until recent days. The local Medical Officer of Health organised the childhood immunisation recall. If there was an epidemic, mass vaccination sessions were held on a Saturday afternoon at the surgery for smallpox and polio immunisation. A local schoolboy was enlisted to act as clerk to take the patients details. Dr Pratt's wife, Dr Barbara Pratt held one clinic a week at the surgery. The practice covered a very wide area which included: Chelford, Snelson, Lower Withington, Alderley Edge, Wilmslow, Mere, Rostherne, Knutsford, Macclesfield, Goostrey, Holmes Chapel, Swettenham, Peover, Ollerton, Marthall, Twemlow, Warford, Nether Alderley, Allostock, Siddington, Marton, Henbury and Mobberley. The practice population in 1954 was 2,157 and rose to 2,372 by 1958. This catchment area was later reduced to a smaller more manageable area.

Following the retirement of Dr Evans in 1963 Dr Roger Roycroft joined the practice, taking up residence at 'Roadside House'. Dr Pratt and Dr Roycroft continued to run the practice from the 'Green Hut' but felt that the premises needed modifying, owing to the rapid increase of administrative work and an increasing practice population. The first modification was to have running water put in the surgery, then shortly afterwards the premises were altered. The waiting room was divided into a waiting room and reception area. In the summer of 1964 a nurse, Mrs Anne Wood, was employed to help with the administration and nursing duties. An appointment system was introduced in October of that year and , with the assistance of a part-time receptionist, reception duties were covered during surgery hours.

Dr Stanley & Barbara Pratt's Retirement

During the 1970's a major housing development was begun in Chelford and the population of the village more than doubled within a few years. The 'Green Hut' was no longer big enough and a new purpose built surgery was built, the practice moving to Elmstead Road in February 1983. Mrs Wood became the Practice Nurse and Practice Manager, Mrs Kath Snelson joined the practice as Receptionist and Assistant Dispenser and Mrs Wendy Burcham as secretary. This was the beginning of the employment of a number of ancillary staff by the practice.

Dr Peter Madden joined the Practice on the retirement of Dr Pratt in 1984. In 1989 he was appointed a member of the Local Medical Committee and soon became their Secretary, a position he still holds. Dr Madden, like Dr Pratt and Dr Roycroft before him, is a G P trainer, giving doctors their twelve months general practice training before they move on to practice on their own. Dr Catriona Forrester has been with the practice for many years. Dr Roycroft introduced the first computer system to the practice in 1985 for the registration of patients and generating prescriptions. The surgery building was again becoming too small so an extension was added in 1993. At that time a corporate logo was quietly introduced in the form of a weather vane on the new extension. It passed without any local comment and a few years later a sign was added in front of the surgery, suitably protected from the attention of vandals. It is a humorous representation of the typical (non-extended) English family, consisting of father, mother, and 2.3 children – but is yet to attract any attention. So much for the British sense of humour.

In 1994, after over 30 years of working every other night and weekend 'on call' Dr Roycroft decided to reduce his official hours to give him more time to concentrate on his involvement in Medical Informatics. It was then that the practice acquired its first lady partner with the arrival of Dr Helen Thomas who joined the Practice to work half time.

Just what the coming millennium holds for small country practices is unknown. It may well be that, just like village Post Offices and village grocers, they will become a thing of the past, their place being taken by the equivalent of medical supermarkets now being developed as 'drop-in centres' in the local towns. As with all things in any community it will be the pressure and interest of the local population – or the lack of it – that will decide.

Jessie Gledhill, Chelford   *July 1908*

Do what you can, being what you are;
Shine like a glow worm, if you cannot be like a star,
Work like a pulley, if you cannot be like a crane,
Be a wheel greaser, if you cannot drive a train.

THE OLD SURGERY (Green Hut)

THE OLD WAITING ROOM & RECEPTION

Nurse Hulley

District Nurse – 1903 – 1929

Little Orchard as it was then

Nurse Hulley lived at the Cottage and was the district nurse and midwife, caring for people and delivering the babies in the area. Maybe you were one of the babies delivered by her.

Below is the Cottage as it is today (Little Orchard).

CHELFORD'S FAREWELL TO DR AND MRS EVANS
A report from the County Express – 10th January 1963

Chelford Parish Hall was packed on Friday evening although snow was falling outside, the occasion being a social evening in honour of Dr. and Mrs. E.S. Evans, who are leaving Chelford to live in Lurgashall, Sussex. Dr Evans has been in practice in Chelford for more than 30 years. Mrs Evans has also been a prominent local figure, and they were the recipients of a cheque for £375 and a 400-day clock among other gifts.

The evening began with an entertainment. Edwin Massey playing well-known tunes on the piano accordion and Miss Nancy Hope singing two songs, accompanied by Mr D. Pickard.

The Vicar of Chelford (the Rev. Cyril H. Lee) then invited Dr. and Mrs. Evans, their younger son John, and their housekeeper, Miss Maggie Tickle on to the stage. Dr. and Mrs. Evans being seated on a settee in the centre.

Addressing Dr. and Mrs. Evans he said: 'Before you take your leave of Chelford a very large number of people wish to pay tribute to your life of service in our midst, and this we propose to do by a spoken biography of your lives. Dr. and Mrs. Evans: "This is your life."'

161

After telling about Dr. Evans childhood spent at Bidston, Bilton Grange and Charterhouse, reference was made to the first visit he made to Chelford, when at the age of seven he was a pageboy at a wedding.

Flourishing the marriage register, the Vicar announced that, although the wedding was duly recorded, there was no mention of the pageboy! The only person who could have recalled that occasion, Mrs Coombes (Miriam Slater) had unfortunately been taken ill and was unable to be present.

After three years war service with the Cheshire Regiment, E.S. Evans had been wounded on the Marne and had to spend more than a year in hospital. This helped him to decide on his career. His training took place at Gonville and Caius Cambridge, and St. Thomas' Hospital, London. His first experience was as a ship's doctor. Mrs Sparrow then came on to the stage and told of his coming to Chelford in 1929 as assistant to Dr Shepard, his brother-in-law.

The Vicar mentioned the childhood of Dorothy Swettenham and told how she acted as principal boy in a pantomime written and produced by Daphne Peel (now Mrs Berkley), in which the young doctor was the King.

Mrs. Russell (Betty Armitage), who had travelled from Wales for the evening, told of another production, "The Plumber's Mate", and how they came together.

Finally the Vicar spoke of Dr. and Mrs. Evans' two sons, Edmund was now a fully qualified doctor specialising in ophthalmics at St. Thomas' Hospital where his father had been trained, and John was well known locally for following in the family tradition in amateur theatricals.

Mr. Tom Newton, who had been co-Warden at Chelford Parish Church with Dr. Evans. and the Rev. J.S. Gamon, (Rector of Tattenhall and the former Vicar) spoke of Dr Evans as a leading churchman in the neighbourhood.

Mr. Ernest Pimlott announced that a special peal had been rung in the tower by local ringers on Wednesday night in honour of Dr. and Mrs. Evans, and spoke of the care he had for his patients.

The Vicar recorded Mrs. Evans great service to the community, producing and acting in plays and pantomimes, being a school manager, President of the Women's Branch of the British Legion and of the Womens' Institute, organising R.S.P.B. film shows, helping the District Nursing Association and the R.N.L.I., the local church and the parish hall, as well as teaching art.

Mr. J.P. Jackson recalled how Mrs. Evans drew portraits at a garden party.

Mr. S. Potts then came on the stage and presented Dr. and Mrs. Evans with a 400-day clock from the Chelford Cricket Club.

Dr. S. Pratt told the gathering how much he had appreciated working with Dr. Evans and the Vicar said that the previous day he took a tape recorder to one of Dr. Evans patients to record a message – Dame Lilian Bromley-Davenport.

Her reply came from the back of the hall! She had flatly refused to send a recorded message, sprang a surprise on the gathering and went forward to the platform.
Receiving a great ovation, Dame Lilian paid tribute to Dr. and Mrs. Evans in glowing terms, and also to their sons and housekeeper, and then on behalf of their many friends and admirers she presented Dr. Evans with a stainless steel meat dish and a cheque for £375.

After Dr. and Mrs. Evans had expressed their thanks for the gift and the tributes paid them, refreshments were served. There followed an entertainment by Franki Woods and finally dancing to the Alpines Dance Band.

The refreshment helpers were Miss L. Tickle, Mrs. T. Newton, Mrs. Slater, Miss Turnock, Miss J. Taylor, Mrs. Blomfield, Mrs. C. Worthington, Mrs. Camm, Mrs. F. Worthington, Mrs. Sutcliffe, Mrs. H. Bradley, Mrs. Forrester, Mrs. W. Lowe, Mrs. G. Shelton and Mrs. Yates

THE VILLAGE POLICEMAN

The village policeman has only a relatively short history, the Cheshire Police being formed in 1856. Prior to this date the responsibility for law and order was with the village Parish Constable appointed by the Court Leet in medieval times and later by the vestries. There appears to be no record of a Parish Constable in Chelford, the village probably being too small to warrant such a position.

One of the Parish Constable's duties was to supervise the stocks which only became extinct in England in the middle of the 19th Century. There is no evidence of any stocks in Chelford though they probably did exist as most villages used the stocks until comparatively recent times.

Throughout the first half of the 19th Century the Parish Constable's status declined rapidly and eventually only the unemployed took the position. As a result most Constables were illiterate, and in some cases, disrespected, holding a position that nobody else wanted. It was against his background that the Police Act of 1856 compelled counties to establish forces in all towns and villages.

The 'new' constables were to be intelligent, able to read and write, active, of a strong constitution and certified free of bodily complaints, at least 5'-7" tall and not more than 40 years old. They were to be of good moral character and connections. However, there were considerable draw backs. Discipline was very strict, the work was hard and wages only on a par with those of unskilled agricultural labourers. They were expected to attend church on Sunday and, in some cases, some Police Chiefs limited a Constable's family to two.

A Victorian country policeman worked a seven day week and a ten or twelve hour day in two shifts. By the 1870's conditions improved to one rest day in every four weeks and an annual unpaid week's holiday. Most of his working time was spent patrolling on foot, on rough country roads. In the Chelford area he would have been on the look out for common offences like 'riding without reins, cattle-stealing, petty stealing, drunkenness, poaching and vagrancy'.

The first reference to a Policeman in Chelford is in the 1851 Census which shows an Abram Lawton, Lodger, Unmarried, aged 36, County Police Officer who was living with Timothy and Elizabeth Locket in School Lane, probably at Yew Tree Farm as Timothy Locket was a farmer of 12 acres.

Village policeman early 20th century

The 1861 Census records George Dalton, aged 24 born Staffordshire married to Ellen, as a Police Constable.

By 1871, according to the Census of that year, the Police Constable was Thomas Gibbons who lived with his wife and young family in Station Road.

Between 1871 and 1881 the Constable had changed at least once as the 1881 Census lists John Alexander aged 28 born in Scotland as the Police Constable. His eldest son, Edgar aged 3, had been born in Chelford and his father must have been the Chelford 'bobby' in 1878 if not earlier. The family lived in Station Road.

The same house (presumably) in Station Road must have been a police house as the 1891 Census shows Thomas Bowyer, aged 33 as Police Constable, living with his wife, Sarah and two daughters, in Station Road.

Throughout the 20th Century there has always been a Police presence in Chelford with a Police House/Station being built in Knutsford Road. The building remains along with the local *'Bobby'*. However, in recent years there have been significant changes in the village and society generally. For example, the village has expanded, better roads and more cars have led to traffic problems, easy access to the area and increased affluence have attracted travelling criminals and the growth of telephone usage creates a demand for the Police to respond faster and more often. The local Officer is therefore now supported by Officers from nearby Knutsford.

This article is reproduced following permission granted by Superintendent D. A. Barnett, Divisional Commander, Macclesfield Division.

CHELFORD AND DISTRICT FARMERS BALL

It was on an autumn day in 1936 at Heath Farm, Snelson, the home of farmer Alan Massey. The traction engine and threshing box arrived to thresh the corn. It was Jim Dakin of Manor Farm, Over Peover who blew the whistle on that day to start his day's work. During the 'baggin' time break which consisted of toasted cheese and fried onions, it was decided by Alan and Jim to 'Have a Ball', and a good social get together. They decided to ask their friends Arthur Turnock of Yew Tree Farm, Lower Withington, Rex Massey of Brook House Farm, Lower Withington and Rex Walkley of Mill Lane Farm, Capesthorne to join them. A committee was formed, Jim Dakin was elected to be the chairman, Alan Massey the secretary and each person donated 10s 0d (ten shillings) to a fund to open a bank account. The Ball was to be named Chelford and District Farmers' Ball.

The first Ball was held in the Chelford Village Hall on the last Friday evening in January 1937 and is still held today on the last Friday evening in January. The tradition was to keep it a Ball with evening dress, black tie for the men, ball gowns for the ladies. Local people have catered for this event, the first caterers being Hides of Chelford followed by Mrs Bates of Goostrey and Actons of Wilmslow.

During the Second World War 1939 - 1945 food was on ration but the caterers always seemed to provide enough, maybe helped by the committee members. It was at about this time that Wilf Massey was elected to the committee; he joined at a very difficult time. No Ball was held in 1941 due to the war and the blackout regulations.

Menu and price of a 1950 meal by Actons of Wilmslow: -

7.30pm	Main meal	cold meats, green salad and a sweet	5s 0d
10.30pm	Supper	sandwiches, sausage roll and a cake	1s 0d
Midnight		Ice Cream	0s 6d

| Hire of the Hall | £2 5s 0d |
| Flowers for decoration (Daffodils and Mimosa) | 5s 0d |

The committee members and their wives or friends decorated the hall. Balloons were blown up and put into a large net hung up in the ceiling. They were released just before the last waltz onto the heads of the dancers. The price of the ticket at this time was 10s 6d.

No bar was ever provided in those early years but certain people sneaked away during the interval to the Dixon Arms to quench their thirst!

In the 'Swinging Sixties' the dress for the ladies changed, long ball gowns were out and shorter skirts were the 'in' thing. This picture taken on 29th January 1964 shows the shorter dress length. The price of the ticket for this Ball was 15s 0d; Hire of the Hall was £3 10s 0d and the Kath Jones Dance Band charged £9 0s 0d. There was a big change on the 27th January 1967 when the Ball was held for the first time away from Chelford. The venue was the newly built Lower Withington Parish Hall. This was the first time a hot meal was served and the first time a bar was provided. The caterers were Boyles from Stockport. The price of the ticket was £1 2s 6d. The Jay Leslie Dance Band played for £21 0s 0d and the hire of the Hall was £7 10s 0d.

Front Row: Freda Massey, Doris Read, Susan Ryder, Christine Barber, Christine Turnock, and Joan Massey
Centre Row: Ethel Walkley, Mona Turnock, ..., Vera Stanier, Evelyn Venables, Margaret Venables, Josie Parfitt
Back Row:......... Wilf Massey, Rex Walkley, Arthur Turnock, Edwin Massey, Marie Foden, Judith Oliver, Peter Clarkson .... Brian Clarkson, Bill Venables ....
Ernest Pimlott, Dennis Parfitt

No Ball was held in 1968 due to the foot and mouth outbreak in cattle. It was a very sad time for those farmers who lost all their cattle.

For 27 years the Ball was held in the Lower Withington Parish Hall. The 40th, 50th and 60th Anniversaries were celebrated there. The tickets show the date, price of ticket and the band that played for the dancing.

In 1972 Arthur Turnock was elected as Chairman. He introduced the singing of the old folk song 'Farmer's Boy' and he led the singing. It is still sung at midnight at each Ball. Special guests on the 30 January 1981 were the Mayor and Mayoress of Macclesfield, Councillor and Mrs Ernest Coppock.

THE FARMERS BOY

The sun had set behind yon hills,
Across yon dreary moor,
Weary and lame, a boy there came
Up to a farmer's door.
'Can you tell me if any there be
That will give me employ,
To plow and sow and reap and mow
And be a farmer's boy?'

'My father is dead, and mother is left
With five children, great and small;
And what is worse for mother still,
I'm the oldest of them all.
Though little, I'll work as hard as a Turk,
If you'll give me employ,
To plow and sow and reap and mow
And be a farmer's boy.

'And if that you won't me employ,
One favour I've to ask; -
Will you shelter me, till break of day,
From this cold winter's blast?
At break of day, I'll trudge away
Elsewhere to seek employ.
To plow and sow and reap and mow
And be a farmer's boy.'

'Come try the lad,' the mistress said,

168

'Let him no further seek',
'O, do, dear father, ' the daughter cried,
While tears ran down her cheek.
'He'd work if he could, so 'tis hard to want food,
And wander for employ;
Don't turn him away but let him stay,
And be a farmer's boy!'.

And when the lad became a man,
The good old farmer died,
And left the lad the farm he had,
And his daughter for his bride,
The lad that was the farm now has,
Oft smiles and thinks with joy
Of the lucky day he came that way,
To be a farmer's boy.

For the 50th Anniversary on 29th January 1988, Mrs Rachel Whittaker of Knutsford baked a delicious 14-inch square fruitcake, iced and decorated to perfection.

It was all change again on 28th January 1994 when the Ball was held in the newly modernised Chelford Village Hall. Farmhouse Fayre of Ullard Hall Farm, Toft, Knutsford provided the hot meal. In 1997 the ball was again held in Lower Withington Parish Hall. The 60th Anniversary on 30th January 1998 was celebrated at Lower Withington Parish Hall. The delicious fruitcake was baked by Mrs Heather Pearson of Lower Peover, and an abundance of good food was provided by Farmhouse Fayre.

Menu

Vegetable Soup with roll and butter
Roast Beef with Yorkshire pudding
Hot potatoes with parsley butter
Roast potatoes
Carrots with parsley butter
Cauliflower cheese.
Choice of four sweets.
Cheese and Biscuits
Coffee or tea and mints

Dance Bands through the years:

Paramount Players	£16 0s 0d
Victor Green Ballroom Orchestra from Crewe	£19 12s 0d
Kath Jones Dance Band	£ 9 10s 0d
Mabel Smith Dance Band	£21 0s 0d
Ray Peters Dance Band	£11 11s 0d
Les Gatley Dance Band from Northwich	£ 8 10s 0d
Alphine Band	£10 0s 0d
Eric Pep and His Music from Warrington	£20 0s 0d
Jay Leslie Dance Band	£21 0s 0d
Bert Grange Band	£25 0s 0d
Dane Valley Dance Band(1969-1987)	£16 0s 0d to£90.00d
Sounds Easy Dance Band (1988-1999)	£90.00 to £150.00d

Barmen who have quenched our thirst:-

Mr Peter Cookson, Snelson, Chelford
Mr Williamson, Macclesfield
Mr Harry Drew, Commercial Hotel, Macclesfield
Mr Harold Ryder, The White Bear, Knutsford
Mr Geoff Irlam, The Dixon Arms Hotel, Chelford
Mr Robert Hollinshead, The Royal Oak Hotel, Worleston, Nantwich

Caterers who have provided good food:

Mr Hides, Chelford
Mrs Bates, Goostrey
Mr Joe Acton, Wilmslow
Boyles of Stockport
The Corner House, Alderley Edge
Mrs Brown, Congleton
Bakers of Leek
Mrs Cynthia Dale, Congleton
Ridgeways of Leek
Farmhouse Fayre, Knutsford

Committee members past and present:

Alan Massey	1936 - 1967
James Dakin	1936 - 1972
Arthur Turnock	1936 - 1990

Rex Massey	1936 - 1976
Rex Walkley	1936 - 1982
Wilf Massey	1938 -
William Buckley	1947 - 1961
Alan Baskerville	1961 - 1970
Peter Clarkson	1962 -
Edwin Massey	1963 - 1983
Alan Barber	1967 - 1992
Paul Massey	1982 -
Steven Massey	1983 -
David Venables	1990 -
Andrew Barber	1992 -

The committee members 1999

Wilf Massey - Secretary and Treasurer, longest serving member, secretary 30 years
Steven Massey, Chairperson
Peter Clarkson, Vice Chairperson and past Chairperson
Assisted by Paul Massey, Andrew Barber and David Venables.
The next Ball will be held on 28th January 2000 - The Millennium Year

60TH ANNIVERSARY OF FARMER'S BALL 30 JANUARY 1998

60TH ANNIVERSARY OF FARMER'S BALL 30 JANUARY 1998

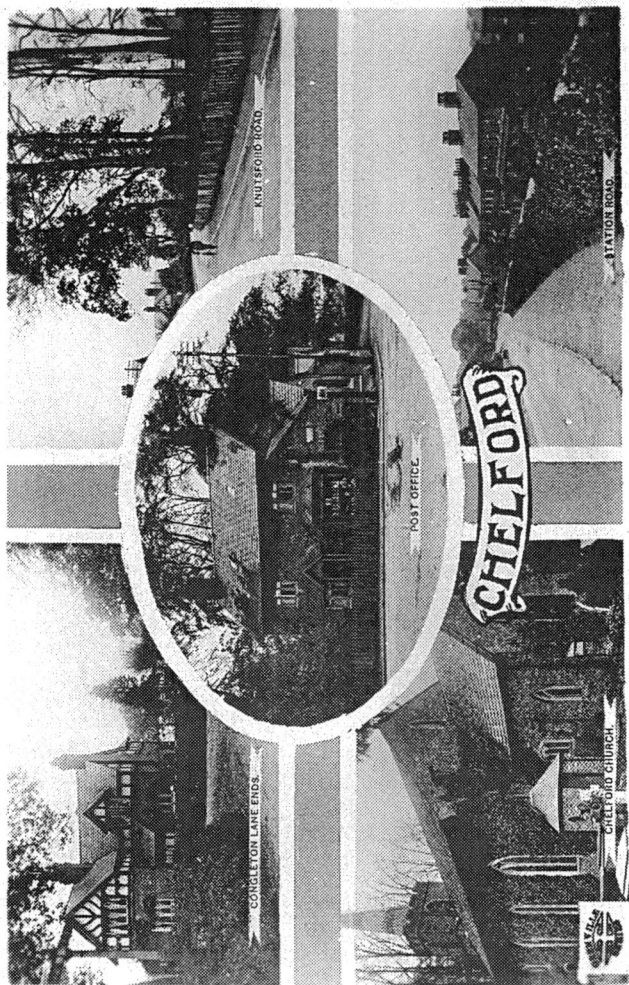

Top left: Congleton Lane Ends, Top right: Knutsford Road, Bottom left: Chelford Church, Bottom Right: Station Road, Centre: Post Office.

173

MEREHILLS   c1930
Merehills was situated in the area of the junction of Dixon Drive, Knutsford Road and Pepper Street.

174

KNUTSFORD ROAD - CHELFORD (Date not known)

175

HOLMES CHAPEL ROAD – CHELFORD c (Date not known)

POST OFFICE & BLACKSMITHS (Date not known)
Extension on Post Office used as Sorting Office

177

CHELFORD CORNER (Date not known)
Smithy approached from Holmes Chapel Road.

Chelford, The Village

APPROACHING CHELFORD STATION (Date not known)
Garage on right hand side is no longer in existence

179

Chalfont Dene Roundabout
CHELFORD ROUNDABOUT – PRE 1959 (Date not known)

POST OFFICE – CHELFORD CORNER (Date not known)

Telephone post in centre of picture was used to tie horses and was reinforced with hard board strips to prevent horses from chewing the post. The post is still in the same position. Man in centre of road could have been RAC Scout on point duty. (See memories by Katherine Tomlinson.)

STATION ROAD-DIXON ARMS ON RIGHT HAND SIDE (Date not known)
Building on extreme right hand side of picture was sub branch of Westminster Bank

CHELFORD STATION (Date not known)
Date unknown but when we had railway workers

183

SHOP IS NOW MR & MRS CHAN, GREENGROCERS *(Date not known)*

THE GRANGE - CHELFORD

The home of the Shiers family in 1871, the Howarth family in 1881 and the Cook family in 1891.

185

ASTLE HALL *(Date not known)*

186

ASTLE LODGE (Gamekeeper's Cottage)
Possible site of original school room.

187

THE EGERTON ARMS IN 1954

AERIAL VIEW JAMES IRLAM & SONS c1990
Showing Dixon Arms in right hand corner and Station Road bottom left

189

CHELFORD CRICKET

Chelford's connection with cricket goes further back than most villages. In 1861 Thomas Nixon left Oxford to take up a permanent engagement with the Cheshire County Club at Chelford. He quickly established a cricket ground adjacent to the Dixon Arms Hotel on the site at present occupied by the Haulage Company, James Irlam & Son.

Thomas Nixon was born in Nottingham on 4 June 1815 becoming, as so many others in that town, a lace worker. He was also involved in the emerging game of cricket, being a slow round-arm spin bowler. It was said that he acquired both accurate length and that quick 'lift' from the pitch, which makes slow bowling effective. He spent 1837 with the Southwell Club but only remained there for one season. There was a great deal of competition in Nottinghamshire at that time and the tall but sparsely built young man (he was 5'10½" in height but only weighed 10 st.) had little to recommend him for a place in the Nottinghamshire team. Even though his slow bowling was very effective he was neither a batsman nor a reliable fielder.

Throughout his life he was inventive and very early in his career recognised that with increasing bowling speed, protective armour would soon be in general demand. In fact he devised cork pads in 1841 and throughout his life he was a foremost designer of cricket assessories.

NIXON.

Reproduced by kind permission of M.C.C.

190

The following year he played for the Slow Bowlers against the Fast Bowlers at Lords, a match as low scoring as one would expect from a game featuring bowlers only. He was out for a duck in both innings. He did however take three wickets in the Fast Bowlers' first innings. A number of well-known names featured in this particular game including Felix, A Mynn, F Pilch and W Lillywhite.

When in his early thirties he obtained an engagement at Stourbridge where he took a number of wickets in matches against Wolverhampton, Worcester and Birmingham. In 1847 he played for 22 of Birmingham and District against an England X1, contributing to a five run victory by taking 14 wickets. Some further successes led to him being borrowed by the Gentlemen of Worcester to play against I Zingari at Himley, a match in which he took 8 wickets.

In 1850 he spent one season at Layer-de-la Haye in Essex. He continued to develop his bowling skills (but not his batting) and in 1851 he was engaged at Lords, taking nine wickets in an innings when playing for the MCC against Middlesex. In July 1851 he played for England against Kent, taking the wickets of Fuller Pilch, Felix and Alfred Mynn in the second innings.

In that year, he also assisted Nottinghamshire in their first match against Surrey at Kennington Oval taking the notable wickets of Julius Caesar, Martingell and Felix.

Between 1851 and 1853 he appeared four times for the Players against the Gentlemen, recording his best performance in the second fixture at Lords when he accounted for three batsmen in the first innings and five in the second.

Nixon's engagement at Lords enabled him to develop his inventive skills and in 1853 he introduced skeleton pads followed by cane-handled bats. As he approached his forties he must have realised that his ingenuity as a manufacturer promised a more secure future than playing so in 1856 he set up in business at Oxford. A year later he resigned his post at Lords, having become landlord of the Old White Horse Inn, which had a cricket ground attached to it as well as a racket court.

He then took up a post with the newly formed Cheshire County Cricket Club and on his arrival at Chelford he established, in conjunction with his two sons, a Cricketing Outfitters.

According to contemporary opinion if he had been a better batsman and fielder, he would have been chosen for more representative games and possibly have become a regular in the England team. As it is, his position in the game's history is probably more renowned for his inventive enterprise with cricketing equipment rather than his prowess on the field.

Prior to moving to Chelford he devised and patented a bowling machine called the Ballista, one of the first (if not **the** first) machines of its type in the UK.

The Commercial Directories of the time carried an advert covering his outfitting enterprises.

T. NIXON & SONS,
CRICKETING OUTFITTERS,
CHELFORD, CHESHIRE.
Cobbett's and Dark's very best Cane Handle Bats, 15s. each.
All other First-class Articles at reasonable prices.
Wholesale Manufacturers of their newly invented Broad Cane Double-quilted Leg Guards.   Price Lists Free

---

He lived with his wife Phoebe, his two daughters Ann and Phoebe, and his two sons Henry and Reuben, at one of the houses in Station Road.

Thomas died on 20 July 1877 and was buried at Chelford.

The Cheshire County Cricket Club's first season was 1861 but few county games took place.   Most games were against town clubs and wandering players. Subsequently, a number of games against representatives of County Clubs did take place but by the late 1870's the club was having great difficulty in raising eleven players.   Consequently in 1882 the Cheshire County Cricket Club was re-formed and, in 1883, amalgamated with the Stockport club so that gate money could be collected for an enclosed ground.

During the period when Cheshire County played at Chelford, i.e. 1861-82, a number of players from the Astle Park Club represented Cheshire including the following: -

Name		No. of Matches
Leonard Peel Andrews	1876-78	5
Willoughby Andrews	1881-82	4
Alfred Ashton	1881	5

Rev Colin Edward Beever Bell (Vicar of Chelford 1907-1914)		1880-81	4
Walter Arthur Bromley Davenport		1882	1
Brg. Gen. Sir William Bromley Davenport (Also played soccer for England)		1881-82	5
Arthur Edward Caldecut		1874	1
Harold Carlisle		1874-78	2
Samuel Carlisle		1873-74	8
Richard Louis Crankshaw	(Lived at Dalefields)	1880-82	13
Sir James Stewart Davy		1880	2
Frederick Parker Dixon	(Lived at Astle Hall)	1872-81	5
Lt. Col. Sir George Dixon	(Lived at Astle Hall)	1865-82	16
John Wykeham Dixon	(Lived at Astle Hall)	1861-62	3
William Arthur Tatton Dixon	(Lived at Astle Hall)	1873-82	18
Richard Entwisle		1863-74	10
John Baskervyle Glegg	(Withington Hall)	1865-70	3
William Baskervyle Glegg	(Withington Hall)	1874	2
Radclyffe Radclyffe Hall		1882	1
Sir Arthur Percival Heywood		1868-69	2
Leyland Langton		1871-82	20
William Heywood Langton		1867-81	5
M. McKenzie		1875	2
J. S. Manor		1881-82	4
William Henry Baker Medd		1878-81	9
James Henry Murray		1867-77	10
St Aubyn Henry Player		1875	8
Rev Alfred Littledale Royds	(Vicar of Chelford)	1882	8
Joseph Shiers	(Lived at The Grange, Chelford)	1870	1
George Edward Solly		1874-82	27
Edmund Swinburn		1863-82	23
Charles Edward Thornycroft		1870-81	5
Rev John Mytton Thornycroft		1877-81	9
Edmund Gannon Winstanley		1874-81	11

In addition to the above Rueben Nixon played in 8 matches between 1863 and 1882 and Thomas Nixon one match in 1861.

The above information has been reproduced by kind permission from Tony Percival from his publication 'Cheshire Cricketers 1822-1996'.

The old County ground at Chelford was retained for matches played by the Gentlemen of Cheshire and continued to be used by this club until the Second

World War when the ground was taken over by the Ministry of Food and a storage depot built.

The present Chelford Cricket Club was founded in 1948, the first captain of the club being Stan Potts who on the 25th anniversary of the club gave the following description of the early years.

It all started on a pleasant morning in 1948. Mrs Evans, wife of our local doctor and the live wire of the village, gave me a hail as I went by on my pushbike. "What we want in this village" she said, "is a cricket team". "Well you're the very person to start one", said I, knowing full well that once Mrs Evans got her teeth into a project it would succeed even if she had to move mountains.

Enlisting the help of Col. Fox, who had just moved into the village, and any other interested or half-interested parties who could be press-ganged into action, we set about looking for a ground. Cricket was nothing new in Chelford. In Astle Park the village team had played for over 50 years and in the Church cottages still lived Mr G Steele, veteran of the 1920's, who had himself taken all ten wickets in a match.

Prior to the Second World War, and in the village itself, the Gentlemen of Cheshire had their lovely ground. However, the troops recently demobbed from HM Forces found things somewhat changed from when they went away. A large cold storage factory had been built on the Cheshire Gents ground with a railway siding sliced through the middle of six of the finest tennis courts in the country and continuing straight through the centre of the soccer pitch on the Dixon Arms field. If this was not enough, the ground in Astle Park had disappeared, ploughed up in the "Dig for Victory" campaign.

Nothing daunted, Mrs Evans visited Mr Fred Hope who farmed Abbey Farm, and the outcome was that he was prepared to let us play on the field behind the Post Office.

Came Saturday afternoon when all the volunteers and pressed men assembled at the ground and in through the gate we trooped. A depressing scene met our eyes. Long dank grass covering an uneven field, a large hump at one side and a ridge running straight down towards the brook. A variety of ancient and unpruned blackcurrant bushes, brick ends, bits of pottery and several sheets of rusted corrugated iron littered the side of the field by the Church road. Thistles, docks and a large variety of weeds completed the picture.

194

On that day I am sure that had not Mrs Evans been the CO, ably supported by the Col., her working party, daunted by the enormity of the task to be done, would have melted away. However, with spade, shears, scythe, the good doctor's lawn mower (slightly past its prime), we moved in and the first swathe was cut on what is now a delight to the eye, a cricket ground of character, beauty and fair wickets.

Memories abound: catches in the slips; Arnold Cookson enjoying every minute and a delight to watch with a bat, Joe Callwood bowling like a two year old and producing a "shooter" out of the back of his hand almost at will, and many, many more.

Of Prof. Lovell, having brought along a Russian celebrity or two were visiting Jodrell Bank, trying to explain the game to them, and why, having erected three stumps at each end and walked out into the field, did we then immediately return and proceed to sit in the pavilion for the rest of the afternoon. I have a feeling that these mystified gentlemen returned to the Soviet Union firmly convinced that the British were quite mad. I am sure they did not believe that the rain had anything at all to do with it!

The existing pavilion was erected in 1963 and in 1990 a score box was built alongside.

In its early years the club played frequent games against other Cheshire village teams until 1974 when Chelford became one of the 14 founder members of the Cheshire Cricket League and are currently in Division 1 of The Mellor Braggins Cheshire County League.

One of the features of the club is the annual competition for juniors. This event started in 1984 and comprises 8 teams of under 13 years playing 10 overs each in a knock-out competition.

The club has always been interested in developing young local players and, in the very early days, Mrs Evans encouraged any scouts who expressed an interest, to join, a few of the earlier players were, Eddie Hobbs, Lawrence Bailey, Peter Newton, John Oliver, Peter Robertson, John Evans, Edmund Evans and Harold Ryder.

Early Senior players included

Don Bloor
Ashton Bloor
Tommy Bloor
Colin Bloor
Arnold Cookson
George Barber
Lawrence Bailey
Walter Bromley Davenport
William Bromley Davenport
Arthur Dakin
Lawrence Dunning
Alan Henshall
Eddie Hobbs
Fred Potts
Stan Potts

Peter Newton
Bill Merchant
Roy Merchant
Peter Robertson
Arthur Street
Len Rowlands
Michael Coates
Joe Callwood
Harry Drew
Rev Gamon
Dr Fox
Dr Hill
Ken Kirk
Frank Potts

At a later date they were joined by:

Prof. Lovell
Edmund 'Ebb' Evans
Alan Gresty
Don Wright
Bob Farnon
Nigel Ryder

John Evans
Robert Newton
Richard Duckworth
Rod Davies
Harry Newton
Derek Barber

The present president of the club is John Oliver and the chairman is Rowland Diggle. The first team Captain is Mike Shenton.

The authors would like to thank Mike Shenton for the loan of his 'scrap book' in the preparation of this chapter and various members of the club who have lent photographs. Thanks are also due to the MCC for permission to include information relative to the Nixon family

CHELFORD PAST ELEVEN PLAYING THE PRESENT XI – JULY 1973

Back row left to right: Peter Newton, Harold Harding, Joe Halsall, Peter Robertson, Ken Kirk, Brian Cope (in suit) Front row: Don Robertson, Ashton Bloor, Professor Sir Bernard Lovell, Rowland Diggle, Geoff Marsden.

CHELFORD CRICKET CLUB LATE 1950'S

Back Row: William Bromley Davenport, Rod Davies, Stan Potts, Don Wright, Ken Kirk. Front row: Richard Duckworth, Harry Newton, Sir Bernard Lovell, Peter Newton, Derek Barber, Bob Farnon

198

PEOVER – V – CHELFORD 1950

Top row: Mr White, P Robertson, P Newton, L Rowlands, M Cookson, K Kirk, W Baskerville, S Poole, C Blain, P Robinson, J Briscall, T Evans, L Jervis, J Baskerville, T Slater. Bottom row: L Bailey, N Dakin, F Potts, H Drew, M Coates, Dr Hill, Mrs Kirk, Mrs Blaines, I Wright, T Walton, H Newton, D Mallineax.

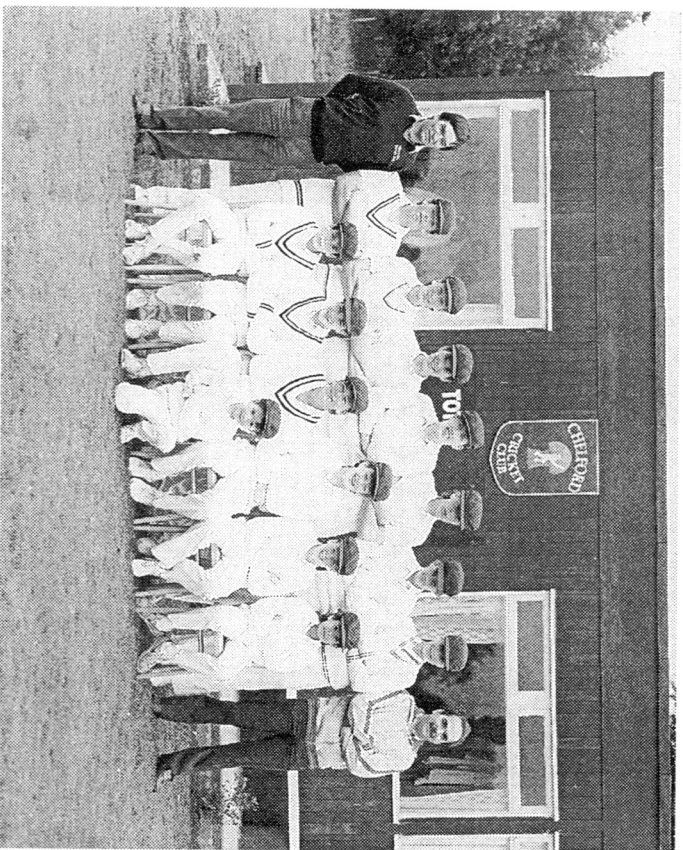

CHELFORD U15-1985

Back row, left to right: - Derek Higgins (Manager), Christian Smith, Adrian Smith, M Wattason, C Hibbert, M Walker, R Jones, G Evans and Paul Heath (Coach).

Front row, left to right: - Rick Shenton, Peter Campbell, Rob Higgins, Rick Dean, Tim Maxwell, Douglas Salto and Paul Rushton.

Sub Title – If you cannot win – wear a big hat.

Chelford Cricket Pitch – (Date not known)

Dixon Arms on left hand side – pitch used by Cheshire Gentlemen Cricket Club

ALEHOUSES OF CHELFORD

It is known that Chelford has had three Alehouses; (four if you include The Egerton Arms which technically is in Marthall,) plus possibly another, The Cat & Fiddle, Church Cottages, memories of which have been passed down through generations of villagers. It must be said at the outset that no documentary evidence has, as yet, come to light relative to this mystery alehouse.

Public houses constructed and licensed specifically for the purpose of selling alcohol only dates back to the 18th century. Prior to this date village communities were served by a range of drinking establishments, each fulfilling a different function. The most common of these alehouses were domestic houses where people could buy home-brewed ale or beer. Some of these houses were identified by a large broom protruding from the outside wall.

A Licensing Act of 1552 stipulated that anyone who wanted to sell ale had to apply for a licence at the Quarter Sessions. The Act was retained until 1828, though over the years there were many amendments to the original statute. However, it was not until 1619 that Registers of the Licenses were kept.

In 1828 a further Act provided a new framework for the granting of licenses but, it was not until 1872 that the keeping of a register of licenses was implemented. These records can be found in the records of the Quarter Sessions under the title of County Licensing Committee.

The earliest reference to Chelford in the registers is a list of licenses given to applicants for the sale of ale though not necessarily through an Alehouse. The list comprises as follows:

Daniel Bartington	1749
Joseph Sandbach	1749-55
Martha Bartington	1755
William Locket	1757

Alehouses known to have existed in Chelford at various times are

Archers   Red Lion   Dixon Arms

Archers

The Archers Alehouse was what is now Ivy House situated on the left hand side of Macclesfield Road as it leaves the village roundabout. The following information has been established.

Licence given to Thomas Potts	1762 - 86
Licence given to Thomas Snelson	1787 - 89

The 1789 map of Chelford shows a bowling green in the area of the present Ivy House and it is probable that at that time the Archers Inn possessed a Bowling Green.

Licence given to George Corner	1793
Licence given to Isaac Massey	1802
Licence given to Daniel Henshaw	1803-26

Sureties for Daniel Henshaw were:

1805	William Davenport & Wm Acton
1806	John Walker & Thomas Rawlinson
1807	Joseph Norbury & Joseph Shotwell
1808	William Mellor & James Mellor
1809	William Davenport & Peter Dumville
1810	Thomas Foden & Peter Dumville
1811	Peter Dumville & Samuel Henshaw

Daniel Henshaw and his wife, Elizabeth, were resident until 1826/7 when William Gilbert took over. Gilbert, with his wife, Ann, appeared in the Parish Registers with the baptisms of their children over the next eleven years. The 1834 Astle Estate Conveyance lists William Gilbert at Archers Inn as does the Register of Electors for that year.

In 1825 the Archers was referred to as the Royal Archers - why is not known - possibly a reference to the Royal Archers who formed part of the Black Prince's army in his wars with the French in the 15th Century and who were drawn from the Macclesfield area.

William Gilbert was buried on 26 January 1840 at the age of 54 and the Register of Electors for 1841 lists a Joseph Kennerley as occupier of The Archers Public House.

In the 1851 Census under the name of Archers Inn, Joseph Kennerley, age 33, is shown as an Innkeeper farming 23 acres. He was married to Margaret and they had two children aged 5 and 2.

The 1860 Commercial Directory and the 1861 Census shows that Archers Inn was occupied by Margaret Kennerley, Joseph having died by that time.

The 1871 Census, the 1872 Ordnance Map and the 1874 Commercial Directory show that Archers Inn had become The Robin Hood Inn and that Margaret Kennerley, age 53, widow, was Publican and farmer of 28 acres.

By 1881 the name had changed again, this time to Moss Grove and was the residence of Samuel Smith, a Surgeon, whose third son had been born in Chelford in 1875, his older sons having been born in Alderley. It can therefore be argued that Samuel Smith took over residence in about 1874 and it is probable that Archers Inn ceased to be an Alehouse at that time.

The 1897 Ordnance Map indicates a further change of name and the house is now known as Ivy House.

IVY HOUSE

204

Henry Lupton was the first of a series of medical practitioners resident in Ivy House. He was followed in turn by Mr S Smith and Mr H H Ballachey. It was Mr Ballachey who named the property The Ivy House.

Kelly's 1906 directory lists the next doctor in the Ivy House as Mr A H Shepard, joined some years later by his brother-in-law, Dr Evans.

During the Second World War Canadian Officers were billeted there and when the war ended one of them purchased the property. After a short period of being passed off as Chelford Place, it reverted to The Ivy House.

The present owner is Mr David Sutton.

Red Lion

Licenses given covering the Red Lion Chelford comprised the following:

Joseph Forster	1762	
Joseph Taylor	1765	
Joseph Ffrost*	1766	* (possibly Forster)
Joseph Forster	1774 to 1789	
James Lowe	1793 - 1806	

The sureties for James Lowe in 1805 were Wm Davenport and Wm Acton and for 1806 John Walker and Thomas Rawlinson.

There do not appear to have been any further licenses granted and therefore the Red Lion must have ceased operation as an alehouse sometime around 1806/7.

So where was the Red Lion? The last known licensee was James Lowe in 1806 and prior to that Joseph Forster. The Land Tax Returns for 1785 list a Joseph Forster with a tax assessment of 10s 1d. The 1795 Land Tax Returns list James Lowe at the same tax assessment of 10s 1d. It is therefore probable that these returns refer to the Red Lion. The 1825 returns list a Job Dale at a tax assessment of 10s 1d and his residence as a farm. Job Dale was buried in 1832 having died aged 54 of "Affliction of the bowel[1]".

The Recapitulation Apportionment taken on 19th March 1834 when the Astle estate was sold to Henry Dixon show a Widow Dale resident at a farm on the site

---

[1]   Chelford in the 19th Century by W Keith Plant

at present occupied by Knowsley Farm on the right hand side of Macclesfield Road as you leave the village. On the other hand the Recapitulation also lists a property in Astle as belonging to the late Job Dale. So was, what is now Knowsley Farm, originally the Red Lion, or was it on the site of Church Cottages under the name of Cat & Fiddle?

Cat & Fiddle

Tradition in the village has it that a further alehouse or beer shop existed, situated on the present site of Church Cottages and probably one of the existing cottages. It is supposed to have catered for the lower class of customer and to have been merely a converted cottage and also a house of dubious reputation. Relicts connected with an Alehouse have been found on this site. During the early part of the nineteenth century the Cat & Fiddle is said to have been closed down by the Stanley family, with two possible explanations as to why. The first is that a drunken horseman knocked over and killed a pedestrian. The second is that the Stanley family (who presumably owned the property) did not approve of the consumption of alcohol[2].

Whether there was an alehouse called the Cat & Fiddle cannot be confirmed. To date no documentary evidence has come to light confirming its existence.

According to Melanie Bouskill who used to live in the cottage supposed to have been the Cat & Fiddle, the house is now two half-timbered cottages and was at one time a single building with twin gabled dormers in black and white. Furthermore it had been known as the Cat and Lion as well as the Cat and Fiddle. It is therefore possible that the Red Lion and the Cat and Fiddle (or Cat and Lion) are the same.

It must be remembered that Knowsley Farm was in the Alderley parish which was very much under the influence of the Stanley family whereas, Church Cottages, as far as is known, had no connection with the Stanleys family. If the supposition is that the Stanleys had some bearing on the closing of the Red Lion/Cat & Lion/ Cat & Fiddle, it is more likely to have been Knowsley Farm than Church Cottages.

Perhaps when the Red Lion closed down, trade transferred to an unlicensed pub in Church Cottages under the name of Cat & Lion or Cat & Fiddle.

Alternatively, the Cat & Fiddle may have been an early 20th century hostelry.

---

2   Chelford - the Village and its railway by Melanie Bouskill.

The feeling from the existing villagers is that a public house did exist in one of the Church Cottages and it must be a reasonable assumption that such an establishment was situated on this site.

CAT AND FIDDLE

Dixon Arms

The Parliamentary Electors lists for 1845/6 has no reference to the Dixon Arms, the first years list containing the name of Dixon Arms being 1847/8. Therefore it was presumably built in this period. Obviously it was built to meet the needs of the railway. The first owner was Thomas Gledhill who, in the 1851 Census, is referred to as a Coach Proprietor and Innkeeper farming 17 acres and employing seven labourers[3].

It is interesting to note that the 1848 Slaters Commercial Directory refers to the Dixon Arms as an Inn and Posting House whereas the Robin Hood (Archers) was only referred to as a Tavern & Public House. Obviously the Dixon Arms was considered 'up market' at that time. By 1860 the Inn was run by Mr William Adams. The Commercial Directory of that year[4] contained the following:

"The Dixon Arms Railway, Commercial and Posting Hotel is situated close to the station. The house is fitted up with every

---

3   Chelford in the 19th Century by W Keith Plant

4   White & Co History, Gazattee and Directory of Cheshire

comfort and convenience for visitors. Post horses and carriages may be had on the shortest notice by application to the proprietor, Mr William Adams".

"Omnibuses operate from Dixon Arms & Railway Hotel:-

To Knutsford at 9.00 a.m., 2.30 p.m. and 6.00 p.m. daily

(except on Sunday when it leaves at 10.20 a.m.) to meet the trains at the above mentioned times to forward passengers to Knutsford.

To Macclesfield, Tuesday and Saturday at 9.00 a.m. and return at 4.00 p.m.

In 1871 and 1881 the Innkeeper was Alfred Claxton who was married to Anna both being natives of Norfolk. However, by 1891 Thomas Gledhill (the grandson of the original proprietor Thomas Gledhill) had taken over the Inn. He was married to Sarah and at that time they had seven daughters. According to the 1891 Census the family had a nurse, a general servant, a barmaid and an ostler.

Mr Gledhill brewed his own beer on the premises. "A brewer from Congleton called Jess Dale used to live in the pub during the week to make the beer. There was a lovely smell on brewing days. Gledhill;s ale was real strong stuff".

The Gledhills also ran a meet curing business in the Dixon Arms, and kept their own pigs. Sides of bacon and hams could be seen hanging in parts of the pub. This all came to an end after the First World War when George Henry Dale became the landlord. He ran his own taxi business and the Westminster Bank occupied the old coach house (now demolished to make the car park). Mr Dale was succeeded in 1936 by Mr & Mrs Nield. At that time the Cheshire Gentlemen had a cricket pitch alongside the railway. Hockey was played there in the winter and there were two bowling greens at the back. The years before the Second World War were recalled as being hectic. One night some 40 charabancs were on the car park having brought trippers to the cricket and ballroom.

By the 1920's the Dixon Arms had become a popular place to visit by organisations such as Unions, Companies, Cycling clubs etc. The picture below was taken from the September 1928 issue of the Amalgamated Society of Woodworkers Monthly Journal. The Cricket Pavillion is shown in the background.

The District Committee this year selected the Dixon Arms Hotel, Chelford, Cheshire, as the venue for the annual outing for our superannuated members, and on Saturday, 21st July 1928, 50 veterans, together with a number of stewards, the District Committee and its officers, and our Assistant General Secretary were present. It turned out to be a beautiful day, and the best part of it was spent in the open air. A bowling match also took place for which prizes were given.

DIXON ARMS c1900

In 1943 Mr & Mrs Woodward took on the licence and remained until the 1970's. For a few years the pub was run by managers until Mr Alan Large arrived late in 1975.

Egerton Arms

Early licenses for the township of Marthall (in which the Egerton Arms is situated) cover the following:

John Smith	1639-41	Alehouse Keeper
Philip Baguley	1640-41	Alehouse Keeper
Henry Glover	1753	Licence to sell Ale
Samuel Henshall	1753	Licence to sell Ale
Joseph Shotwell	1770-92	Egerton Arms
James Hill	1793-1803	Egerton Arms
Thomas Clarke	1804-1824	Egerton Arms
John Leather	1825-1828	Egerton Arms

Whether the references for 1639-41 refer to the Egerton Arms or some other alehouse on the same or a different site is not known. The references for 1753 are probably licenses for beer houses.

On the Marthall Tithe Map of 1847 the Apportionment for the area at present occupied by the Egerton Arms is shown as Ref. No. 367 House & Yard, occupied by John Chadfield, owned by Wilbraham Egerton Esq. and   - A 1R 28P in size.

The 1851 Census for Marthall includes[5]:

Egerton Arms	John Chadfield	Head	Mar	50	Innkeeper and Farmer 20 acres	bn Derbyshire
	Catherine "	Wife	Mar	49		bn Wincham
	Sarah "	Dau		7		bn Marthall
	Robert Daniel	Serv	Un M	24	Servant	bn Marthall
	Sophia Davies	Serv	Mar	32	House Servant Inn	bn Peover

---

5   Census Returns – CRO - Chester.

Based on the census returns for 1861 the Egerton Arms was probably taken over in 1857 by William Moore, the 1861 Census showing[6]

Egerton Arms William Moore		Head	Mar	44	Veterinary Surgeon Farmer 48 acres employing 1 man	bn Cambridgeshire
	Margaret "	Wife	Mar	36		bn Bollington
	William A "	Son		5	Scholar	bn Rostherne
	Margaret "	Dau		4	"	bn Marthall
	John "	Son		3		bn Marthall
	Richard "	Son			10 mth	bn Marthall
	Eliza Brown	Serv	Un M	18	Dairy Maid	bn Toft
	Jane Bowers	Serv	Un M	14	General Servant	bn Ollerton
	James Sumner	Serv	Un M	28	Carter	bn Mobberley

From this census return it can be shown that in the 10 years between 1851 and 1861 the Egerton Arms had grown considerably. It was now a farm of 48 acres.

There is no reference to the Egerton Arms in the 1871 census, but that of 1881 contains information showing that William Moore now called himself William Dalton Moore and in addition to a farmer, now listed himself as a Licensed Victualler. He had four children living at home, John and Richard, his two sons, running the farm. There was a Dairymaid, Mary Ann Ware, born in Peover, showing that at that time the farm was still a dairy farm.

By 1891 the Egerton Arms is listed as Mere Hills, William was a widower and the farm was run by Richard. Resident on the night of the census was a housekeeper, a domestic servant, a farm servant and a farm labourer.

Kelly's Directory of 1910 lists James Brown of the Egerton Arms. James was still resident there in 1934.

---

6   Census Returns – CRO - Chester
                                    .

EGERTON ARMS ABOUT 1915

Shown above are James Brown, Mary Hannah Brown, Sydney Brown and Hilda Brown. They came to the Egerton in 1901 from Moulton and left in 1933, moving to the house opposite, next to the farm. A man called Richard Knowles then moved in and after him came Dick Tyldesley who played cricket for Lancashire.

CHELFORD CATTLE MARKET

The Chelford Cattle Market Company Limited was formed in 1910 with forty-five shareholders holding fifty shares, with £450 issued of an authorised capital of £600. A half-acre plot of land, presently the site of the vegetable shed, was rented from Sir George Dixon and livestock pens erected.

The Market opened in 1911, selling fortnightly on Mondays. The first chairman being Thomas Wilson with John E Braggins as managing director.

The company banked with the Manchester and Liverpool District Banking Co., which operated, from the front room of a house in Chelford.

The founder of the present Company operating Chelford Market, Frank R. Marshall, at the age of 13 years, joined the late John E Braggins, who ran the then Market Company, in 1917. At this time Cheshire and the surrounding area was served by Cattle Markets at Crewe, Congleton, Knutsford, Beeston Castle, Macclesfield, Malpas, Chester, Frodsham, Marple, Northwich, Warrington, Norton Arms (Warrington), Altrincham and Stockport.

From 1916 to 1921/1922 livestock was the subject of Ministry of Food control, with most Markets operating as grading centres, all having to open on a weekly basis. Just as control was removed, Foot and Mouth disease broke out, between January 1922 and May 1924, with 1,075 cases and a further 362 cases by December 1924. During most of this time the Market was either completely closed or partly restricted.

After the foot and mouth outbreak was over, the Market began to expand and develop with the Limited Company buying the Market site in 1926, together with 500 wooden pens for holding poultry, for the first Christmas sale in 1928. Competition had also developed however, with more markets opening at Wilmslow, Handforth, Holmes Chapel and Winsford.

Heck of a noisy mart at **CHELFORD**

/

What with the jabbering of the poultry and the auctioneer

I've been bidding against him for the last five minutes!

The buyers don't stand a dogs chance.

In 1933 John E Braggins purchased the assets of the Chelford Cattle Market Company Limited, taking Frank R Marshall into partnership in 1935

At the outbreak of the Second World War, control was again imposed, and Chelford was used as a grading centre until 1954. In 1946 Mr Braggins retired and, with the purchase of the goodwill of the Livestock and General Business, and the Chelford Cattle Market, on 9th May 1947, Mr Marshall established the present company.

The Hay and Straw Market was started by Mr A J Newton, late of Haymans Farm, Nether Alderley, and the Market site was added to by the acquisition of 1,854 sq. yds. from Sir John Dixon in November 1950, together with 1,560 sq. yards and another 550 sq. yards from General Refraction. Knutsford auction closed and the shedding and sheep pens, together with some pens from Altrincham Market were purchased and re-erected at Chelford where they served faithfully until 1981.

Whilst Chelford continued to grow in size, it was not until the end of another outbreak of Foot and Mouth disease in 1967/8 when the market was closed for 11 weeks, that its full potential was realised. Being one of the first markets allowed to re-open, Chelford received – and absorbed to everyone's satisfaction – a great influx of stock which had been held on farms pending the restoration of normal trading activities, and such was the service offered by the Company that a dramatic growth in throughput ensued.

Chelford Market now occupies a site of approximately 10 acres, and whilst the number of markets in Cheshire has been reduced to only 5, major advances in road systems and heavy haulage have greatly increased the competition between such markets, and thereby ensured the farmer/producer of the best returns possible.

Demand from vegetable growers wanting to sell home produce at Chelford led to the first designated produce and horticultural sale in October 1976 and this area of the company's activities has continued to grow. It now includes, in addition to vegetables, flowers, pot plants, trees, shrubs, eggs, fruit, dressed poultry and game. Chelford is now the largest horticultural auction market in Great Britain.

The market was extended further in 1979 when a new calf sales ring formed the first phase of accommodation for 1200 calves. Mr Frank Marshall (pictured next page) took the bids in the first sale and the buyer of the first calf was presented with a bottle of champagne to commemorate the occasion.

214

Chelford's reputation over the years has been built on the foundation of providing its customers with an efficient service. There is a continuing commitment to development and growth to cater for an increasing market.

The above article has been prepared from information provided by Gwyn Williams of Marshall Chartered Surveyors and the authors would like to thank him for his help.

A 'young' Nicholas Winterton. MP. presenting the award for the Champion Steer to Ernest Webb of Plumley at the Christmas Show 1978.

Miss Greswell, Marthall Vicarage, Knutsford
July 1908

Its the little things which tell!
Adage true; like many others.
If you don't believe it, well –
Ask big sisters with small brothers.

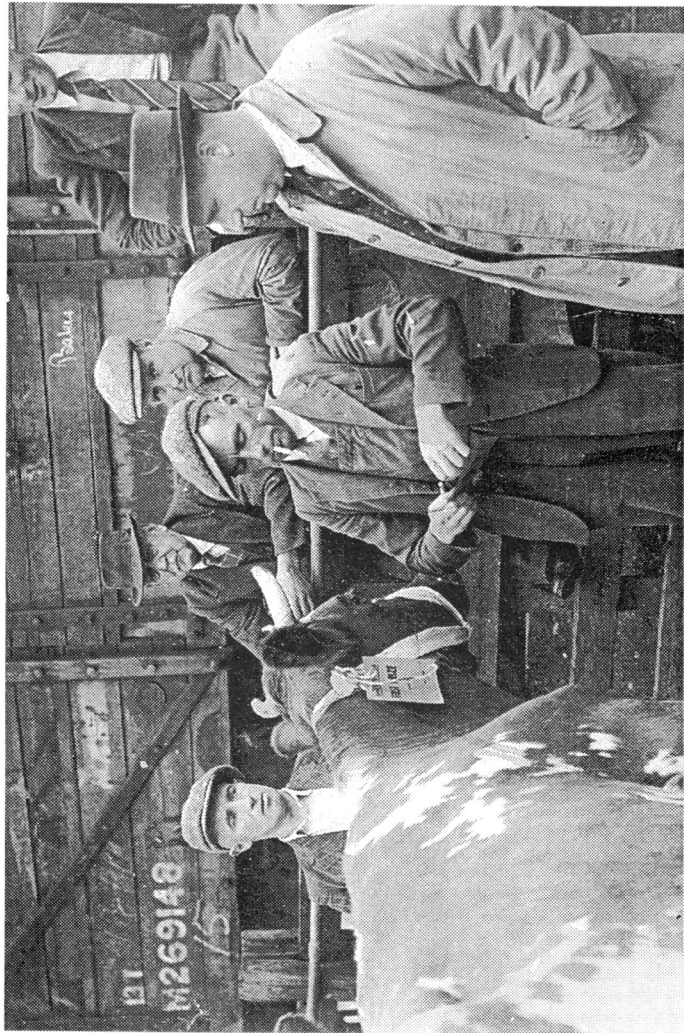

CHELFORD MARKET c1955 – DAIRY SHOW

George Ball (herdsman to Len Ford), Arthur Massey (Common Farm), Len Ford (Home Farm), Cecil Robinson, Frank Marshall, Harold Kennerley (Broad Oak Farm

217

CHELFORD PARISH COUNCIL

In 1894 an Act of Parliament decreed that Parish meetings should take place in all the parishes in the country. Chelford held their first Parish meeting on Tuesday 4th December 1894 with the option of forming a Parish Council. The guidance stated *'The Parish Council will come into office on the 13th December 1894 if no poll is held for the election of councillors and on the 31st of the same month if a poll takes place. It will continue in office until the 15th April 1896 and subsequent years the date of 15th April will be the date of the coming into office of the Parish Council".*

The first minute book recorded that on 24th November 1894 notice was posted that the Parish Councillors, numbering seven, would be nominated on the 4th December 1894 at 6.30 p.m. at Chelford School. Mr James Callwood, the overseer, nominated Colonel Dixon JP to chair this meeting. After addressing the electors and explaining the purpose of the meeting and method of procedure, the chairman proposed Mr Elijah Page as his clerk. The chairman then commenced receiving nomination papers from the clerk, numbering them as he received them and reading out the names of the candidates, with their proposers and seconders. The seven candidates with the highest number of votes were: -

Mr James Callwood	Roadside Farm
Mr Thomas Wilson Jnr.	Sunny Bank
Mr Thomas Gledhill	Dixon Arms
Mr Thomas Basford	Astle Farm
Mr Joseph Bill	Station Road
Mr John D Haigh	Post Office
Rev. Alfred L Royds	The Parsonage

Thus the Parish Council was born:

The newly formed Parish Council took responsibility for the Charities belonging to the Ecclesiastical Parish of Chelford which were distributed on or about Christmas Day 1894. The following account was entered in the minutes:

Receipts	£	s	d
Balance in hand from 1893	1	9	3
Received through the bank from Charity Commission on account of: -			
Wm Smallwood Charity	5	6	0

218

a/c of Hardy's Charity	1	7	8
a/c of Brooke's Charity	5	13	0
from Chas A Brady of Stockport			
on a/c of Roger Holland's Charity		6	0
Total	14	1	11

Deposits
Paid to:

11 householders in Chelford @ 12s each	6	12	0
3 householders in Old Withington	1	16	0
6 householders in Snelson	2	1	11
Total	14	1	11

The charity donations continued until the 1990's when it became more costly to administer the gifts than their value.

The Parish Precept is the amount of money allocated from the Parish rate payers to fund the activities of the Parish Council. In April 1899 the minutes of the Parish Council meeting read: *"The estimate for the Parish Rate for the current ½ year was brought before the council and a rate of 1s 8d in the pound, namely 1s 8d for buildings and 10d in the pound for land would meet all expenses".* The precept is set annually continuing to the present day.

There was growing concern about the safety of the cross roads near the vicarage and on 1st August 1908 (Saturday) the Parish Council minutes read: *"The subject of providing special danger posts at the crossroads near the vicarage was brought up by the chairman who suggested that posts should contain words, 'Very Dangerous' and 'Drive with Extreme Caution'. After some discussion and seeing that the County Council declined to do anything in the matter, it was proposed and seconded and carried that the clerk write to the Automobile Union asking them whether they would kindly put up these proposed posts, or at any rate bear some of the expense".*

In November of that year the clerk was to write to Cheshire County Council asking them to provide 4 speed limit posts to be erected at certain places in Chelford. The speed limit not to exceed ten miles per hour!

As the village evolved and throughout the minute book one finds in 1912 the request to owners of properties in Chelford for subscriptions towards the cost of a proposed sewerage scheme in the village. In 1930 in view of the benefits likely to be derived, the approval of the conveyance of electric power through a portion of the district was agreed. The question of a water supply to the village was discussed in 1934, but it was proposed that such a scheme was not required as the cost would be prohibitive and a great deal of hardship on the ratepayers, especially the poorer class. But in 1935 a special rate was to be levied on the parish in respect of the water scheme, which would not exceed 1s in the pound per annum. In 1937 the minutes recorded the commencement of a fortnightly refuse collection in the village of approximately 80 houses and the product of 1d rate per year would fund this venture.

The Parish Council minutes of 15th August 1927 record the following: - *"On Monday 1st August (Bank Holiday) a motor car and two charabancs travelling from Knutsford in the Macclesfield direction had in error taken the Station Road, narrowly escaping going over the milk dock on to the railway".*

War time was recorded in the minutes in May 1938 when a meeting of about 50 people attended to discuss (a) Air Raid Wardens, (b) First aid and casualty service, (c) Rescue and demolition service, (d) Decontamination service, (e) Dispatch notes and messages, (f) Clerks. Other wartime topics discussed were Blackout, Spitfire Fund, War Weapons Week, the appointment of salvage stewards, fruit preservation schemes, Empire Air Raid Distress Fund and then post war housing programme.

The work of the Parish Council escalated as a result of increased parish activity. A number of council houses were built and then in 1961 a large residential development was proposed on about 75 acres of land adjacent to the Egerton Arms, and spreading back into the village to link with the cattle market and council houses. As well as the regular problems of street lighting, grass cutting, footpath maintenance and speed limits, the Parish Council act as guardians for the community and ensure every effort is made to protect the village for present and future generations. The proposal for a prison on the edge of the village; the continuing destruction of the landscape through sand quarrying; the major development of houses; the heavily trafficked road through the village with the added problems of speed and accidents, all take time and dedication from the Parish Councillors. Where they do not have the ability to stop the tide of change, they ensure that the views of the residents are made known and that negotiation with the Parish Council takes place. The Parish Council have fought strongly to make sure that all aspects of village life are looked after. For example, by their persistence over 20 years they have ensured that Chelford has a new village school and that the requirements of the elderly for housing in the heart of the village have been met.

Note: *From the minutes of the Parish Council it is possible to establish that facilities in the village were provided on the following dates:*

Sewerage	*1912*	*Electricity*	*1930*
Water	*1935*	*Refuse Collection*	*1930*

From other sources it is known that the Telephone was provided in the early 1920's and gas in 1991/2.

Emily Hague, Fallows Hall, Chelford
July 1908

Be unto others kind and true,
As you would have others be to you.

T Hope, Marthall, Knutsford   July 1908

Cheer up! 'tis no use to be glum boys,
'Tis written, since fighting begun,
That sometimes we fight and we conquer,
And sometimes we fight and we run!

Blague, Chelford   July 1908

Desire not to live long, but to live well;
How long we live, not years, but actions tell

WOMENS INSTITUTE

On Thursday 27th July 1922 a meeting was held to consider the setting up of a Women's Institute in Chelford. The meeting was held in the Parish Room, Chelford and Mrs Crowther, the Secretary for Cheshire Women's Institutes addressed it and explained the W.I. movement. At the end of the address Mrs Crowther asked the meeting if they were in favour of starting an Institute in Chelford. All those present, numbering about 30, were unanimous in wishing to do so. Mrs Crowther expressed her pleasure at the decision and suggested that the Institute should be called the 'Chelford Women's Institute' and that a committee should be formed at once.

Thus the Chelford Women's Institute was born on 27th July 1922 the first committee comprising:

President	Mrs Donner	Mere Court	Chelford
Vice President	Mrs Wilson	Sunny Bank	Chelford
	Mrs Bythel	The Grange	Chelford
Secretary	Miss Dixon	Astle Hall	Chelford
Treasurer	Mrs Brodie Hoare	Dalefields	Chelford
Committee	Miss Baskervyle Glegg	Astle Hall	Chelford
	Nurse Hulley	Little Orchard	Old Withington
	Mrs Naylor	The School House	Chelford
	Mrs J Barber	School Cottages	Chelford
	Mrs Dakin		Old Withington

At the first meeting, held on 30th August 1922, 51 members were enrolled, and by the middle of 1923, 110 members had been enrolled[1] and a wide variety of speakers had presented talks.

The very first talk was given by a Miss Pollock on 'Fur Craft' followed, at monthly intervals by, Mrs Hopwood on 'Hat Covering' and Miss Wilks on 'Icing Cakes'. The first Christmas social was held on 27th December.

The main event in 1923 was the Garden Party held at Astle Hall on 27th June, the total attendance being 350, made up of members from Prestbury, Goostrey, Peover and Swettenham as well as from Chelford. Tea was served in a tent in the Park at a price of 1/- per head.

---

1   Chelford Women's Institute Minute Book

Up to the 1970's meetings were held during the daytime but it was then decided to hold the summer meetings in the evenings. By 1980, in order to meet the needs of working women, all meetings were, and still are held in the evenings.

The outlook of the Institute has changed since the early days. No longer do they only know how to make jam. It is worthwhile considering the part that Chelford W.I. played during the Second World War. According to Miss Audrey Walsh, (unfortunately no longer with us) members of Chelford W.I. used to visit the Manor House and fold strips of silver in a special way. The strips were then packed, despatched to the Royal Air Force and dropped over Germany to confuse the German radar. The members' efforts earned them a Certificate of Honour in the Wings for Victory National Savings Scheme.

In addition to the usual activities associated with the W.I., Chelford has had a drama section, and a handbell ringing section good enough to visit other institutes and take part in competitions.

On 27th July 1972 the W.I. celebrated its Golden Jubilee with a party in the Parish Hall.

CHELFORD W.I. - GOLDEN JUBILEE

27th July 1972. Two of the longest serving members, Mrs W Stanier and Miss A Walsh, cutting a Golden Jubilee cake.

The Diamond Jubilee celebration was held on Tuesday 27th July 1982, again in the Parish Hall

REUNITED at the celebrations are six of the women who attended the first meeting of Chelford Women's Institute back in 1922. Miss Walsh and Mrs. Stanier (left), are still active members of the Chelford Institute. They meet up again with Mrs. Callwood, Miss Baskerville, Mrs. Venables and Mrs. Hocknell.

Re-united at the Diamond Jubilee celebration are six of the ladies who attended the first meeting of the Institute in 1922. Miss Walsh and Mrs Stanier (left) meet up again with Mrs Callwood, Mrs Baskerville, Mrs Venables and Mrs Hocknell.

A further celebration took place in 1992 to mark the 70th birthday. To commemorate the occasion, a clock was presented to the Parish Hall Committee for the new hall, together with a suitable plaque.

In 1997, the 75th anniversary was marked by a quarter peal of bells followed by a party and entertainment by Fred Treesider with stories from his dual roles of actor and undertaker.

President, Joan Mills, cuts the 75th Anniversary cake watched by, from left to right, Lesley Shimell, Joyce Richardson, Anne Hornby, Jean Worthington and Edwina Oldham.

Over the years the Institute has continued to flourish, entertaining a wide variety of speakers and raising a considerable amount of money for various good causes, as well as taking an active part in village activities. The Institute is still in existence meeting every month on the first Wednesday.

It is hoped that the Institute will continue to play an active part in the activities of the village. It is continuing to adapt to meet the requirements of a changing society and to make a useful contribution to village life in the 21st Century.

Women's Institute Meeting held at the Manor House c 1965

Chelford Women's Institute members celebrated their Diamond Jubilee at the parish hall on Tuesday 27th July 1982 and Mrs Winnie Stanier and Miss A Walsh are pictured cutting the anniversary cake.

227

SUE COULING AND BARBARA MANWARING "Two Mrs Mops" at Knutsford Road Bus Shelter which the Women's Institute members took turns to clean from time to time.

THE EMBROIDERERS' GUILD

The Guild exists to encourage the study of contemporary embroidery and other textile arts, and to awaken interest in and appreciation of the history of embroidery and textiles. Josephine Robinson of Sunnybank Farm formed a local branch in October 1991. The early meetings were held at Sunnybank Farm (with Josephine as Chairman, Anne Hornby the Vice-Chairman, Barbara Mainwaring the Treasurer and June Hakami as Secretary) but soon the membership outgrew the room and the meetings were moved to Goostrey Village Hall in June 1992. Since September 1998 the Chelford Branch of the Embroiderers' Guild has been happily settled in Chelford Village Hall where they meet every month.

The meetings continue to go from strength to strength, attracting excellent and well-known lecturers. All aspects of the embroiderers' art have been demonstrated, including needlework, quilting, patchwork , and creative embroidery. These topics can all be followed up by attending the day schools, enabling the student to progress further with the help of the tutor.

Presently the Chelford Branch has sixty members, with Anne Parker being Chairman and Judy Hargreaves, the Secretary. Hilda Lowe was elected Life President in June 1992 in view of her long experience of all aspects of needlework and for her creative embroidery.

The Special Events are of particular interest. They are essentially an exhibition of the members' work and displays from other branches, together with stalls from where sewing items may be purchased. These events attract friends from a wide area; indeed the very large car park gets full to overflowing.

Hopefully the membership will continue to grow as more friends come along to join, relax, have pleasure, and enjoy 'THE ART of the NEEDLE'.

1ST CHELFORD SCOUTS

Based primarily on information provided by Peter Robertson

Scouting in Chelford has played a very important part in the lives of many boys from Chelford and the surrounding villages. The group was founded in 1934, the prime mover being Roger Walsh.

In the early 1940's, the troop was thriving and it was about that time that the Vicar of St Lawrence's Church Over Peover, the Rev. George Cyril Green asked Roger (Skip) to help him set up an Air Scout Troop in Over Peover. This lasted until about 1947, when it was disbanded and all the members wishing to continue joined Chelford Scouts. It was with the Peover troop that I (Peter Robertson) started my scouting and we had patrols such as Eagle/Falcon/Owl and Kestrel and we wore grey shirts. The change meant discarding the grey shirts and donning the khaki ones of the Land Scouts, and joining patrols such as Hound, Fox, Badger and Otter.

Members of the early 40's/late 30's included:

David Harradine	Ronnie Capper
Harry Newton	Ken Kirk
Stan Potts	Wilf Baskerville
John Dale	Geoff Boon
Dick Boon	2 Benson brothers from Holmes Chapel

And following the disbandment of the Peover group in 1947:

Colin Stayley	Dean Johnson
Alan Derbyshire	Alan Tomkinson
Derek Briscol	Keith Carter
Tony Ward	Ken Clarke
Peter Green	John Green
Peter Robertson	

The above information was provided by Peter Robertson and the authors express their thanks for permission to include in the publication.

Between 11944 and 1968 the following Scouts have achieved Queen Scout Awards.

1944	Harry Newton	1945	Dean Johnson
1953	Tony Harrison	1963	Brian Harradine
1965	David Peake	1966	Brian Ranson
1968	Roger Burgess		

By the mid 1970's the original Scout Hut, built in 1934, had become rather dilapidated. Under the leadership of Brian Harradine, plans were made for an new Scout Hut to be built which had the backing of the whole village in raising money for this necessary venture. The Scout Hut was duly funded and built adjacent to the Village Hall and has provided a meeting place for not just the Scouts, but also for the Cubs, Beavers, Guides, Brownies and Rainbows.

The Opening of the New Scout Headquarters

Opened by Miss A.C. Walsh (centre) on September 19th 1978

"Before opening this building I would like to say a few words about my brother Roger, or 'Skip' as he was called by the Scouts. As a baby he had to have an operation which left him partly deaf. My mother used to say that he was a cheerful little boy, and if he could not hear, when anyone spoke to him, he would turn to me and ask "What did they say?" – which he did for most of his life. During the 1914-18 War he joined the army and was stationed in 30 different places on the East Coast and finished at Limerick in the Irish Troubles.

It was about 1934 that he was asked to form a Scout troop, and to 1974, the year that he died, he devoted himself to this work – though he had never been a Scout. I think he did his best.

My sister, brothers and I are proud and touched that the plaque in this building should bear his name.

And now a word to the Scouts and Cubs. Remember your Scout Promise –

"I promise to do my best to do my duty to God and the Queen, and to help other people, and to keep the Scout Law"

Look after this building - keep it nice and clean - be proud of it, and enjoy the time you spend in it."

The new headquarters had been under construction for over two years and owed its existence to a tremendous effort in fund raising and the sterling work of the construction team led by Mr Peter Robertson (second from the left). Also present were Canon Henry, Councillor Denzil Kingston (Mayor of Macclesfield, Dr J.F. Wilkinson (The District President – second from the right), and Mr Harold Horry (District Commissioner – far right)

The highlight of every year at Chelford is the Summer Camp, which, despite many wet and cold camps, has never dampened the fun and enthusiasm of the Scouts and their Leaders.

Camp at Llandrillo 1949.

From Left to right

Peter Robertson, Nigel Ryder,
John Gresty,
Wilf Dykes

The original Scouter, Mr R C Walsh (Skip), who founded the Troop in 1934, was a familiar figure at the Friday evening Scout meetings for many decades.

When 'Skip' retired in 1966 the following appreciation was given: -

"More than 130 Chelford Scouts, guides, ex-scouts, and friends were at Chelford Parish Hall on Saturday night (1966) to pay tribute to the man many of them have known during the past 30 years simply, but affectionately as 'Skip'..At the age of 68 he has just retired from the movement and after the scouts and guides Christmas party a presentation was made to him, by one of the youngest boys of a bicycle and, by the present scoutmaster, of a cheque on behalf of the many people who had subscribed."

His real name is Roger Walsh and he has been scoutmaster and group scoutmaster at Chelford since January 1934. The District Commissioner thanked Mr Walsh for all the work he had put into the Scoutinng Movemenrt over the years, especially during the war, when he had worked single-handed with a troop swollen by evacuees to 45 members. A book token was also presented to Mr Walsh's sister Miss Audrey Walsh, who had been a badge-examiner for the boys for the past 30 years.

Mr Walsh, a poultry smallholder, whose interests are mountaineering and walking still maintained a strong association with the Scouting movement long after his retirement

In 1984, as well as being the Golden Anniversary year, it proved to be one of the most successful years relative to achievement with thirty-nine proficiency badges being gained in addition to four Scout Standard badges, two advanced Scout Standard badges and two Chief Scout awards.

1st Chelford Cub Scouts

In 1971 Brian Harradine who was Scout Leader at Chelford, heard that Gwynneth Shemilt had been a Cub Scout Leader at Silverdale, Stoke-on-Trent. He persuaded her to start a Cub Pack in Chelford, with his wife Jean being an assistant Cub Scout Leader. When Angela Robertson brought her elder son to Cubs, he was not very happy to stay so Angela stayed with him and became involved with Chelford Cubs for the next 20 years!

Over the years many people have become helpers and leaders at Chelford Cub Pack. Some of those were Heather George, George Preece, Richard Hindley, Tony Sullivan (who later became Scout Leader), Janet Williamson, Alison Shemilt, Bill Nellist, Judith Annikin, Lisa Dean, Jane Williamson, Andrew Barber, Liz Barker

233

and Karen Butler. Not forgetting Camp Cooks Hilda Lowe, Pat McNish, Janet Goldstraw and Andrea Wardell.

As Chelford Cubs approach their 30th Birthday, it is heartening to know that there is always a full and enthusiastic pack of Cubs benefiting from their founder, Baden Powell's aspirations for young boys of every generation.

CHELFORD GUIDES

The Guide Troop in Chelford was started in 1929 and, with one pause, has run ever since. It has proved to have a powerful influence on both the feminine youth of the village and their adult helpers. The first meetings were held in a room over the garage at 'The Grange' though today they share the facilities at the Scout Hut near the Parish Hall.

The activities of those early Guides are delightfully set out in words, photographs, and sketches in their splendid collection of Guide Log Books. There follow some extracts from that very first log book – written by the girls themselves.

<u>The Log Book, 1929-1933.</u>   "Our first Meeting" March 9th 1929

Our first meeting was exciting. None of us had been Guides before and we all longed to be. Our Captain, Miss Bythell had been a lieutenant in the Mobberley Company, and our Lieutenant had also been a Guide.

We arrived at a quarter past two and went up into the Guide room. It is a very jolly room over the garage at 'the Grange'. You go up some steep wooden stairs, and then you find yourself in a big airy room with two large windows. We have a stove to heat the room with, and it is very useful for cooking.

At the first meeting there were besides Captain and Lieutenant, Rene Drew aged fifteen, Marjorie Dale who was twelve, Beryl Dixon who was also twelve, Evelyn Wright, Joyce Thompson and my sister Jean who were thirteen and myself, aged sixteen.

We began dividing everyone into patrols, we were going to have two patrols. Evelyn Wright was leader of one and I was the leader of the other. Evelyn, Joyce, Jean and Beryl were in one patrol which we decided to call the Bluetits and in my patrol were – Rene and Marjorie, and Captains sister, Alison, who was at school. My patrol was called the Kingfishers.

Captain began by giving us an address on Guiding, which made us still more keen. She explained how jolly Guiding was and how useful. She told us tbat she wanted us to call her "Captain"'as she did not like being called "Miss Bythell". We were to call Miss Wilson "Lieutenant".

After Captain's address Lieutenant taught us the whistle signals. We made awful mistakes at first, Evelyn and I always forgot "leaders come here" and everyone rushed about wildly. At last we managed to grasp them more or less, so we put the "leaders come here" into practice and did patrol drill and roll call out in the yard. It is amusing to look back on our struggles. How when Captain said "by the left two paces extend!" we both moved two places!

After wrestling with drill for a short time, we did something less serious. We had ball and hopping relays and all got thoroughly blown and excited.

To cool us down we went indoors and learnt some knots from Lieutenant. We first tried the reef, most people thought they could do it, but nearly everyone tied grannies! We next wrestled with the sheet-bend which most people, who had been studying their test-cards, called a sheep-bend! or a sheep-shank! This proved even more difficult than the reef. The Fisherman's knot was fairly easy, but the clove-hitch took a lot of mastering. All the chairs in the room were commandeered and their legs ornamented with clove-hitches (more or less!)

When the knots had all been unravelled and the chairs restored to their proper places we suddenly heard a terrific stampede coming up the stairs, and in rushed the three Mobberley patrol-leaders who dumped down an enormous parcel and fled before we could say a word! Captain opened it amid great excitement. It was a beautiful picture illustrating the Guide-law with all the famous knights in olden days all round. This beautiful present was given a place of honour on the wall by the fireplace.

After the excitement had ended about the picture, we went out into Lieutenant's field and played games. We played zig-zagging first and then a message game, in which a message was passed down the patrol, and the last person's message was never the same as the first, which looked as though the future 1st Chelford Company was stone deaf!

The next game was a leaf game. The patrols numbered and when Captain called a certain number the people had to run to her and she told them to bring a special leaf to her. It was surprising how few people seemed to know an oak leaf! Some people rushed wildly half way across the field, only to find the leaf they wanted was almost under their feet!

After racing about for a long time we went back to the Guide room. We then practised the drill that we had learnt outside. Fairly successfully the patrol leaders fell in and the company marched round into horse-shoe formation. Captain then taught us the song that Guides always finish up their meetings with. It is called "Taps" and the words are:-

Day is done,
Gone the sun.

236

From the sea, from the land, from the sky.
All is well.
Safely rest.
God is nigh.

When we had sung this, holding hands, Captain gave the order to dismiss. We could not salute yet as we were not yet enrolled.

We left at a quarter past four, having thoroughly enjoyed the afternoon and all thrilled by Guiding and determined to work hard to pass our tenderfoot test and become Guides as soon as possible.

Margaret Brodie Hoare

Monthly enrolments followed and on June 14th 1929 the Guides took part in Knutsford May Day where Princess Mary was present.

"It was a terrible day and it rained in bucketsful and thundered and lightened ,…. We all got soaked …After the presentation to Princess Mary we sat on benches in the pouring rain, but we had to smile and make the best of it to follow out the Guide Law."

In August the Guides visited the World Scout Jamboree in Arrowe Park, Birkenhead.

"What a sight met or eyes! Thousands and thousands of tents were clustered together, with their country's flags flying in the breeze. All around us were Scouts in their different uniforms. The South African Scouts wore ostrich feathers in their hats and the Indian Scouts wore turbans. Then there were the Scots Scouts in their gaily coloured plaids and our own English Scouts in the uniform we know so well. We saw the Japanese Scouts cooking and eating their dinner and altogether having a jolly time for although we could not understand their language, one cannot mistake a laugh!. We watched the grand parade of all the Scouts before the Chief Scout and then the entertainments. Altogether we had a very thrilling and enjoyable day and I don't think any of us would have missed it for anything.. It gave us such a feeling that Scouts and Guides are good comrades all over the world and made us more than a little proud".

Hilda Ford

In January 1930 the Guides presented "The Princess in the Sleeping Wood" at the Parish Hall to a good audience and made £10 from the tickets. It was divided thus:-

£2- 5-0 in expenses.

£3- 0-0   to the new Imperial Headquarters in London
  10-0   to the S.P.S for Girl Guides in India
£1- 5-0   towards the new stage curtains for the Parish Hall
£1-11-0   put into company funds

"and we had enough to buy our own Union Jack of which we are very proud."

In March there was a very successful first birthday party and a third enrollment and in June Astle Park was the site of the 1st Cheshire Post Guide Camp for crippled and handicapped Guides, may of whom were in wheelchairs. Each day the Chelford Guides went to help and join in the evening camp-fire celebrations.

In July the first Chelford Guide Camp was held jointly with the Toft group at Wray Castle on Lake Windermere and on December 18th came a performance of "A Christmas Carol", followed two days later by a party given by the Guides for the future Brownie pack.

> *"... the Guides were hurrying about getting tea, and to my surprise they were laying it on a green carpet on the floor. It was very dark outside but they did not attempt to turn on the lights. They had laid the things in a huge ring and decorated round with crackers, then in the centre of the ring they placed a beautiful cake covered in white icing and the words "Welcome Future Brownies" were written on it in silver balls."*
>
> *Mary Fisher*

The highlight of 1931 was the County Rally at Chester on May 30th when 8,000 Guides from all over Cheshire met together before Princess Mary. From Knutsford a special Guide train took the girls to Chester where they marched through the streets and down to Chester Racecourse. After the service came the march past and then the pageant where the Chelford Guides represented "Alice in Wonderland". Many people wrote of what the Rally meant to them. From the Nightingale Patrol: -

"The most thrilling moment of all was when, marching eight abreast, we came up to Princess Mary and we turned, four to the left and four to the right. To think that she was saluting each one of us. That moment I am positive was the most thrilling I have ever had in Guiding."

August saw a week-long Camp at Tatton Park with the Mobberley and Knutsford Guides begun 'in boiling sunshine'. Every page of the log book is filled with their activities but, perhaps inevitably at the end the rains came." It was impossible for the ground to dry so each Guide emptied the straw out of her mattress, and packed up her things...."

238

1932 began with a production of 'Robin Hood' in the Parish Room which raised the sum of £7-17-2 of which £4-0-0 was profit and was disposed as follows:-

£1- 7-0	*to the London H.Q.*
£2- 1-0	*for a World Guide Flag and a cover*
5/-	*for the cost of a railing put up the Guide Room stairs, and*
7/-	*given to the Brownies pack.*

A rally was held in Tatton Park to mark the 31st birthday of Guiding and on the following Sunday, May 29^{th,} all the Guides in the Knutsford Division attended Guide Sunday at Knutsford Parish Church where the colours were dedicated. The Chelford colour bearers were Evelyn Houldsworth and Amy Slater, and the escorts Muriel Barber, M Gould, and M Drew.

That summer the annual camp was held at Gayton on the Wirral and this time it began in pouring rain and ended in sunshine.

1933 saw the unveiling in April of a seat which the Chelford Guides and Brownies had presented to the village. It bore a brass dedication plate and was probably placed at the village bus stop but no further reference to it has been found.

Summer camp in August was at Caldy Manor, with a visit to Hilbre Island when every day was hot and sunny !

And so it went on, and still does thanks to the devoted work of the Guide Leaders and of those parents who support their activities. It spread too, first to the Brownie Troop who are mentioned as about to be formed in 1930 in this first log book.

Following an inactive period after 1950 the Guides were restarted soon after Canon and Mrs Henry came to Chelford. After a meeting of parents in September 1965 the first Guides were enrolled on January 10th 1966. The early Guiders were Mrs Henry and Rosemary Pell who were followed by Nesta Worthington and later by Dr Bess Barry from Mobberley. The early Brownie Guiders were Elsie Henry, Helen Mills and Jane Dale, and their first Brownie enrolment took place on October 15th 1966

BROWNIES

1st Chelford Brownie Pack is probably very little younger than the Guides. There is mention of a party given by the Guides for the Brownies in 1930 – but records from the early days are missing. The only documentation relates to when the unit was 'reborn' in the early 1960's after temporary closure – presumably because of lack of leadership.

There's little danger of today's unit fizzling out. In June 1999 the Pack closed its membership at a record 30 girls, with other would-be Brownies put on a waiting list to join. Run by mother and daughter partnership Muriel Preece (Tawny Owl) and Alison Richardson (Brown Owl), the pack currently has Brownie mother Jane Williamson as a unit helper known as 'Barn Owl' and also a' mascot', Alison's three-year-old daughter Elizabeth, affectionately known as 'Baby Owl'.

The Pack retains strong links with Chelford Church, mustering some willing Brownies to attend the monthly Church Parade. The Brownies also put on maypole dancing displays at the Church Garden Party and nearby school fetes. Another welcome contribution is the Brownies' harvest baskets for the Church Harvest festival.

The annual weekend Pack Holiday away is eagerly anticipated. 1999 saw the Unit go to nearby Ashley Activity Centre with an 'Alice in Wonderland' theme.

1st Chelford Brownies is the largest Brownie unit in the Alderley Edge Division, and was delighted to claim the Brownie trophy at last year's Divisional Swimming Gala – 'Splash Night' – at Wilmslow Leisure Centre4 (believed to be the first time the pack has won!)

The Chelford Brownies were out in force at the retirement of Drs Stanley and Barbara Pratt in 1984.

240

Regular Tuesday evening meetings, from 5.30pm to 7pm in Chelford Scout Hut, are filled with interest badge activities, craft-making, and regular features of the Brownie 8-point programme.

In more recent years the 1st Chelford Rainbows were formed to produce an onward path, where girls join at five and then progress to the Brownies. The Guides, and then the Rangers to become, one sincerely believes, far more focussed and caring adults than might have been the case if time and school had been their only mentors.

RAINBOWS

The Rainbow Section of the Guide Association for girls aged 5 to 7 years began in 1987. The First Chelford Rainbow Group was started in January 1992 by Sue Roycroft and Sarah Byrom, who were working for their warrants as the unit opened. They were initially assisted by Alison Cartwright, as a Unit Helper, followed by Lizzie Slater, who was helper for two years when she was working for her Duke of Edinburgh Gold Award. Since 1997 Charlotte Slater, Lizzie's sister, has been unit helper but she is soon to receive her own warrant to become a Guider.

The 18 Rainbows follow the same eight point programme as the Brownies and Guides. Their one hour Monday evening meetings follow themes which include crafts, games, singing and a host of varied activities.

One highlight for the Rainbows in the group is the Annual Sunshine Day held in May or June. On that occasion they meet, together with the Rainbows from Lindow and Alderley Edge, for a day of fun, with a picnic lunch held (hopefully) out of doors. The theme for 1999 was 'The Owl and the Pussycat' and all the crafts and games were based on this. Another special occasion is Thinking Day, which is held on the joint birthday shared by Lord and Lady Baden-Powell, our founders. In 1999 the Thinking Day celebration and service was held at Manchester International Airport with all the Lindow, Alderley Edge, and Chelford Guide, Brownie, and Rainbow units travelling there together by train. Everyone took part in an international quiz and the Thinking Day Service led by the airport Chaplain. This was followed by refreshments provided by the airport personnel before the return journey home. The event was a tremendous success and thoroughly enjoyed by everyone.

In the autumn the Rainbows take part in the District Splash Night, together with the Brownies and Guides. Last year Chelford Rainbows won the Rainbow trophy for the second time. Twice each year there is a joint evening meeting with the Chelford Brownies so that the Rainbows can observe and get to know the group they will be moving on to. The three guiding sections also come together each month for Sunday Church Parade where the service is specially adapted for them to participate. At Harvest Festival the girls put tremendous effort into preparing their Harvest Baskets which are dedicated at the Harvest Service. On the Monday evening these gifts are taken by the whole unit to the senior citizen's accommodation around Astle Court and Elmstead Road where they are delivered personally by the girls. A mixing of the generations that proves universally popular.

Each year a charity event is organised in which all the girls take part in order to raise money for specific causes. In 1999 the 'Red Nose' charity was chosen and a small mountain of 'Red Nose Buns' were made, sold, and eaten – all in record time. Last year the Rainbows, and their guiders, all 'walked-a-mile' (or more) in support of the Macmillan Nurses fund.

This year of 1999 has just seen the celebration of 70 years of Guiding in Chelford. At the party and the church service which followed on April 25th were to be found again some of those who featured in that first log book; and who were able to re-live and share the memories of those first formative years.

Back row: (with the married name in brackets)*Edna Dale (Hallam), Betty Camm (Stanier), Phyllis Snead Pugh), Margaret Drew (Alwly),Mary Gould (Williams), Beryl Taylor (Callwood), Nora Burgess (Whitehurst)*
Front row: *Evelyn Wright (Stevenson), Bessie Worthington (Henshall), Muriel Barber (Kellett),Evelyn Houldsworth (Walton), Jean Bloor (Pearce)*

242

HOMEWATCH

The growth of criminal activity has, in recent times, been facilitated by the availability of the motor car and the development of motor (or free) ways. No wonder that "Neighbourhood Watch Schemes" began in the United States of America.

The first scheme in the UK was started by the villagers of Mollington near Chester in 1982 following a spate of burglaries and soon thereafter burglaries reduced. Cheshire Constabulary supported this initiative and in 1983 they promoted and supported the development of Homewatch Schemes throughout the County. There are now 4357 such schemes in Cheshire.

Chelford's Scheme was introduced in May 1985 by Mrs Coghlan of Hitch Lowes, fully supported by the Police and the Parish Council.

To match the growth of population in the village there are now forty one Homewatch Co-ordinators who, together with the residents and the Police, are working together to keep Chelford crime free – through constant vigilance, security and good communication.

CHELFORD BRIDGE CLUB
By David Sutton, Ivy House

We started out with the intention of being a friendly and relaxed club for people to play properly but not too intently. An indication of our success in this aim is that quite a few members have been to virtually every meeting. A further principle is that we specifically do not require people to come in pairs and we encourage individuals to come whether or not accompanied by a pre-arranged partner. The organisers ensure no one who comes misses out, by themselves playing or not as the numbers dictate. We feel that this has contributed to the fact that many new friendships have been formed over the years and other clubs and social bridge circles have formed as a result of introductions made in the club.

As the aim is to play and be sociable at the same time, we arrange play to move people around the room to meet as many others as possible. According to numbers a pairs or teams movement is arranged, at other times we may simply play chicago.

The club's first meeting was held on 17th September 1991 and has met regularly ever since. We now meet in the small room in the village hall every Friday, except when the hall is required for some other major event. Everyone who comes receives a list of meeting dates for the coming year. The annual subscription is £3 and table money is £1 for members and £1.50 for visitors.

THE THURSDAY CLUB

The club was formed in 1968 by Mrs Elsie Henry, the wife of Canon Henry who was the vicar at that time, with the help of a committee formed from members of the St. John's Churchwomen's Fellowship. The full and resplendent title of the club is - The Chelford, Lower Withington, Over Peover, Ollerton, and Marthall over 60's Club, and it meets on the second Thursday of each month (excepting August). Not surprisingly it is always referred to as 'The Thursday Club' and anyone over 60 in the parishes mentioned is eligible and most welcome to join.

Initially the response was so great that membership soon reached 100 and a waiting list had to be formed. The vicarage proved too small for so many people and so the meetings moved to the Village Hall. The club badge was designed by one of the members, and a band of volunteer drivers regularly brought members to and from the meetings.

Over the years, with far fewer people living in isolated places, the membership has decreased and at the club's Thirtieth Anniversary in 1988 the roll was down to 40 members. Yet the interesting and varied programmes continue, as does the companionship, and the delicious afternoon teas!

Unfortunately the Annual Produce Show (cookery, handicrafts and horticulture), the Club Holiday and the Christmas Carol Service no longer take place. The Spring Fair is still enthusiastically supported by the members and the committee and raises money to keep the club funds healthy – to pay for the hire of the Hall, speakers at meetings, an excellent Christmas Party and entertainment. An annual outing is still arranged, but after thirty years it is becoming difficult to think of new places to visit!

Sadly, there are no founder members left, but some of the original committee still serve the club.

A warm welcome awaits every eligible person, and it would be lovely to restart those events which have lapsed; to clean and polish the trophies, and once again to be able to present them to the Show winners!

The original committee comprised: -

Mrs Henry	Mrs Dale
Mrs Day	Mrs Sutcliffe
Mrs Henshall	Mrs Barlow
Mrs I Newton	Mrs Richardson
Mrs Boyling	Mrs J Irlam
Mrs I Irlam	Mrs S Newton
Mrs C Gledhill	

CHELFORD AND DISTRICT LADIES BOWLING CLUB.

The two founder members of the club were Freda Massey of Snelson and Elsie Plant of Over Peover. One summer's day in 1962 they met at the Dixon Arms and decided to ask the Landlord, Geoff Woodward, if they could bowl on his bowling green. He allowed them to do so. They used the old woods from the bowling hut which seemed to go in any direction, so they decided to buy some woods of their own and form a Ladies Bowling Club.

Previous to this in 1958 the members of the Dixon Arms Men's Club invited the ladies to bowl for a 'Cup'. Mr Fernie donated this 'Cup' which was called 'The Ladies' Cup'. The first winner was Freda Massey and it was bowled for on one afternoon only during the year.

In 1962 after the final of this cup, an independent unit was formed. The first committee meeting was held on October 8th 1962. Elsie Plant was elected chairman, Betty Harding secretary, Freda Massey, treasurer, assisted by Mary Pimlott and Freda Turnock. Financial arrangements were discussed with Mr Woodward and a fee of £5 was agreed for the year for the use of his bowling green on two afternoons each week.

It was decided not to bowl in a league but only to bowl in friendly matches against the ladies of Foden's Sandbach, Mary Dendy Warford, Cranage and Wilmslow.

Seventeen members attended the first general meeting, paying a subscription of 10s to join the club. Barbara Camm was elected captain - Betty Bradley and Lena Newton joined the committee to raise money for the club and a Whist Drive was held in the Village Hall.

The first Presentation Dinner was held on October 16th 1963 at the Dixon Arms Mr and Mrs Woodward provided the meal the price of the ticket being 17s 6d.

The competitions held during the season are the Cup, Shield, Rose Bowl, Merit Trophy, Joyce Dakin Memorial Doubles Cup and the Outings Prize. Outings to Swettenham Bowling Club and Siddington NFY Bowling Club are looked forward to and enjoyed. A picnic tea is served at the end of these days, each member taking some food.

Some of the members must have very happy memories of the outings especially to the Red Lion Hotel, Little Budworth when Wilf and Audrey welcomed them with their good food. Also picking strawberries on the way home from Malpas after bowling with the Malpas Ladies and the delicious tea they made for us all.

The outing to Fleetwood on our 25th anniversary in 1988 and the fresh Fleetwood fish we all enjoyed. The celebration cake was made by Sheila Read. To Waterloo, Blackpool on our 30th anniversary in 1993 with our friends from Alderley Edge.

Today friendly matches are played with the ladies of Wimboldsley, Wilmslow, Alderley Edge, Byley and Swettenham. We also bowl to raise money for the MAST appeal (Million Action Scanner Trust) for the Macclesfield Hospital Scanner. In 1997 we made it into 'Cheshire Life' with a photo of the Chelford Ladies Bowling Club in an article called 'Chelford Village Life'!

25th Anniversary – 4th November 1988

Left to Right: Freda Turnock, Betty Harding, Mary Moulton, Barbara Camm, Elsie Plant, Freda Massey, Betty Bradley, Barbara Kitching.

Picture taken at The Lymes, Sandbach (18th July 1984)

Front Row: Brenda Coutts, Elsie Plant, Evelyn Venables, Freda Kerrigan, Brenda Burgess, Alice Wain, Margaret Brown, Mary Boyling, Josie Perratt, Ethel Bennett, Mona Norbury, Bessie Coppack, Joyce Edwards, Betty Bradley.

Back Row: Betty Harding, Freda Turnock, Yvonne Ball, Barbara Camm, Margaret Venables, Flo Stanier, Freda Massey, May Acton, Vera Clarkson, Margaret Hankey.

248

Original Group 1964

Front Row: Betty Harding, Freda Massey, Betty Bradley, Susan Bradley, Sylvia Massey, Julia Massey, Gail Burgess, Andrea Kitching, Susan Kitching, Sheena Burgess.
Middle Row: Lizzy Tickle, Mary Moulton, Freda Turnock, Mary Pimlott
Back Row: Mrs Christie, Barbara Kitching, Edith Wilkins, Mrs Broughton, Lena Newton, Nora Presley

Presentation (Dixon Arms 13th June 1981)

Mr Herbert Dakin who gave the Joyce Dakin Memorial Double, Brenda
Couttes and Freda Massey winners

CHELFORD AMATEUR DRAMATIC SOCIETY

Just when Chelford Players actually began is a matter of considerable mystery. As with most village communities there were frequent amateur dramatic productions and the first one that we know of was held at Chelford School in January 1896. A monologue entitled "A Woman of Courage" was delivered by Mrs Adrian Hope and followed by a two-act comedy, "The Chimney Corner" by H T Craven. No press cuttings are available but the cast list was formidable, four of them being sons of a stipendiary magistrate resident in Chelford. In their own rights they were a knighted Lieutenant Colonel, a Brigadier General, a senior civil servant and a Housemaster at Eaton.

In 1953 'The Chelford Amateur Dramatic Society' presented "Murder in the Vicarage" with the vicar, his wife, and the village doctor 'perfectly type cast' according to the press.

In 1954 the offering was 'Arsenic and Old Lace' for two nights at the Village Hall with the following cast list: -

Dorothy Evans, Ernest Dickens, Ernest Evans, Arthur Beckley, David Parrish, Bee Gamon, Nary Boughyt, Mark Tully, Edmund Evans, Jack Gamon, Geoff Gee, Harold Jones, William Carruthers, George Shelton, and Robert Tully. The producer was Edith Whiteside. One press report declared that she had done a remarkably good job as producer and was presented with a bouquet when the curtain fell. (Dr) Ernest Evans also received a large Victorian posy - with a cauliflower as a central feature!

In 1955 three one-act plays were offered, and in 1956 the Emlyn Williams comedy "The Late Christopher Bean" was very well reviewed. Later in the year the Womens' Institute put on an excellent production of the same author's "Night Must Fall".

1957 saw "See How They Run" produced by Dorothy Evans and Geoff Gee receive a rapturous reception. In December they also presented "Gaslight" with very good reviews.

What happened in 1958 is not known but in December 1959 there was a hilarious production of "The Little Goose Girl" by Wilfred Millar. In 1960 "Sailor Beware" was a tremendous success and in 1961 Jeffrey Dell's play "Payment Deferred" was 'very well received'.

January 1962 saw the CADS production of "Babes in the Wood" given to a 'large and appreciative audience'.

After each production Dame Lilian Bromley-Davenport wrote a splendid letter of appreciation to the producer and in only one was there a criticism – of the audience. It really is worth quoting.

"Your audience needs a bit of shaking up – why can they not show their enjoyment?
For there is no doubt they <u>do</u> enjoy it.
Television teaches people to do nothing but stare!"

THE (present) CHELFORD PLAYERS

Chelford had not had an amateur club for some years until Mrs Joyce Williams, who had been deeply involved in the amateur theatre for many years, moved here in 1978 and decided to start a drama group. She found that another Chelford resident, Mrs Judy Parrack, was a well known amateur actress and so they called a meeting in November 1978 which was attended by about 30 people. As a result a society was formed and was called the Chelford Players, with Mrs Williams and Mrs Parrack as joint Chairmen.

The first production was an Old Tyme Music Hall held in the Ballroom at the Dixon Arms on 17th March 1979. A number of social events were held in the ensuing months but a year passed before the next production, "Toad of Toad Hall", which took place in the Village Hall in April 1980.

With the passage of time, members tended to form two informal groups within the society, those who acted and the "Minstrels", who gave many performances for various organisations in the district. This group renamed themselves "Melodyline" some 10 years ago.

Stage productions took place in the Village Hall, usually two per year though there were delays when a producer could not be found and when the Hall was being rebuilt. Since 1991 the Players have settled down to a programme of three productions per year – usually a pantomime or other suitable play before Christmas which has a number of parts for young people, - and one 'straight' play and one musical or revue type of show.

The productions have been: -

	Apr 79 – Mar 89	Apr 89 – Mar 99
Christmas shows/Pantomimes	6	7
Plays	8	11
Musical	1	4

The Christmas shows have included "traditional" pantomimes such as "Aladdin" and "Cinderella", more modern themes such as "Santa in Space", and some less obvious choices like "Dracula" and "Sweeney Todd"! Plays have ranged from one scene from Shakespeare (!) via "Month of Sundays" to Habeas Corpus", and have included works by Priestley, Maughan, Christie, Durbridge, Ayckbourn, Oscar Wilde and others. Musicals have included two productions especially compiled for the company; and in recent years occasional review and music halls with a fish and chip supper in the interval have proved popular.

The Players are in a healthy state financially, and have invested in a commercially built stage extension and basic lighting set. There is still the major problem of storage of equipment, props and costumes, but having a unit at the rear of the Village Hall could solve this, and a Planning Application for the unit has been made.

The society has a committee who meet regularly, and has had five Chairmen since Mrs Williams and Mrs Parrack retired in 1983. Unfortunately it has not proved possible to continue to hold a busy social programme for club members, perhaps because the number of members is fairly small, and because the calls on their 'spare' time are greater than 20 years ago. Indeed times have changed and it may be that such social events are not the flavour of the late 90's. However, although the membership is smaller than desired, their great enthusiasm and talent perhaps makes up for the lack of numbers and the group have been fortunate in attracting members of other amateur companies to come and act with them on many occasions.

What of the future? In the long term it is hoped that the Chelford Players will continue to attract those who wish to act, and in so doing, provide live entertainment, which seems to be very popular in the village and district. More immediately, it is appropriate that their 50th production at the beginning of December 1999 will coincide with the Society's 21st birthday and with the 225th anniversary of the rebuilding of the Chelford Church.

CHELFORD PLAYERS MID JULY 1991
Chelford Players are pictured above during rehearsals for "A Comedy Tonight" which was performed last Friday and Saturday at Chelford

CHELFORD VILLAGE - PRE-SCHOOL

Originally the 'Chelford Village Pre-School' was known as the 'Chelford Under 5's Playgroup' and there are minutes recorded from meetings as early as February 1978.

On the suggestion of Mrs Elsie Henry, the Playgroup was founded in 1975 by Mrs Anne Hornby, Mrs Jenny Lomas, Mrs Pauline Hallam and Mrs Sue Barber.

At that time the 'Playgroup' was held at Marthall Village Hall and later had the use of a 'shed' placed nearby to store equipment and toys that were used by the group. There were about 20 children involved and the 'Playgroup' met on two mornings each week.

There was clearly much input from the mothers who were involved with the organisation and tireless fund-raising to bolster up the funds to keep the Playgroup going.

By November 1979 plans were afoot to change the venue of the group's meetings from Marthall to Chelford Village Hall. There was still a need for the shed as there wasn't enough storage space at Chelford, so the shed was put on top of a trailer and transported by tractor to Chelford.

The Playgroup ticked over for the next 2/3 years, managing to survive on the endless raffles, sales and fund-raising events organised by the mothers.

During 1982 there were discussions about opening the playgroup for 3 mornings each week, and after the summer holidays that year the 3 day week began.

By November 1983 it was suggested that a fourth day should be considered for the following year, albeit on a trial basis to start with. The monies needed to run the Playgroup successfully continued to be a nightmare and the perpetual fundraising had to be undertaken.

The Playgroup had to be re-housed whilst the re-building of the Village Hall took place, so a move to the scout hut had to be faced. The 'shed' was still needed but by now it was becoming worn-out and in need of drastic repair.

By the time the Playgroup opened for the September 1991 term it was established in the re-furbished Village Hall. Extra space and storage was now available so at last the shed was no longer needed.

Towards the end of 1993 the Playgroup decided to open every morning and was listed as a 'Registered Charity'.

The supervisor and deputy, plus the assistants, were starting to attend appropriate first-aid courses and the Playgroup was being inspected by C.C.C. Money was still very tight and the inevitable fund-raising continued.

By 1995, the idea of a uniform if Sweatshirts and T Shirts was high on the agenda - to be bought by parents in order to make a small profit to help with the funds.

At a meeting held in September 1995 there were discussions about whether the name should be changed and, if so, to what. It was finally agreed that the group should be re-named 'Chelford Village Pre-School'! This new name was registered with the Pre-School Learning Alliance and the C.C.C.

Currently the 'Pre-School' employs a Supervisor, Deputy Supervisor and an Assistant. The staff are assisted each day by a mother on a 'rota' basis. The staff are encouraged to attend all relevant courses to broaden their skills and knowledge in the field of pre-school teaching requirements.

The Pre-School is inspected annually by OFSTED and their report is available for all parents to see.

Children can attend from 3 years old until they reach primary school age, although there are one or two children $2^1/_2$ years old. The fees are kept to a minimum to make the Pre-School available to all children in the village. The hours are 9.15 a.m. until 11.45 a.m. Monday to Friday.

Looking back through the records there is clear evidence that brothers and sisters follow on at the 'Pre-School' and some family names are recurring over a number of years.

The 'Pre-School' is advertised on all the village notice boards with contact names and telephone numbers.

CHELFORD BADMINTON CLUB

The Badminton Club was founded in 1972 by Mrs Sheila Roycroft, herself a keen player, with one court in the Parish Hall and approximately 20 members.

The Club has always been run with friendly informality and for many years has been popular with families – parents perhaps returning to the game, or taking it up for the first time, with their teenage children.

Small Badminton Clubs have lost some support in recent years since the provision of excellent sports facilities at the local Leisure Centres but Chelford still has a small band of enthusiasts who are always keen to welcome new members.

ASTLE PARK TRACTION ENGINE RALLY

In Astle Park, just once a year,
The sound of engines trundles near
The shrill steam whistle, with its familiar sound
Echoes the excitement of villagers around

We welcome visitors from near and far
To Chelford they come on bike and in car
They enthuse at the engines and remember their names
of Winnie, Stanley Monarch, George V and Little Mac
Each year they come and we welcome them back.

We never forget the people past
Who started the rally and caused it to last
'Twas their enthusiasm, generosity and giving
That keeps the hearts of our villages living.

The first Traction Engine Rally to be held in Astle Park took place in 1965. The seed had been sown three years previously when a group of local traction engine enthusiasts with Lower Withington Parish Hall Committee held their first Traction Engine Rally in Mr Ted Moston's field in Lower Withington. This was on 6th & 7th October in 1962 and was called Jodrell Bank Traction Engine Rally. The second rally, on 28th & 29th September 1963, was held to raise money for the building of the new village hall in Lower Withington.

Little did the organisers of the first Astle Park Traction Engine Rally in 1965 know that the rallies would still be in 'full steam' as an annual event in Astle Park today, 33 years later. Going back a little further, the original local traction engine enthusiasts from 1962 would never have dreamt that their inspiration would continue for over 36 years. These engine enthusiasts consisted of Mr John Alan Barber, of Chelford, Mr G Lea of Snelson, Mr Jim Bostock of Lower Withington, Mr Jim Dakin of Goostrey and Mr Colin Dale of Congleton. The sons of these enthusiasts (except Mr Bostock) still attend the Traction Engine Rallies today with their own engines. Mr Fred Dibnah, the steeplejack of TV fame has attended the Traction Engine Rally for many years, bringing his own traction engine and living van. He attended some of the very early Traction Engine Rallies before his TV fame and still just blends into the scene along with all the other engine drivers.

The first Astle Park Traction Engine Rally was held to raise money for Chelford Parish Hall. In 1966 Lower Withington Parish Hall, in conjunction with the enthusiasts, took over the running of these events to raise money for improvements to Lower Withington's new Parish Hall facilities. In 1989 Mr Frank Lythgoe, himself a traction engine enthusiast, took over the rally when the Parish Hall committee decided to call it a day.

Over the 23 years that Lower Withington Parish Hall committee and the group of local enthusiasts organised the rally, it went from strength to strength. Not only did the rally raise money for Lower Withington, but Chelford raised money through draws for the Church and the Scouts, Steam Preservation Societies raised money for their causes and the event itself gave great pleasure to over a million people. The park itself owned by Henshaws Institute for the Blind was given a donation for the use of the land for each rally. Regularly there were over 30,000 visitors over the rally weekend enjoying the nostalgia of the smell of warm cylinder oil, the lingering clouds of smoke, the sound of the fairground organs and the pulsating of the engines whilst they awaited their proud procession around the arena. The land is now owned by Mr Alan Baskerville and the organising of the event is done professionally, but thankfully the event continues.

Stanley Monarch Burrell 8 NHP single crank engine purchased 1961 by Alan Barber and still in working order. Jim Bostock on left hand side with Alan on right. The engine following is a Foden compound 6 NHP also owned by Alan Barber

Ford Truck owned by John Lawton of The Crown, Goostrey alongside William V Showman engine owned by Alan Barber. Taken in front of Jodrell Bank Telescope.

261

Traction Engine

Left to right: - Alan Barber, JT Barber, Peter Holden, Jim Dakin, Terry ?, and two unknown engineers from Holmes Chapel.

William V Engine

August 1983 – Astle Park Traction Engine Rally
Sarah Barber and Charlotte Slater pictured by the Steam Carousel

'Ode to Steam'

This cavalcade of steams great might
Presents to us a wondrous sight.
Of engines now resplendent made
From years of harbouring in the shade.
They came from yard and field and wood
And in their twilight silent stood.
With rusting motion and boiler cold
It was for scrap that they were sold.

Then in the summer's sweltering scorch
Their end it was the burners torch.
But some from this great fate were taken
The slumbering giants gently awaken.
With lavished care from owners new
They are but now the chosen few.
That represent a lost great power
which we present to you this hour.

The Grand Parade it must not vary
Upholds tradition of Supremacy and Queen Mary
The Clayton and Foden wherever they roam
to Burley return for that is home.
A Barrel Tractor named 'Peter Pan'
Displays the work of a Norfolk man.
The Foster 'Winnie' from Lincolnshire
With chime whistle we all must hear.
Pays tribute to the Sandbach breed
For Fodens still are great indeed
North Western black of 'Evening Star'
Shines like that body from afar.
For she was the last of John Fowler's long breed
with steam plough and showman all in the lead.

The Clayton roller immaculate green
Must be admired when it is seen.
From years of toil and roadway duty
She still upholds her grace and beauty.
The Fowler traction from Whitney on Wye
was nearly left for it to die.

So now with portable in tow
They come to make a splendid show.
But pride of place for Salop men
The Sentinel it was for them.
This silent power of years long past
was made with skill that was to last.
For as the joy of Shrewsbury Town
It never let their masters down.

The great event we herald today
Close by the Bishop's Castle Railway
Alas no more 'Carlisle' steams past
with driver Cadwalider and whistle blast.
The train it had a friendly way
But sad to say it did not pay.
The wake of progress it thought proved
The 'Iron Horse' must be removed.
So after silence of may a year
King Steam returns for all to hear
With flashing rods and vapour cloud
They are but now to please a crowd.
So let us rejoice these machines from the past
Made by the men whose work was to last.
They made them strong to give of their best
In ageing years they do not rest.

Printed by kind permission of Mr D J Bradbury who wrote this poem in 1983 and
who is a regular participant in the Astle Park Traction Engine Rally.

CHELFORD AND DISTRICT BRANCH OF THE RNLI

Although the waterways of Chelford hardly merit a rescue boat, there has been an active local RNLI support committee since 1927. Formed in the February of that year and known as the Chelford, Goostrey and Holmes Chapel RNLI Branch, the officers were Mrs H Stockton and Mrs B Russell. In March 1943 Goostrey and Holmes Chapel separated and it became the Chelford and District Branch. Unfortunately it is not known how long this committee lasted, nor how much money was raised in those early years. In 1962 a new committee was formed under the chairmanship of Mrs J Morris assisted by Mrs D Evans and others. That year a coffee morning was held at Chelford House.

In 1970 it became necessary to reform the committee and in April Mrs Moody became Chairman, Mrs Hugill, Secretary and Mrs Measures, Treasurer. (Mrs Hugill and Mrs Massey, who also became members, are still serving at the present time). Their first event was a coffee morning and Bring and Buy sale. In 1972 the committee was more ambitious and a Wine and Sherry evening with a Tombola raised £138. In 1973 they reverted to the Coffee morning, with an entrance fee of 10p. The following year a service was held in Chelford Church to celebrate 150 years of the RNLI.

The membership of the Committee gradually changed, and in 1976 Mrs Walsh took over the Chairmanship and Mrs Day became Secretary. They, together with Mrs Hugill and Mrs Massey are the longest continuously serving members and have each received a Certificate of Thanks from RNLI. The finances of the Branch have always been in the capable hands of a local or retired National Westminster Bank Manager.

Coffee mornings have proved to be the most popular events and until 1992 were always at the home of a committee member. Since then they have been held in Chelford Village Hall on the Wednesday of the Autumn half term, with an entrance fee of 50p which includes coffee and biscuits. The profit has steadily risen from £110 at the first recorded event in 1960 to £1420 in 1999 and arises from stalls of home made cakes, produce, Bring and Buy, a Raffle and from the sale of RNLI cards and gifts which greatly boost the result.

In 1999 the Committee members were entertained by the Mayor of Macclesfield at a reception to celebrate 175 years of the RNLI, and a celebration dinner, organised by several local branches will be held in the autumn.

It is hoped that the people of Chelford and district will continue to generously support the vital work of the RNLI.

RNLI COMMITTEE 1995 AT PRESENTATION OF LONG SERVICE AWARD TO PAT HUGILL AND FREDA MASSEY

Left to right: Vivienne Chesters- Thompson, Mrs Trish Hugill, Mrs Rosemary Smart, Mrs Jane Ainsworth, Mrs Audrey Walsh (Chairman), Mrs Shirley Thomas, Mrs Audrey Moor, Miss Hilda , Mrs Minty Day (Secretary), Mr Bernard Hindley (Treasurer), Mrs Judith Towers, Mrs Josie Parfitt, Mrs Helen Skelton, Mr David Cashell (RNLI Area Organiser), Mrs Freda Massey and Mrs Elvis Burgess.

MEMORIES
By Alan Barber

The Barber family has been associated with Chelford for a considerable period of time, the name appearing in the 18th century records.

Alan has lived and worked in Chelford all his life (apart from 5 years in the Army during the Second World War). He has served on the Parish Council for 50 years and has been responsible for many improvements carried out in the village. On his retirement in May 1999 his daughter, Julia, joined the Parish Council to continue the family interest and concern for the village and its future.

His father was John Thomas Barber who was born in Chelford and then, as a boy, lived at Mere Farm, Nether Alderley where he became a keen apiarist and member of the Cheshire Beekeepers Association. He then took over the coal and lime business which his father, Edward Barber, had founded at Chelford railway station. This business was carried out for many years by his son Alan and grandson Andrew.

Mr J.T.Barber was living at the Cottage, Chelford when he married, and during the 1914-18 war he drove a threshing machine, which was also used for the transport of timber from Capesthorne and Astle Parks. Known as 'J.T.' in farming circles he was also an insurance broker, founding the business in 1882, which continued until 1985 and was known as JT Barber & Son. During his very active life he became an authority on Epyphiliums and Succulents and was a member of the Cactus and Succulents Society.

Both 'J.T.' and Alan Barber were members of Chelford Parish Hall Committee.

Alan remembers Miss Hewitt who was the infant teacher at Chelford School which he attended. She lived in Davenham near Northwich and during the week lodged in the village. Every Monday morning she cycled from Davenham to Chelford, returning on Friday afternoon after school closed for the weekend. If it happened to be raining she would arrive at school like a "drowned rat". On many occasions he remembered her drying her skirt in front of the school fire.

During the war evacuees from Manchester and London arrived in the village together with their teachers. Lady Dixon distributed the evacuees around the village - no consultation, you just had to accept whoever you were given. Occasionally parents of the children visited them in their new surroundings - usually very traumatic for all concerned - children, parents and villagers looking after the children.

269

When Astle Hall was purchased by a Manchester solicitor named Provis in 1926 and converted into a Nature Cure Home, the news spread around the young men in the village that it was actually a nudist establishment. As a result, groups of young men could often be seen peeping through the rhododendron bushes surrounding the estate.

During, or soon after the war a quantity of explosives were buried on a piece of land adjacent to the lake walk overlooking Astle Lane. Willow trees were planted to act as stakes to hold crates filled with various types of explosives. Some time later a friend of his was asked to dredge the lake. On arrival with two ploughing engines he was warned to be very careful where he positioned the dredge as explosives were buried somewhere in the vicinity of the dredging operation.

Western Command had been contacted and said that there was nothing dangerous and the village policeman seemed happy enough. However, just before the operation was about to start, fire engines and ambulances invaded the area. The crates of explosives were located and moved to the back of the Hall, where a group of Royal Engineers and demolition workers blew them up splashing phosphorous over the whole area until it looked as if a bomb had actually hit the area.

During Alan's time in the Army, during World War II, he spent a number of years in East Africa and the following is a report from the Evening Chronicle dated Tuesday 15th August 1950.

The Omukama

The visit to this country of the Omukama of Toro, Christian ruler of half a million people in Uganda, brings back memories to Mr Alan Barber of Ash Lea, Chelford, Cheshire.

Four years ago Mr Barber was one of two English soldiers who were privileged to attend the celebrations connected with the Omukama's accession.

"I was a sergeant-major at Nairobi at the time" Mr Barber told me. "With a friend I went on leave to Uganda, where to our surprise we were invited by the Omukama to attend the festivities. My friend, Sergeant 'Mac' Macombie, played the organ at the accession service." They had tea with the new

*ruler in the garden of his hilltop palace, set against the
towering background of the mountains of the Moon.*

*Now Mr Barber is hoping to arrange a meeting with the
Omukama and his wife during their four-day tour of the
Manchester area this week. They will be in the city on
Thursday and Friday.*

"The Omukama of Toro and his wife did make contact with me and they agreed
to come to tea at Ash Lea with my wife Elsie and our baby son, Andrew," Alan
remembers.

The presence in the village of the 'Barber' family is still strong. Alan and his
wife, Elsie, and son Andrew and daughters, Julia and Carole all live in the
village. Andrew runs his business 'Ashlea Mobiles' in Chelford and Julia is the
Practice Manager at the Chelford Surgery and is also one of the authors of this
book.

'Steam' has always been in the blood of the Barber family. Alan was one of the
founders of the Traction Engine Rally (mentioned in this book) which raised
money for the building and maintenance of the Parish Hall in Lower Withington.
The influence of the traction engines in Chelford is evident in the Chelford
School Emblem.

Edith Gledhill, Chelford   *July 1908*

*Those love truth best who to themselves are true,
And what they dare to dream of, dare to do.*

J H Jones, Chelford   *July 1908*

*The world would be a better world,
With joys more thickly strewn,
If folks cared less for others' faults,
And tried to mend their own.*

Cottages on Alderley Road c 1910
The Holly Tree was chopped down sometime late 1950's early 1960's.

MEMORIES
By Alan Barber

FRANK FINDS A HURDY-GURDY IS NOT WHAT HE EXPECTS

What is a Hurdy Gurdy? Well after the weekend one person who remains perplexed is Australian singer, Frank Ifield. He came to Chelford on Saturday to have a series of photographs taken of himself and that mysterious machine for the sleeve of his latest record to be released at the end of that month – Hurdy Gurdy.

"I always thought it was some kind of carousel," he told me. "Certainly that's the picture that's conjured up in the song."

Frank Ifield pictured with Rosemary Bloor during visit to Chelford, March 1972.

However, I was quite definite. "A Hurdy Gurdy, in my opinion, is the same thing as a street piano; a barrel organ." And that's just what he had his picture taken with.

Frank had come to Chelford from Eccles where he was appearing at the Talk of the North nightclub. After a short break he was off to his native Australia and later, Las Vegas. While he chatted about his job and his plans I could see that he was still a little upset about the Hurdy Gurdy and I thought I knew what he really had in mind.

And it just so happened that I had the very thing – a mammoth 86 key fairground organ, a giant of a thing. "Now that's more like it," commented the singer, colour rushing back to his cheeks, "that's just the job."

And so on Monday he came over to Chelford again and had his photo taken with the fairground machine.

The little street piano – though not as spectacular as its big brother – has had its fair share of public appearances and some years ago was loaned out to the 69 Theatre

Company, Manchester, as a prop for their presentation of "Erv".

"There are not a lot of them about. They've either been broken up or are in the hands of collectors".

"I have always had a fascination for these old music machines and other hunks of ironmongery from yesteryear. In addition to the two organs, I have a Burrell Scenic Showman Road Locomotive called William V, a Burrell Aagricultural Engine and, along with my son,

Andrew a Saunderson Agricultural tractor."

"They are my pride and joy and, in fact, the pride and joy of all Chelford when they turn out at Astle Park Traction Engine Rally."

But back to Frank and that – for want of better words – Hurdy Gurdy. It was love at first sight and what was to have been a brief visit to Macclesfield lasted all afternoon.

Amy E Jones, Rose Bank, Chelford
July 1908

To think kindly of each other is good,
To speak kindly of each other is better,
To act kindly one towards another is best of all.

THE STRANGE STORY OF ABRAHAM STREET OF CHELFORD
By Sylvia Baguette

Abraham Street was born at Church Cottages, Chelford on 29 January 1886. He was the son of William Street (also known as Ward) the local postman, and Emma Dunn. He worked as an agricultural labourer until the First World War.

He joined the 14th Battalion of the Cheshire Regiment as Private Abraham Street 36183. In 1916 he was at Prees Heath Camp, Whitchurch, Shropshire. He was transferred to the Isolation Hospital, Sealand Road, Chester and died there of Cerebro Spinal Fever on 6 May 1916. He is buried in a war grave in Chelford Churchyard.

The short history above sounds like the sad but ordinary end of a serving soldier.

However, the family story I grew up with is slightly more dramatic!

When Abraham enlisted he was sent to Shropshire and whilst there was inoculated for service abroad. After over 100 men had been inoculated it was discovered they had been injected with "spotted fever" and that the doctor was a German, working as a spy. One aunt who is still living, Nora Blomfield, aged 86 years, remembers one of the men who survived - he had a fear of inoculations and somehow avoided it. He lived in Chelford for years afterwards. She thought his name was Massey.

Abraham's parents visited him at Chester Isolation Hospital and said he was a terrible sight. They could only look at him through glass. He died on 6 May 1916.

My grandparents, Peter and Annie Street, went to Chelford for the funeral. Peter was Abraham's eldest brother. Abraham's body was sent by train to Chelford in a sealed coffin. When the undertakers, Aaron Cooper, came to collect the body it had someone else's name on the lid. It transpired the other coffin was in South Wales. The funeral was postponed to the next day while the first coffin was returned to South Wales and the correct one sent. My grandparents had to telegram relations to explain why they could not return. The relations were looking after their 3 year old daughter, who was my mother, Lilian Street. The railway van was isolated in the sidings at Chelford overnight with the second coffin in, until the funeral could take place the next day. Abraham's mother, Emma (Dunn) Street, said she would never be sure if it was her son that she buried. The coffin could not be opened for fear of infection and no one was sure if it was just the lids that had been mixed up. However, the funeral took place and a war grave headstone was erected in Chelford Churchyard.

A sad, intriguing story but no proof it ever happened except the word of elderly relatives. However, that was not the end of the story!!

In the late 1940's my mother, Lilian Street, (Abraham's niece) was returning to Manchester from a funeral in Chester of a relation of her husband. She had married a man called William Lomas, from Chester, and lived in Manchester. A cousin by marriage of William Lomas travelled home with them, someone they hardly ever met. The conversation turned to wartime experiences and strange incidents. My father was discussing the 2nd World War because he was not born until 1912. However, this distant cousin, Tom Dutton, said he'd had a disturbing experience in the 1st World War. He had been stationed "somewhere in the Midlands". (My mother can't remember any more). He was a sergeant and one day volunteered to escort a prisoner to London, accompanied by another soldier. The prisoner was handcuffed to them but never spoke. On reaching the capital they had been instructed to go to the Tower of London. They handed their prisoner over and gratefully accepted a meal before the journey home. During the meal they heard shots and were alarmed. They were told it was the firing squad dispatching their prisoner. They were shocked but were told "He was a German doctor who had been poisoning our boys and killed over 100 before he was caught".

So over 30 years after the event, the Street family found out the end of the tale. What had been a story handed down in one family was corroborated by someone who had never heard their story. People had not believed Tom Dutton when he told his story about his special duty. The only link between the two families was my mother who had not married until 1941. My mother told Tom Dutton about Abraham only after he'd finished his story.

My mother, Lilian Street, worked for Ferranti's at Chadderton in the late 1930's. A woman who worked with her told her an uncle had been injected and killed by a German doctor during the 1st World War.

The story sounds unbelievable but something must have happened. There are too many people involved, with nothing to gain by lying.

Six years ago, in 1992, I asked a genealogical researcher to try and find out exactly what had happened. We didn't get very far. A Major Astle of the Cheshire Regiment was adamant there were no executions at the Tower in the 1st World War. A Mr Crump, a military historian recommended by Major Astle, assured me German spies were shot at the Tower and there is a photo of the firing range where this took place.

After some weeks of work by the genealogist, Mr Hammersley, he wrote back to say that he believed official secrecy would hamper any progress under the 100 year rule. The cost would be prohibitive to a private individual. However, people he'd consulted said from the circumstantial evidence "it has a ring of truth about it".

The most important aspect to me is that I have talked to people alive when this happened who were told all about "poor Abraham". They have always said he was poisoned by a German doctor, no doubts. That's what they were told and men who returned to Chelford told the same tale. My mother and Aunt Nora are the last two links I know of, people alive at the time and told the facts by Abraham's closest relations. I tried to find the truth for their sake but it looks as though the truth about poor Abraham is buried deeper than he is.

Sylvia Baguette's grandfather was Peter Street, the elder brother of Abraham Street.

Abraham Street

MEMORIES

By Stan Potts

See also Chelford Cricket.

Stan Potts' family have been associated with Chelford for a hundred years. His grandparents, George and Sarah Potts, together with their son, David (Stan's father) are recorded in the 1891 Census returns[1]. For 25 years Stan played for Chelford Cricket Club, often as first team captain. During the war he served in the Royal Navy where he met his wife, Charlotte, who was a nurse aboard ship..

Both now retired they live in Robin Lane, Chelford.

I remember my father telling me of the village flood in 1872. Apparently, due to the lake breaking its banks, a tremendous volume of water came down the two brooks, the waterfall collapsed and someone was despatched to warn the people of Bate Mill of the surge.

My father told me that there was a pub called The Cat and Lion in one of the Church cottages. He also said that some of the pub fittings were there for many years after the owners of the land closed down the pub.

During the war the Army used Astle Hall. Henshaws Blind Institute had bought the Hall and Park intending to use it as small workshops but never developed it and, after the war, it deteriorated until it was knocked down.

I remember going to the Hall before the Second World War to attend some event (I cannot recall what) and when walking round the grounds by the brook, finding a hand mill and a plaque which turned out to be Roman. The original village was where the shrubbery was when the Hall was there and Mill House (knocked down when Astle hall was built in 1749) was more or less where the pool is now.

During the early part of the war, I think around Dunkirk time, cases of rifles were buried on the estate. Nobody seems to remember where and as far as I know they are probably still there.

---

1   Chelford in the 19th Century by W Keith Plant.

The cricket ground was alongside the railway and during one game a hit from one of the batsmen cleared the ground and ended up on a passing goods train finishing up at Carlisle. The longest recorded hit on the ground.

A Chelford Bachelor   *July 1908*

Wanted – A wife, who can handle a broom,
To brush down the cobwebs and sweep up the room
to make decent bread that a fellow can eat –
Not the horrible compound you everywhere meet;
Who knows how to boil, to fry and to roast,
Make a good cup of tea and a platter of toast,
A woman who washes, cooks, irons and stitches,
And sews up the rips in fellows old breeches;
And makes her own garments – an item that grows
Quite highly expensive, as everyone knows;
A commonplace creature, and still with a mind
To teach and to guide- exalted, refined;
A sort of an angel and housemaid combined.

Two of the authors would be interested in finding out who the above Bachelor was and whether he found a wife to meet his requirements.

MEMORIES

My time in Chelford and Lower Withington 1945-1946
by Vera Ridge (Nee Rowlinson)

I was working in a factory making parachute cases and when the contract was finished the firm closed down. It was called Plyformers. My friend and I decided to join the Land Army. We both applied and were sent for a medical and then awaited the results. I was over the moon when I heard I had passed and could not wait to be posted. I was just seventeen years old. My friend also passed the medical but as she was only four foot eleven inches tall, she was too small to work on the land and had to work in the Land Army Hostel.

My posting was to Chelford and I was living in Sale at the time. My father took me to Manchester to get the train to Chelford. This was April 1945. I arrived in Chelford and made my way to the hostel[1] that was five minutes from the station, just by the Dixon Arms. I was introduced to the Matron who would be in charge of us, and Mona, the housekeeper, and the girls who were all very friendly. I can't quite remember whether we were kitted out at Chester or the hostel. We had cream shirts, green sweaters, hats, brown-laced shoes, beige socks, jodhpurs, dungarees and topcoat that was camel coloured. My first posting was working for a farmer called Jimmy Jamieson in Over Peover. I was taught to milk a herd of Ayrshire cows, which used to kick me off my stool. I remember planting seed potatoes going up and down fields all day. One day a huge dragonfly stung me. I had a big lump on my arm. In the summer I helped with haymaking, walking behind the machine that was throwing out the hay or corn and I had to pick it up and tie a sheaf knot around the corn and stand it up in the field. After doing this and during the heat of the day without a hat on, I went back to the hostel for dinner and passed out. Matron got the doctor and I had to go to bed because I had sunstroke.

Another job I used to do was deliver milk. I had one of those old order bikes that butchers used to deliver meat. I had a churn of milk with a ladle and used to go to houses and the people used to come to their doors with a jug and say how much milk they wanted. It was all right when the churn was full but on the way back it was empty, I made a right racket with it bouncing up and down as I went down the lanes.

---

1   The Woodland, Chelford.

I worked with a farm labourer called Jeff; he lived with his wife at Peover Lodge. I remember Mrs Jamieson with her long dresses and pinafores. For bagging, which is the name for food you had for your break in the morning, she used to bake lovely scones but, if she had none left, she used to give us bread and jam with biscuits. I used to feed the hens and collect the eggs. One morning as I was unlocking the door of the shed to let them out, I didn't get out of the way quick enough and a hen that was flying out caught me beneath the eye with its beak. I think I was lucky I didn't lose my eye. Mr Jamieson was always telling me to get to work by 8.00 a.m. but it always seemed to be 8.03 a.m. when I arrived, so he sacked me.

I then started work on another farm in Marthall just down the road from Chelford. We all had bicycles to get to work. This farm was owned by a gentleman farmer, Mr Walkden, who had a tin factory in Manchester.

A bailiff and his wife, Mr & Mrs Wright, ran the farm. The farmhouse was divided in two parts. Mr Walkden lived in one part and Mr & Mrs Wright in the other. At this farm machines did the milking. They were called Alfa-Laval; I soon got the hang of it and also did the dairy work, putting all the milk through the cooler.

I worked with Mr Wright and a farm labourer. We took it in turns to go in at 5.00 a.m. for morning milking. One morning the labourer didn't turn up and I had to milk them on my own. It was Mr Wright's turn to have a lay-in. In the summer when the cows were in the fields all night I had to go to the field to call them in for milking. Sometimes when there was a mist you couldn't see them. I used to shout, cow-up, cow-up, cow-up, and they would start coming towards me. After milking in the morning we would go into the farmhouse for breakfast which was porridge and a boiled egg. I had to bring a jug of cream off the top of the milk to put on the porridge. After breakfast we had to clean the shippons out and put fresh straw down. We had to put the waste in a wheelbarrow and tip it on the midden. When it got a bit high up, we had to put a plank of wood down. It was hard to try to balance a wheelbarrow on a slippery plank when you were wearing wellingtons. Many was the time I fell off and didn't come up smelling of roses. We had one carthorse at the farm that was used to take the milk down the lane to the main road to be picked up by the milk wagons. It was also used for all the other jobs in the fields. I used to clean the harness.

My friends and I used to go to dances in the village. It was just a wooden hut over the station. They used to have whist drives from 8.00 – 10.00 p.m., then dancing later. We were often told off for coming in late. They had a bedroom in the hostel called The Rascals Room and my friends and I had to move in there. The odd times we came in late, Matron had locked the door so we couldn't get in. We used to throw stones at the bedroom window so someone would come down and open the lounge window. Matron got wise to this and opened the window slightly so we could get in, but locked the door so we could not get up the stairs and had to sleep in the chairs in the lounge. Next morning we were really told off. In the village I was friendly with the porter at the station. His name was Colin Bloor (Station Road). He had a brother called Tommy who was in the navy. I also remember Albert Baskerville, who was a farmer's son. There were German P.O.W's. working on some of the farms and there were soldiers at Astle Hall and also some Polish soldiers. When the hostel was closed down because it wasn't paying as there were not enough girls in it, we had to be billeted out with the villagers. I was with an old couple, they were very nice, but did not like you coming in late after the dances at the village hall.

I can remember when the 1939-45 war was over and we all went into Manchester to celebrate. We were all in uniform; soldiers, sailors, airmen, everybody in fancy hats. We had a wonderful time. After that I decided to go back to my parents in Sale.

After a couple of weeks at home I received a letter from my friend who had also been released from the Land Army. She had found a job at Withington Hall and she said she was lonely and would I go out there to work with her. I decided to give it a go and went to be interviewed by Mrs Baskerville-Glegg. I was picked up at Chelford Station by Mr Kitchen, Chauffeur and Handyman, and taken to the hall. I got the job and two weeks later my friend left and I was on my own. On arriving at Withington Hall, my first impressions going up the long driveway, were the thousands of daffodils that were growing in the huge grounds.

My job at the Hall was; first thing in the morning I had to clean the fireplace out in the dining room, then light the fire, then I made breakfast for Sir John and his wife and took it to the dining room. Sir John was a real gentleman. He always wore breeches and tweed jackets. I had a bedsit and my own bathroom. Sir John and his wife lived on their own in the huge Hall. I can remember the beautiful drawing room with all the lovely carpets, tapestries and paintings. There was a self-contained flat at the back of the hall that was occupied by a family called Normansel and Mrs Normansel used to do the cleaning and vacuuming and I used to help her. She had a husband who worked away from the Hall, also a daughter called Bessie and a nine-year-old daughter called Hilda. If I remember rightly, Bessie got engaged to a farmer's son called Len Massey.

I enjoyed working at the hall but I was only eighteen years old and it was a bit lonely so I decided to go back home. Mrs Glegg found me a nice job as a children's nanny as I was fond of children. I went for the interview to a very nice family and they were going away for two weeks and wanted me to start the job when they came home. I went home, Mr Kitchen taking me to the station. While I was home I went shopping for my mum and met an old friend working in the greengrocer's shop. They were short-handed and asked if I could help out as my first job was working in a newsagent. I went the next day to the shop to help out and the manager offered me a job so I never went back to Chelford.

CHELFORD LAND ARMY 1945

Back row left to right: - Marjorie (Micky), Gladys, Mona (HouseKeeper)
Middle row left to right: - Hilda, Josie - ?
Bottom row left to right: - Vera Ridge with Judy the dog and Dorothy.

Vera Ridge in Uniform

Where are you now girls?

(Photograph reproduced by kind permission from Vera Ridge)

283

MEMORIES
From Sylvia Baguette

Sylvia Baguette is the Great Granddaughter of William Street (also known as Ward) and Emma Street, nee Dunn.

As a young man my grandfather, Peter Street, worked on Piggotts Hill Farm for the Venables family. He lived there and came home twice a week. My grandmother, Annie Murphy, used to visit Chelford cottages with her uncle, William Davies, and although she met all his younger brothers she had never met Peter. However, in May 1910, King Edward VII died and churches all over the land held commemoration services. My grandmother attended the one at Chelford and glancing across the church she saw a man sitting with the Street family. She guessed it must be the eldest son, Peter. My grandfather looked across and said, in later life, he never forgot his first view of Annie. She had a large black straw hat with roses on it, a grey suit and she had such a slim waist you could put your arm right round it. They married in October 1911 at the Albert Memorial Church in Manchester and Peter lived and worked in Manchester although he often visited Chelford.

From Lilian Lomas (nee Street)

Lilian Lomas was born in 1912, the daughter of Peter and Annie Street (nee Murphy).

My grandfather was William Street (also known as Ward) who was the village postman at Chelford for over 40 years. He was born at Over Peover in 1854. He met his future wife Emma Dunn, on Chelford station when he went to meet the 11.00 mail train. She had come from Shropshire to be in service at the Dixon's Arms and asked for directions. William said that if she waited while he sorted the mail he would carry her bag across for her.

When they married on 25 December 1877 they lived at Over Peover for two years and their eldest son, Peter, was born there. When he was twelve months old they moved to Church Cottages. A family called Steel lived in the one adjacent to the church and they lived next door.

My grandparents died in Church Cottages, and their unmarried sons, William and Frederick, lived there till they died in the early 70's. William Street was better known as Billy and he followed in his father's footsteps as the village postman as did his brother, Jack, who later lived at Siddington.

Frances Street (Cissie) married a man called Street (Bill) and they moved into the end cottage opposite the church (now No. 5). This cottage had been a pub. The stone slabs were still there in the pantry that had been used to cool the beer and the step from the living room to the kitchen was worn into a 'U' shape by generations of feet. These features were still in place when the Street family moved in about 1880. At the back of this cottage was the well. It supplied the water for all the other cottages and people came from surrounding properties. I remember as a child seeing a Mr Tomlinson come from Congleton Lane with two buckets on a yoke to get water. People bringing flowers to the churchyard would get water for their vases at the well. Big water tubs would be used to gather rainwater for washday. All cottages had outside toilets, some till the 60's.

One event that had a lasting impression on everyone was the Chelford train crash. Grandfather said it was a terrible night and Emma was getting the tea when they heard a loud bang and crash. Everyone ran towards the noise and when Peter Street got to the station it was all smoke and steam. The dead were put in the waiting office and the injured in the booking office.

Peter Street, my father, worked at Piggott Hills Farm for the Venables family until 1911 and he said on a clear night, with the wind in the right direction, he could hear the banging of the doors on the 10 o'clock mail train.

William Street had only one arm, which meant he could not ride a bike and had to deliver his letters on foot. There were some very clever doctors at the end of the last century. Peter Street, his 15-year-old son, was working in the fields one day when he caught his foot in a threshing machine. His father was summoned from the post office, Peter was put on a milkcart and the foot wrapped in towels. He was taken 6 miles to Macclesfield Infirmary and people said they could see a trail of blood all the way there. At first the doctor wanted to amputate his foot but William begged them to give him a chance so he amputated three toes. Peter stayed in hospital for 15 weeks, made an excellent recovery and walked miles each day most of his life. When he went in hospital in later life doctors remarked on what a wonderful operation it had been for those times.

MEMORIES
by Mrs Katherine Tomlinson

Katherine Tomlinson is married to Paul, the Great Grandson of George and Hannah Tomlinson. George and Hannah had seven children, James (the father of Melburn), George, Henry (the grandfather of Paul), Ernest, Hannah, Nellie and Emmie.

It is believed that the shop/cafe was on the corner of Congleton Lane.

Mr Cragg was the baker who, after the First World War, had a horse and cart with two doors at the back. Uncle Ernest Tomlinson was the gardener at Withington Hall and he got rheumatic fever and had to stop gardening so he started the cafe in about 1924. Granddad Tomlinson painted a notice to go outside for advertising and they built a shop on the end. Mr Cragg gave up baking in Chelford and delivering bread in the local area so Tomlinsons took the round over. Granny did the baking at home at first but the bread became so popular that she couldn't keep up with it so a bakehouse was built with a garage between that and the shop. A baker from Congleton was employed and he cycled to Chelford each day. We think his name was Jack. Uncle took bread round in a Morris Cowley in the 1920's, delivering to local farms etc. Welltrough Farm was the last on the round (it was reputed to be the largest farm in Cheshire then, 240 acres).

As well as bread, there were eclairs, sponge drops, cream horns etc. Uncle had to buy a bigger car, a Morris Oxford, which had shelves constructed on the back seat. The business expanded into groceries, tinned fruit, packed lard, butter etc. All these were hand weighed. They also sold pop, cigarettes etc.

Granny's name was Hannah Tomlinson and her husband was George who was the postman at Withington.

Melburn Tomlinson (the uncle who lives in Sleaford now) used to help in the cafe and shop because his parents had died and Granny looked after him. He used to walk to Monks Heath to go to Kings School in Macclesfield every day from Chelford and then used to deliver bread etc., in the evening. They used to deliver as far as the Smithy at Siddington, Jodrell Bank (not the telescope!), Goostrey and also to Sir John Dixon. Chelford used to get deliveries on Saturdays, Withington on Fridays and Snelson on Thursdays as well as going to Bate Mill, Barnshaw and Blackden. Dr Shepard lived at Gledhills Farm next to the Rectory and Sally

Foden lived down Catchpenny Lane, while Rose Robinson lived near Arthur Burgess' garage.

The nurse lived in one of the Church cottages and Bill Street, the village postman, lived in the other one. Another Billy was the RAC man and he was regularly on point duty on Chelford corner while the AA man was at Monks Heath. Drews were the village newsagents, Miss Hubbard, ALCM, was the piano teacher and Charlie Knowles was the butcher opposite Cheshire Farmers in the village. Carters ran the Post Office and telephone exchange. Jack Barber was the local insurance agent and he was also an expert in geraniums and orchids, particularly the old varieties, and he often advertised in Amateur Gardener.

The cafe was sold in 1939.

A typical sales invoice

Corner Cafe & Stores
CHELFORD,...........................**193...**

M. . . . .

. . . .

. . Bought of . .

TOMLINSONS

BAKERS & CONFECTIONERS
FINEST SECLECTED GROCERIES & PROVISIONS

THE NOTES SHOP FOR PURE HOME MADE BREAD

MEMORIES

May Queen Festival – May 1986

The May celebrations in Chelford got off to a fine start recently with the annual May Festival and crowning of the May Queen and Rosebud at the Village Hall.

Floats, vintage cars and the South Cheshire Pipe Band joined in a procession through the village to the festival field where this year's May Queen, Clare

Couling (12), of Oakleigh, Knutsford Road, Chelford, was crowned by the former vicar of Chelford, Maurice Henry, who made a welcome return to the village from his retirement in Plumley with his wife, Elsie.

Clare's attendants were Emma Boyling and Andrea and Wendy Hope and her crown bearer was Martin Bilsborough.

This year's Rosebud Queen was 11-year-old Lucy Grace, of Drumblefield, Carter Lane, Chelford, whose attendants were Katy Lowe and Katie and Louise Robey. One of the stars of the day was Lucy's three year old crown bearer, Alexander Oxford.

Both Clare and Lucy are members of the 1st Chelford Guides who formed a guard of honour for them.

Ending their year of office were the retiring May Queen, Dawn Boyling, and the retiring Rosebud Queen, Emma Hamlin, and there were six visiting queens from neighbouring parishes.

Visitors were treated to a full range of stalls and games throughout the afternoon and were entertained to May Pole dancing by the Chelford Brownies. The South Cheshire Pipe Bank also played during the afternoon.

The highlight of the entertainment came with the first ever Chelford 'It's A Knockout' competition between four family teams. The entrants first had to dribble balls and then had to complete a tricky barrel snake game.

It was in the third game that the spectators got more enjoyment and the participants got wet when they had to carry buckets of water and transfer them over a six foot fence. And in the final game water was also a strong feature with contestants carrying tennis balls on spoons across a beam while being pelted with wet sponges by opposing teams.

The competition ended in a narrow result. The Lomas and Sullivan families were equal in points but an extra game made the Lomas family the winners.

The first Rose Queen was crowned on 29th June 1934 and is still resident in the village, namely Mrs Joan Sutcliffe.

Chelford's crowning glory at this year's May Festival will be Jane Williamson who has been chosen as the village's May Queen. Jane, aged 12, is pictured in the centre with her attendants, Nigel Chorlton, Rosemary Camm, Lindsey Annikin, Sarah Wheldon, Caroline Orr and Guy Camm.

MAY QUEEN – MAY 1991

Chelford's May Queen, Lindsay Annikin, was crowned by last years Queen, Jane Williamson at the highlight of the Festival.

291

CHELFORD DIALECT WORDS

During her lifetime Miss Audrey Walsh collected words associated with the Chelford area of Cheshire.

Adlant	-	the head of the field, where the plough turned.
Asker	-	a lizard (either a land or water newt)
Backend	-	Autumn
Baggin-time	-	a meal taken in the middle of the morning.
Barley me	-	I claim.
Beesom	-	as in 'The young beesom' a young madam.
Black Jack	-	a black beetle.
Boggart	-	a ghost or goblin.
Buckle to	-	to get to work.
Cank	-	having a good gossip.
Chunner	-	to have a good grumble.
Clack	-	to have a good chatter or gossip.
Craddy	-	as in finishing my craddy – i.e. the job I have set myself.
Dumberdash	-	a sharp sudden shower of rain.
Fash	-	nonsense.
Hatch	-	a small gate
Keckling	-	unsteady or falling over.
Kench	-	a knock.
Moithering	-	bewildering.
Mizzle	-	very fine rain.
Nacky	-	very handy, ingenious.
Nesh	-	tender, delicate, unable to stand physical pain.
Screetch	-	to shriek out
Thritch	-	as I'm all thrutched up – squeezed up.

18 May 1900

<u>Remarkable Wedding</u>

"May and December have once more been united in holy bonds of matrimony – contracting parties on this occasion being Miss Clare Thomas, an attractive young lady of 26 summers, and Mr Henry Clark, who we are informed has seen 83 winters but might easily pass for one considerably less advanced in years. After the ceremony, which took place at Lower Withington on 10th inst., the happy pair received the congratulations of friends."

<u>"Furious driving from the station.</u>

At Wilmslow Petty Sessions yesterday, Algernon Dale, farmer's son of Chelford, was charged with furious driving at Chelford on the 14th May. PC Jackson deposed that he was near his station when he saw the defendant drive his milk cart from Chelford station. The horse was on a wild gallop and the witness shouted but the defendant took no notice and drove on in that way for about 2 miles. The witness followed him on a bicycle. Many complaints had been made about this furious driving on the way from the station. Defendant said he could not hold his horse – Chairman: "You think that it was running away?" – Defendant: "Yes!" –Chairman: "Did you see the Officer?" Defendant: "No." - The Bench considered the charged proved and imposed a fine of 5s and costs."

---

25 May 1900

<u>"School Neglect</u>

Daniel Massey, farmer of Lower Withington, was summoned to the Macclesfield County Session on Tuesday on a charge of neglecting to send his children regularly to school. Mr S Downs, school attendance officer who prosecuted, stated that the defendant's girl had attended Chelford school and during the last year the child attended 311 times out of a possible 441 and from the beginning of this year until the present month she was absent 51 times. The matter had been before the committee. "She had really", set the committee, "at defiance." Mr Downs also mentioned the case of another child of the defendant. The Bench ordered the usual fines to be paid."

---

2 August 1901

<u>"The Day Schools</u>

We take the following from the current issue of the Parish Magazine. 'It is with much regret that we have to announce the resignation of Miss E M Bishop as Assistant Teacher of

Chelford School. Miss Bishop has been a member of the school staff since March 1898 and during that time she has done her best to promote the welfare of the school in every way. The Managers are very sorry to lose her services and they hope that the new work that she is to take up would be for her advantage. The subscriptions to Chelford School have been coming in more rapidly during the last month. The receipts have been sent to all subscribers but it may be as well to print the name of those who have supported the school this year. There are others whose subscriptions will doubtless be received before the school year ends. Subscriptions have been received from: - Messrs. H R Sykes, H F Hayhurst, Alfred Bloar, D Phillips, T H Basford, T Wilson Junior, S Downs, Lewis, Holmes, Hardwick, Reaves, J O Clark, Fryer, S Bloar, Gleave, Walsh, Tatton, Newton, W H Cooke, E Johnson, J Callwood, J D Haigh, E Barber, Dr Shepard, Mrs Grant, Mrs Barber (2 years), Mrs Dakin, Mrs Moors, Mrs Venables. Donations have been received from Mrs W H Cooke, The Astle Park Cricket Club and Mrs Snelson's bible classes. Total amount comes to £29."

21 August 1903

"Asleep in charge of a horse

At the Wilmslow Police Court yesterday, Percy Wilkinson, farmer, was summoned for being asleep whilst in charge of a horse and lorry at Chelford on the 6th. He pleaded guilty. PC Jones deposed that at 11.35 p.m. he was on duty on the Macclesfield Road when he noticed a light some distance away. On going to the place he found a horse and lorry laden with hampers of potatoes drawn across the highway with apparently no one in charge. He shouted and, not receiving any answer, he looked over the lorry where he found the defendant asleep on one of the hampers. On being roused up Wilkinson said he must have gone off all at once. Defendant now explained that he had been up 3 nights and had lost his rest – The Chairman (Mr Gregg) said the case was a serious one and the defendant had rendered himself liable to a fine of £30. It was a great danger to the public – Mr Yates; "Was the defendant sober?" Officer; "Yes." A fine of 10s and costs was imposed."

14 September 1906

"Late Milk Galloping to the Station

At the Wilmslow Petty Session yesterday Ed Baddiley, farm servant at Chelford, was summonsed for driving a horse at a furious rate at Chelford on 14th September. PC Houlgrave said the defendant was taking milk to the station at the time and he nearly ran into 2 cyclists. The horse was galloping and going at quite 12 miles an hour. Witness had received numerous complaints about this fast driving to the station. When spoken to the defendant said he could not pull up, but that was not correct as witness saw him urging on the horse. The bench fined the defendant 5s and costs and intimated that if any further cases occurred the employers would probably be prosecuted against for aiding and abetting. The Chairman said that the farmer was to blame if he was late with his milking and the servant was compelled to drive at a dangerous rate to the station, he was really the chief defaulter."

---

19 October 1906

"Football – Chelford Lads

Chelford Lads met the Wilmslow Juniors at Chelford on Saturday last.

Visitors were about the best team they had met, in fact they were too good for them as a result of 7-0 proved. Chelford, winning the post, played with the wind but up to half time had 5 goals scored against them. They were out weighed and out mixed yet they played a plucky game and had one or two hard lines in not scoring. In the second half though, the home teams forwards got to their opponents and now and again towards the finish work fell on the defense. Bob Haigh, Jacky Burgess and Billy Ward were however the stalwart trio and did some exiting saves. The lads have a lot of open dates.

The paper continues to report during 1906 on all Chelford Lads' games of which most were lost.

TRAGEDY AT CHELFORD

The report below was included in the Advertiser of Friday 1ˢᵗ May 1914 and deals with a murder carried out at Knowsley Farm the previous Wednesday, 29ᵗʰ April..

Pig Dealer's Battered Body found in Yard

A terrible tragedy was reported from Chelford on Wednesday. When the village postman was on his rounds he was horrified to find the battered body of William Reeves, a pig dealer, lying in the yard near the side door of his residence, Knowsley Farm, a small building situate a mile from Chelford on the main road to Macclesfield. When the police visited the premises they found the wife in a demented state in the house, and as foul play was suspected she was arrested and conveyed in a motor car to Macclesfield. Reeves, who was 71 years of age, was well known through this part of the country.

The farmyard presented an amazing spectacle. Blood was bespattered everywhere, there were patches on the doors, smears on the windowpanes, floors, and on the brickwork, and on the small red railings near the back door.

At about 11.30 on Tuesday night, a neighbouring farmer declared that he heard shouts coming from the direction of Knowsley Farm as if some person was demanding admittance. Then everything went quiet. The body when found presented a terrible spectacle. There

were a number of wounds on the head, and the man had a number of severe cuts on his wrists, evidently caused by a knife, which was found on the premises by the police.

There was a pool of congealed blood on the flags, and the immediate vicinity of the scene of the tragedy presented a ghastly appearance. Blood was besplashed on the walls, on the pillars, on the doorway, doorsteps, and over the small wooden rails, painted a light red, were dyed deep with the blood of the dead man. The windowpanes were also smeared with blood, as if the man had reeled towards them and had weakly tried to draw attention by knocking on the glass.

In the kitchen one of the chairs was bloodstained, and there was a pool of blood on the stone floor.

It is presumed that Reeves was seated in an armchair in the kitchen when he was attacked by some person with a knife, and that such force was used as to practically sever the wrist. It is surmised that he staggered for safety to the door, where he was again attacked, and then left to bleed to death.

Reeves' wife, a tall, powerful woman, sat before her arrest on a couch in the farm kitchen entirely unconcerned, and drummed her fingers on the table. When asked to put on her bonnet, and to accompany the police officers, she made no comment but jumped in the taxi and was driven away.

Police Court Story

Wife Charged with Murder
And remanded in Custody.

"At noon yesterday, Eliza Reeves (65), was brought before Colonel W W Stancliffe at the Macclesfield County Police Court, charged that "she feloniously, wilfully, and of malice aforethought, did kill and murder one William Reeves, at Nether Alderley, on or about the 29th April 1914."

Prisoner: That is wrong. Read it over again.
Supt. Ennion told the prisoner that she would have an opportunity of speaking afterwards. It would be as well if she did not say anything just yet.

The Magistrates' Clerk (to the prisoner);: Yes, you had better wait.
Supt. Ennion said he only desired to offer sufficient evidence to justify a remand. The circumstances were very sad and distressing. The prisoner was the wife of a man named William Reeves, who followed the business of a farmer and pig dealer, and resided at Knowsley Farm, Nether Alderley. For some years past, he was sorry to say, the deceased and his wife had

lived unhappily together and about nine o'clock on Tuesday night the deceased was seen by an employee to be seated in the kitchen at his residence. At the time the accused, so far as the police were able to judge, was not in the neighbourhood. The man referred to retired to bed, and about eleven o'clock the same night he heard the prisoner and the deceased quarrelling. The man had got so accustomed to this sort of thing, however, that he took no notice of the quarrel, but remained in bed. About the same time a neighbouring farmer, who was returning from Chelford station, in company with his wife, heard some quarrelling at the Knowsley Farm, which continued until about 11.30, when all went quiet.

Postman's Discovery

About 6.15 the next morning a postman named Wm. Henry Ward, of Chelford, went to Knowsley Farm to deliver a letter, and there to his horror he saw the deceased lying dead in the yard near to the kitchen door. He made a communication to another party, and P.C. Moore, of Chelford, having been informed, arrived at the farm about seven o'clock, and he would tell the Court how he found the deceased and where he saw the accused. Subsequently Dr. Shepard, who had been communicated with, arrived on the scene, and pronounced life extinct, stating that the deceased had been dead several hours.

Terrible Injuries

He (Superintendent Ennion) was apprised of the affair, and reached the farm about 8.10 a.m. After having the body removed into the house he made a search, and found a certain instrument, which would be produced in due course, and with which no doubt the crime was committed. He also found a certain article of wearing apparel, which the accused admitted she was wearing on Tuesday. Later in the day the prisoner was conveyed to the Macclesfield County Police Station, where, after being duly cautioned, she was charged with the capital offence, and made no reply. He might mention that Dr Shepard's examination of the deceased went to show that there were a large number of cuts on both hands and the back of the head, the wounds having evidently been caused by a knife. In addition, the left wrist was practically severed, as were also several arteries and tendons, and death was apparently caused by shock, due to haemorrhage brought about by the wounds so inflicted.

What the Constable Found

P.C. Moore, of Chelford, said about 6.50 a.m. on Wednesday he received certain information, in consequence of which he proceeded to Knowsley Farm, Nether Alderley. On his arrival there about seven o'clock he saw the deceased, William Reeves, lying dead in the yard near to the kitchen door. There were a lot of bloodstains about the place. Deceased was cut about both hands and the head, and the left hand was partially severed at the wrist. Witness saw the accused in the kitchen, and having said something to her, he asked if she knew how it happened. She replied, "I know nothing about it. I have been in bed all night, and I was the one who found him." Witness subsequently took her into custody, and conveyed her to the Macclesfield Police Station in a motor car. After being cautioned, she was charged with the capital offence, but made no reply.

On this evidence Supt. Ennion asked for a remand until after the inquest, which he said had been fixed for Friday afternoon, at the Chelford Parish Room. He had mentioned the matter to the accused, told her the time and place of the inquest, and asked her if she would like to attend, but she seemed undecided on the point. He had also asked her if she would like a solicitor to take up her case, and she seemed undecided about that also.

Prisoner: I am undecided because I don't know any solicitor.

The Superintendent said he would help her in any way possible.

Prisoner: I have no money for one thing, and it is difficult to get a solicitor without money..

Asked if she had anything to say why she should not be remanded, prisoner replied: "It is no use my saying anything, if I had."

Prisoner was then remanded, in custody, until Saturday morning.

Note: The Macclesfield Courier and Herald of 25th July 1914 reported that: the verdict on Eliza Reeves, aged 72, had been changed from death by hanging to custody for life.

JAMES IRLAM & SONS LTD
KNUTSFORD ROAD CHELFORD

James Irlam arrived in Snelson with his wife and five young children in 1949. Originally from Ringway, their market garden was taken over by Manchester Corporation for house building. The eldest son, Ken, now the Chairman of James Irlam and Sons Limited had just left school to work for his father in his market garden in Snelson.

All was well until fourteen months after moving to Snelson, tragedy struck. James' wife, who had been waiting to go into hospital for a small operation received her admission letter to Macclesfield Infirmary. She died, aged 45, under anaesthetic – before she had even been operated on. James was left with five children and no wife. Fortunately, a sister who had never married decided to take care of the family and did an amazing job until long after she was needed.

Eighteen months younger than Ken, Gordon left school to join his father and brother in expanding the family business. This was to be the case with all of the Irlam children, as one by one they left school to become market gardeners alongside their father.

In 1962, James made the decision to retire and the business was handed over to his four sons. The company was registered for the first time as James Irlam & Sons Limited.

The brothers were anxious to expand and prosper and in 1963, purchased a retail milk round delivering bottled milk to Chelford, Lower Withington, Marthall and Over Peover residents. Things went so well that soon they had acquired a second milk round encompassing the rest of Over Peover and Ollerton. At 5 o'clock each morning the four brothers, two in each vehicle, would deliver milk to the surrounding areas.

One morning in 1964, Walter Broome, owner of a milk lorry collecting churns from farmers and delivering them to a dairy on the outskirts of Manchester, called to see James Irlam. He had been advised by his doctor to take a couple of weeks off work as he had been feeling unwell. Would one of James' sons be willing to drive for him during his absence? James agreed and Ken was given the job of driving the lorry. Unfortunately, instead of improving, Mr Broome's health deteriorated and he was diagnosed with cancer – a disease which was to touch the Irlam family time and time again over the following years. The Company eventually purchased the vehicle and work from Mr Broome's widow. James Irlam & Sons Limited was now in Haulage.

The Irlam brothers continued with their market gardening and retail milk rounds and in 1966 a new vehicle was purchased, to be used for farm milk collections. Because of licence restrictions, the new vehicle could only be used to carry agricultural products for and to farmers and growers, but in 1968, the Operators Licence came into force with the opportunity to carry a wide range of products.

Because of the pre- 1968 product limitations, Bedford lorries were the only types of vehicle utilised by the brothers. However, when their Operators Licence was granted, they invested in a new Leyland vehicle with the ability to carry 10 tons. The new vehicle and the new regulations opened up new opportunities for the Irlam brothers, although as forklift trucks were not particularly popular, vehicles were loaded by hand and this was sometimes backbreaking work.

It was decided to sell the retail milk rounds when the brothers became more involved in product distribution. Although they continued with the farm milk collections, it became apparent in 1972 that this side of their business was no longer viable. More and more farmers were turning to bulk milk tanks and the utilisations of milk churns had become rare.

It was also in this year that the two younger Irlam brothers, Geoff and John, made the decision to go it alone in the transport business. Ken and Gordon were left to trade as James Irlam & Sons Limited, which they did successfully for the next eight years.

In 1980, Gordon and his wife Irene, achieved their life long goal, buying a hotel in Lynton, Devon. Ken Irlam, left alone, joined forces with his two elder sons, David & Stewart, who had been operating their own small haulage business, and the three of them continued as James Irlam & Sons Limited.

By 1985, their fleet of five articulated and four rigid vehicles had outgrown the small yard at Snelson. It was time to look for new premises.

The refrigerated Cold Store, originally built by the Government in 1941 on the site of the cricket ground adjacent to the Dixon Arms for the storage of mainly beef and lamb during World War II, was set in six and a half acres in the village of Chelford. Comprising of three floor heights with two storage rooms on each level, assessed by three lifts, the Cold Store employed approximately thirty people. All the products were brought to the depot by road and rail and unloaded by hand. Railway tracks within the depot meant that goods could be shunted off the main railway line. Road access was also good. During the war, ration books were stored here, but in the nineteen fifties, the Cold Store was closed as an operating centre. Although one office was utilised by the Milk Marketing Board as an A.I unit in the 1960's, they too found alternative premises and the building remained vacant until 1985.

In this year, the Cold Store was offered for Sale by Tender. The Irlams, deciding that the premises were ideal for their purposes, bid for the property and had that bid accepted.

In the intervening fourteen years, the company has expanded dramatically and has a large blue chip customer base to its credit. From being one of the smallest hauliers within such customers as Britvic Soft Drinks, Coca Cola, Pedigree Masterfoods, Mars Confectionery and Procter and Gamble, James Irlam & Sons Limited is now one of the largest. It is not uncommon for the company to move and distribute over five hundred loads per day – Nationally.

The Cold Store is no longer used as a refrigerated depot but as part of a large warehousing complex, home to many and varied palletised products. New warehouses have been added and storage facilities have been mechanised. Battery operated forklift trucks now carry products via installed lifts to any one of the three floors and the stock control system has been computerised.

The original fleet of nine has now risen to 280 vehicles and over 400 trailers. Two new depots have been purchased, in Normanton, West Yorkshire and Grantham, Lincolnshire – the company also has depots in London, Norwich, Lancashire and Northamptonshire. James Irlam & Sons Limited employs 450 staff including Ken's two younger sons, Michael and Andrew – Operations and Planning Directors respectively.

The road has been a long and sometimes hard one, from the humble beginnings of a market garden in Snelson. However, throughout those years, the family has remained close and committed to achieving success. It was the ultimate accolade when James Irlam & Sons Limited was awarded the title of Haulier of the Year in 1996 by the transport industry and a crowning moment for Ken and his four sons. It was recognition, by those able to judge, of the effort they had put in to their company over many years and since 1996, James Irlam & Sons Limited has continued to prosper and thrive.

In 1999, the Company received yet another award – Lifetime Achievement within the Road Transport Industry. It was a proud moment for everyone but certainly not the end of the road.

The Company ethos is summed up in their mission statement:

"Through hard work, determination, team work and communication – we will achieve success."

They have done and will continue to do so for many years to come.

The above article was prepared by Kenneth Irlam and re-produced with his kind permission.

CHELFORD GREENGROCERS
KNUTSFORD ROAD

The Village Greengrocers on Knutsford Road was taken over by the present owners, Mr & Mrs Chan, in 1985. Prior to that date it had been, amongst other things, an antique shop and for a period of time a hairdressers.

Since the start of trading the shop has offered a warm welcome to all.

The store sells high quality fruit and vegetables alongside a wide range of Asian Cuisine and specialised food. Mrs Chan is readily available to give cooking advice wherever needed.

M G WILLIAMS & SONS
Cheshire's Traditional Grocers

M G Williams & Sons is still a family business established in Holmes Chapel in 1875. We have had a branch in Chelford since 1968 selling quality foods and provisions.

THE PAPERSHOP
by Doug White and David Reading

The local newsagent, in Chelford known as The Papershop, was acquired in 1996 by its present owners, Mr David Reading and Mr Douglas White. An old established newsagent dating back some fifty years, it was set up in the front room of a mid terrace and sold nothing but newspapers and tobacco. Today, however, it has grown as the village has grown, and now has a morning home delivery service of more than six hundred houses from Siddington to Peover and beyond.

Many locals make more than one daily call to the shop, whether it be a small child choosing from the penny sweets or to pick up that birthday card from the ever increasing selection that you nearly forgot, or a quarter of Uncle Luke's to shake off a sore throat, or just even to catch up on the local news. Of course its not just the locals that make regular visits to the shop. Many farmers visiting Chelford on market days have regular orders for farming papers and magazines. So whilst "Mr Farmer" is selling his produce "Mrs Farmer" can be found browsing through our selection of cakes, biscuits, bread, milk and groceries and all the other household items we stock, not forgetting our wide selection of weigh out sweets that everybody likes to indulge in.

So next time you think, ' I've forgotten that thing.' why not call in and be surprised at what you'll find.

HAIRDRESSERS

The Chelford Hairdressing salon was purpose built in 1985. The previous salon was at, what is now, the greengrocer's shop. Originally Mrs Holland, who was followed by Heather Irlam, ran the salon and then Mark Daniel Colman bought the salon. Mark stayed for about 18 months then Alison Gater took over the business $7^1/_2$ years ago. During Mrs Holland's ownership, Liz Dawn (Vera Duckworth) once had her hair done in the salon.

The village hairdressers is now called 'Mulberry Hair Design' and is owned by Alison Gater. Alison has been the owner for over 7 years and employs two full time hairdressers beside herself and one part-time hairdresser. Alison lives in Congleton with her husband, Neil, and her 14-month-old son Ethan. She travels to Chelford every day to run her salon which is well supported not only by the people of Chelford but clients have come from as far away as Leicester, Wales and abroad.

The full-time hairdresser assistants who help Alison are Tilly Clare, who has been there for 13 years and Jackie Stewart, who has been there for 11 years. Liz Jones who is a part time assistant has only been with the salon a short time.

CHELFORD POTTERY
Patricia Higginbotham

Born in Manchester, Pat's passion for studio pottery led her to take part in several ceramics courses, but she would regard herself as largely self-taught.

She originally made slipware in earthy colours, followed later by stoneware domestic pottery with 'landscape' glazing, but alongside her studio work Pat taught pottery in a psychiatric hospital, continuing this rewarding work until the 1990's.

305

She was a member of the prestigious Red Rose Guild of Designer Craftsmen (recently featured in Crafts Magazine) and has exhibited widely in both solo and mixed shows. The fine porcelain produced in the last few years has become eminently collectable, and has been purchased for the permanent collection of Manchester City Art Galleries.

Pat moved to her present studio in the beautiful surroundings of the Cheshire countryside in 1982 where she continues to work and explore her particular interest in fine porcelain vessels and in her more rugged ceramic sculpture for the garden.

Chelford Pottery is situated in one of the Church Cottages, Holmes Chapel Road, Chelford.

Also trading in the village are:

FARM SUPPLIES
HORSE AND COUNTY
ALAN BILSBOROUGH - LOCKSMITH
ASHLEY MOBILES
JEFF BOON – BUTCHERS
FRAME ART

EPILOGUE
By Roger Roycroft

By now our reflection on this Cheshire village is drawing to its conclusion. Still to come is the Appendix wherein are collected names and dates, people and places and data for those who will research in the future. But on the whole these are but dry statistics and to judge a community from such facts would be as hard as to judge a city by reading its telephone directory.

In what has come before we hope to have shown you some of the people and events that made the village of Chelford unique. Unique that is to those who have lived there, but yet ordinary enough in that it reflects the values of any English country village that has endured through this hectic century. A period of enormous change in farming, in industry, in technology, services, communications and transportation. Changes enough to engulf any established way of life.

Change is of course good in any society, indeed positively essential if we are not to stagnate but it needs to be paced lest it becomes not change but rather revolution: for unremitting change is a most erosive force. In this regard Chelford has been no exception. The established order of 1900 is long gone – with undoubted benefits to many, but balanced by what losses? Those who look upon the old photographs of our village always remark on the quiet, peaceful, roads. On the tranquillity and evidence of the unhurried enjoyment of life. Nostalgia blossoms – but set against that what you can not see. The fallen infant mortality rate. The absence of tuberculosis. Unlimited clean water from a tap, light at the press of a switch, warmth in the winter, and the effortless disposal of sewage. Would we really turn the clock back if we could? One doubts it.

Look though not at material things but at human factors. Of people bonding together because they are neighbours. What an interesting word that is – usually thought of as 'the people next door' but better defined as 'persons regarded as having the duties or claims of friendliness and consideration'. Research in any dictionary and the word is synonymous with friendliness. That certainly is something we have lost. Lost, probably, because of that factor of rapid change, of rapid immigration into the village and having a far more shifting population than ever was the case before. Yet were these the only causes we should be able to assimilate and adjust and indeed in many ways we have, but not nearly enough.

Changing work practices and the demands of employers have left many village residents with far less free time in the evenings and at weekends to become involved in village activities, and that we have to accept. Yet again it is not sufficient reason to account for why our village institutions are dying. Rather the final blame must lie in apathy. We care about our homes, our cars, our children, reading the papers, gardening and being – well, essentially selfish. We look inwards, not outward. That must surely be the greatest loss for all of us to endure. Are we all really too busy to help with youth groups? Is it so terrible to support the aims of the Womens' Institute? Are we so pressed that the needs of our senior citizens are left to social workers? Are we, in fact, really neighbours?

Within any society there are many catalysing forces but in any village none so effective as the church – of whatever denomination. Leaving aside the desire for immortality, or even the possibility of it, any coming together of a village population to share in a belief of what might be summated as 'positive forces for good' can not be other than beneficial. One might prefer the term 'Christian belief' but in these days it seems to be regarded as definitely non-trendy – but why?

In relation to church attendance one factor missing now in Chelford is that the village pub is no longer opposite the church. An excellent arrangement which is common in many villages and plainly no accident since it has been long recognised that any attempt to separate the spiritual from the secular must be doomed to fail. Any community needs both to survive.

As we look back and consider how this small village has changed it is natural to also look forward. Where do we want to go, and why? We have, overall, an excellent standard of living. We have security and a stable political climate – though, as ever, not to everyone's taste. But on the distaff side we have an appalling divorce rate. We have disaffected teenagers who have lost their extended childhood as a result of media pressures and a flourishing drug environment. And in the adult world far too high a proportion with a 'look the other way' philosophy who are prepared to let someone else get involved. Will society and the younger generations rebel? Will the pendulum swing back to revive a more ordered society? Certainly there isn't a lot of time left for the 'doers' are all ageing and their successors are yet to appear in any numbers.

We hope our tale of local history will stimulate some. No doubt we may irritate others by our criticism of today's values. Yet all we ask is that our readers reflect on what was, consider afresh what is now, and make a value judgement on their preferred future.

Those who rebuilt Chelford Parish Church 225 years ago had faith and vision. Their building was not a sacrificial offering to God, but a place of education, of enlightenment, of inward reflection and, that word again, of neighbourhood gathering. We have the ability to keep their vision alive as the church moves into the next 225 years. We certainly have the need, and we must sincerely hope that between us we have the will. What we don't have is room for apathy.

GUIDE LEADERS - 1929-1950

Name	Title	Date Joined	Date Left	Address
A P Bythell	Captain	Mar 1929	Oct 1946	The Grange, Chelford
J Wilson	Lieutenant	Mar 1929	Jan 1934	Sunnyside Farm, Chelford
B Dixon	"	Jan 1934	Oct 1936	Astle cottage, Chelford
B Dixon	Captain	Oct 1936	Oct 1951	" "
M Gould	Lieutenant	Oct 1936	Oct 1937	Smiths Green Lwr Withington
J Taylor	"	Jan 1939	June 1945	Thorn Bank, Chelford
M Gould	"	May 1942	Dec 1943	Smiths Green, Lwr Withington
M Haynes	"	Jan 1944	?	Station Road, Chelford
P Lomas	"	Jan 1945	Oct 1947	Stelfox Farm, Soss Moss
H M Bloar	"	Dec 1949	?	Dairy House Farm, Withington
M Hope	"	Jan 1950	?	Bagguley Fold Farm, Marthall

BROWNIE LEADERS – 1931-1948

Name	Title	Date Joined	Date Left	Address
A P Bythell	Brown Owl	June 1931	June 1933	The Grange, Chelford
E Wright	Brown Owl	June 1933	Jan 1938	Station Road, Chelford
P Cash	Tawny Owl	Jan 1937	Jan 1938	The School House, Chelford
P Cash	Brown Owl	Jan 1938	June 1940	" "

Pack disbanded June 1940 Returned October 1946

E Sujanson	Brown Owl	Oct 1946	1948	Leyton Holt, Chelford
Barbara Hodgekinson	Brown Owl	1948	1950	Wilmslow
Mary Dale	Tawny Owl	1948	1951	Chelford

LIST OF GUIDE MEMBERS
1940 TO 1950

Name	Address	Date Joined
Barbara Capper	Bank House, Chelford	June 1940
Nancy Hope	Baguley Fold Farm, Marthall	March 1941
Charlotte Hockwell	Bell Marsh Farm, Goostrey	May 1942
Gwene Lowe	Astle Hall Gardens, Chelford	May 1942
Barbara Burgess	The Garage, Chelford	May 1942
Nesta Worthington	Station Road, Chelford	May 1942
Margaret Hope	Baguley Fold Farm, Chelford	May 1942
Mary How	----	May 1942
Joyce Batiste	----	January 1943
Pamela Pratt	David Lewis Colony, Great Warford	January 1944
Renee Sproston	Astle Farm, Chelford	June 1945
Joyce Wardman	----	June 1945
Doreen Caldicutt	Council Houses, Alderley Rd., Chelford	June 1945
Elizabeth Newton	Council Houses, Astle Farms.	June 1945
Hilda Burgess	Dingle Bank, Withington	June 1945
Nancy Dale	Yew Tree Farm, Chelford	June 1945
Phyllis Hope	Baguley Fold Farm, Marthall	June 1945
Marion Coults	Beeches Farm, Ollerton	June 1945
Audrey Bailey	Astle Hall, Chelford	June 1945
Margery Lowe	Astle Hall Gardens, Chelford	June 1945
Mary Brown	Mere Hills Farm, Chelford	June 1945
Eileen Price	David Lewis Colony	June 1945
Margaret Newton	Roadside Farm, Chelford	April 1946
Nina Burrows	Six Acres, Siddington	February 1946
Olive Cotterall	Mile Lane, Siddington	May 1946
Barbara Buckley	Roadside Cottage, Siddington	May 1946
Jennifer Davis	Dividale, Great Warford	September 1946
Marion Lomas	Soss Moss	June 1947
Jean Lomas	Soss Moss	June 1947
Alice Shufflebotham	Gleads Moss, Lower Withington	July 1947
Doreel Holland	----	September 1947
Irene Drinkwater	----	June 1948
Jean Povall	----	March 1948
Barbara Fisher	The Black Swan, Lower Withington	June 1948
Janet Sinclair	----	June 1948
Hilary Stanier	Marthall	---
Rita Snelson	Brook House Farm, Chelford	March 1949
Brenda Booth	Council Houses, Lower Withington	June 1951
Ruth Gamon	----	----
Shelia Lowe	----	----
Doreen Ryder	----	----

Susan Drinkwater	Ollerton	February 1949
Marie Povall	----	1952 ?
Audrey Rowbotham	----	June 1951
Joyce Elizabeth Kennerley	Deons Rough Farm, Withington	September 1952
Jean Burgess	Oak Bank, Marthall Lane, Ollerton	1954
Jean Brindley	41 Marthall Lane, Ollerton	March 1955
Jean Wright	Ollerton	October 1955
Margaret Sproston	Astle Farm, Chelford	???
Margaret Bull	New Council Houses, Chelford	February 1955

LIST OF CHELFORD RESIDENTS - 1924

Name	Occupation (Where known)	Address
Adams Frederick	Gamekeeper	The Lodge
Adderley James Arthur	Booking Clerk	Station Road
Barber John Thomas	Insurance Broker	Alderley Rd, School Cottage
Baskerville Amos	Plate Layer	Station Rd
Bell Joseph	Signalman	Pepper St
Beswick Thomas	Otter Keeper (Hall)	Pepper St
Bloar William	Plate Layer	Station Rd
Bowyer Edward J	Mfr. Chemist	Woodlands
Burgess Ralph	Blacksmith	Smithy
Burgess Henry	Blacksmith	Pepper St
Dr Bythell William James Storey	Specialist	The Grange
Carter Thos Henry	Grocer & PO	Post Office
Cobbett Richard	Solicitor	Rode Syde
Dale GH & Son		Garage
Dale Frederick Wm	Farmer	Astle Farm
Dale George Henry	Publican	Dixon Arms Hotel
Dean John Foden		Wood Villa
Dixon Col Sir George		Astle Hall
Dorner Frank		Mere Court
Drew Geo. Henry	Newspaper Prop.	Station Cottages – Paper Shop
Ellis John	Porter	Station Rd
Ewen Mgt Ann		Oakdene
Ford Charles		Park Cottages
Callwood Henry	Plate Layer	Station Rd
Gordon William		Station Rd
Gledhill Walter	Farmer	Astle
Hoare Joseph Brodie		Dalefield
Hollins Philip Leslie	Cotton Manufacturer	Chelford House
Hope Henry	Farmer	Abbey Farm
Hubbert William	Refreshment rooms	Congleton Rd
Johnson Thomas		Pepper St
Jones Edward	Farmer	Carter Lane
Knowles Charles	Butcher	Knutsford Rd
Knowles Joseph		Pepper St
Moores Abraham	Coal Agent for Lord Vernon	Station
Moores Joseph	Tailor	Church Cottage

Moss George	Farmer	Yew Tree Farm, School Lane
Moulton William	Chauffeur	Station Rd
Naylor John Warren	Schoolmaster	School House
Newton Arthur	Farmer	Roadside Farm
Norbury Albert Allman		Farm
Parkers Rev. William Herbert MA		Vicarage
Potts David	Assistant overseer	Yew Tree Cottage
Ryder Samuel	Plate Layer	Station Rd Cottages
Shepard Arthur Harold BA	MD	
Sproston John James	Farmer	Astle
Sparrow Major Walter		Manor House
Steele Joseph Silver	Bricklayer	Bank House Knutsford Rd
Taylor John snr	Postman	Yew Tree Cottage
Thompson Ernest	Saddler	Shop Station Rd
Wilson Thomas	Farmer	Sunny Bank Farm

LIST OF RESIDENTS OF CHELFORD AND SURROUNDING AREAS
EARLY 1960'S

This list has been compiled from information provided by Josie Parfitt who, with her husband, Dennis, owned the village shop and post office from 1961 to 1976.

Shops

The Corner Shop and Post Office	Mr & Mrs Parfitt
Newsagent – Knutsford Road	Mr & Mrs Steeple
Manchester – Macclesfield	Mr Newton (Manager)
Farmers Knutsford Road	
Hardware – Roundabout	Mr & Mrs Burgess

Hotels

Dixon Arms	Mr & Mrs Woodward
Egerton Arms	Mr & Mrs Green

Garages	
Roundabout	Mr & Mrs Deaken
Village – Knutsford Road	Mr Blackhurst

Doctors

Roadside, Knutsford Road	Dr Evans
	Dr Pratt

Farms

Astle No. 2	Mr E Dale
Astle No. 1	Mr C Sproston
Brookhouse	Mr Norbury
Knowsley	Mr Gledhill
Abbey	Mr F Hope
House (Withington Hall)	Mr L Ford
Lapwing Hall	Mr N Baskerville
Foden Bank	Mr E Pimlott
Norfolk	Mr A Turnock
Oakwood	Mr J A Bloor
Ainsworth	Mr F Gledhill

Woodend	Mr F Williamson
Sunny Bank	Mr Shenton
Common	Mr Wilf Massey
Heath	Mr Alan Massey
Highfield	Mrs F Stanier
Yew Tree	Mr Dale
Roadside	Mr T Newton
Piggots Hill	Mr Skellern

Small Holdings

Spitted Hall (opposite Lapwing Lane)	Mr Frank Pimlott
Oaklyn	Mr Jackson
Lapwing Cottage	Mr S Shuttleworth
Acre Nook	Mr Evans

Residences

Chelford House	Mr & Mrs Morris
Dalefields	Mr & Mrs C Duckworth
Chelford Place (Now Ivy House)	Mr & Mrs J Harrison
Manor House	Mr & Mrs Shiers
Vicarage	Rev. & Mrs Lea
Withington Hall	Col. & Mrs J Glegg
Farmwood	Mr & Mrs R Lowe
Farmwood Cottage	Mr & Mrs J Barber
Congleton Road Cottage	Mr T Massey
Moss Cottage	Mr & Mrs Barber
Astle Lodge	Mr & Mrs Barrat
Astle Cottage	Sir John & Lady Dixon
Rose Cottage	Mr & Mrs Johnson
Rose Cottage	Mr & Mrs Worthington
Highfield	Mr & Mrs Holt
Astle Lane Cottages	Mr T Newton
Astle Lane Cottages	Mr P Newton
Astle Lane Cottages	Mr Bailey
Tied to Fallows Hall	Mr O'Brien
Fallows Hall	Lady Holt
	Mr Barlow – Tenant
Fallows Hall Cottage (1)	Mr Blinkhorn

Fallows Hall Cottage (2)	Mr Stan Skopanski
Church Cottages	Mr & Mrs Okill
"	Mr & Mrs John Copps
"	Miss Sarah Moores
"	Mr & Mrs J Cheadle
"	Mr & Mrs Geoff Street
"	Mr W Street and Mrs Fred Street
Oak Road	Mr & Mrs A Coppack
	Mr & Mrs Earp
	Mr & Mrs Chadwick
	Miss J Taylor
	Mr & Mrs Egerton
	Mr & Mrs Harold Bradley
	Mr & Mrs J Camm
Robin Lane	Mr & Mrs A Sutcliffe
Council Cottages	Mr & Mrs G Shelton
	Mr & Mrs Lea Eyers
	Mr & Mrs Callwood
	Mr & Mrs R Barlow
	Mr & Mrs J Wright
	Mr H Bell
Knutsford Road	Mr & Mrs J Carter
	Mr & Mrs Hobbs
	Mr & Mrs P Hall
	Mr & Mrs Norbury
Station Road	Mrs Holcroft
	Mr & Mrs Worthington
	Mr & Mrs Brown
	Mr & Mrs Blomfield
	Mr P Newton
Peover Lane	
Kinross	Mr & Mrs J Robertson
?	Mr & Mrs Norberry
Willow Glade	Mr & Mrs H Cluff

Leyton Holt	Mr & Mrs L Dunning
Hinton Cottage	Mrs Pearse
Kennel Bank	Mr & Mrs L Howarth
Astle Hall	Mr & Mrs W Bailey
Astle Hall Cottages	Mr & Mrs Lowe

Also known to be resident in the village were Mr & Mrs G Henshall and Mr & Mrs Heyworth in Peover Lane, plus Lizzie (who lived at Roadside Farm) and Maggie Tickle who was employed by the Doctors.

Apologies to anybody missed off the list or in incorrect residence.

FAMILY NAMES - RESIDENTS OF CHELFORD 1999

Aasht
Ablitt
Adams
Allmand Smith
Anand
Anderson
Annikin
Atkins
Bagnall
Bailey
Baker
Ball
Ballntyne
Barber
Barker
Barnes
Barron
Barry
Basanez
Baskerville
Bates
Beaman
Beech
Beesley
Bench
Bennett
Berry
Billington
Bilsborough
Bilsborrow
Birchall
Blackwell
Blain
Blake
Blomfield
Bluck
Bond
Bonney
Boon
Booth
Bosomworth

Bowen
Bowyer
Bradley
Bradshaw
Bream
Brew
Bridge
Bridges
Brierley
Brighouse
Brindle
Brindley
Broadbridge
Brocklehurst
Brodie
Bromley
Brooks
Brown
Bryan
Buckle
Budgett
Bullock
Burgess
Burke
Burns
Burrows
Buxton
Byrom
Callis
Callwood
Camm
Campbell
Capper
Capps
Carlile
Carter
Cartwright
Casale
Caulton
Chadwick
Chambers

Chan
Chaplin
Chapman
Cheetham
Chorlton
Christiansen
Chubb
Clark
Claxton
Clayborough
Clayton
Cliffe
Collins
Colman
Conn
Conquer
Cook
Cookson
Coope
Cooper
Coppock
Cotterill
Couling
Cowley
Coxon
Crewe
Crimes
Crowder
Cunliffe
Curran
Currie
Cusselle
Dagnal-Kilshaw
Dale
Dando
Dartee
Davenport
Davies
Dawson
Dean
Dean-Smith

Dennis
Derbyshire
Dibble
Diggle
Dilworth
Dingle
Dobell
Dobson
Donoghue
Earl
Earp
Eastaugh
Eastwood
Edward
Edwards
Egerton
Elliott
Ellis
Ellison
Evans
Ewers
Farrington
Fawcett
Ferguson
Fielding
Flattery
Fleming
Fletcher
Flinter
Fogarty
Ford
Forrest
Foster
Foulkes
Freeman
Friedlander
Fryer
Furnival
Gale
Ganguly
German

Gibbs	Harwood	Jump	McArdle
Gilbert	Havill	Kavanagh	McBrinn
Gildon	Hay	Kawa	McDonald
Gill	Head	Kellett	McNulty
Giraud	Heathcote	Kelly	Meadowcroft
Gledhill	Heggs	Kennerley	Medley
Goldstraw	Henriques	Kerfoot	Michell
Goodall	Henshall	Kerr	Miller
Goodman	Henson	Kerrigan	Millward
Goodwin	Hewitt	Kettle	Mitchell
Goostrey	Heywood	Kipps	Monighan
Gould	Higginbotham	Kirk	Montgomery
Grace	Higginson	Kirkham	Moody
Grant	Hillier	Kitching	Morris
Grasse	Hillis	Knowles	Morrison
Green-Buckely	Hindley	Lane	Moss
Greenhill	Hobbs	Langham	Moston
Greenhough	Hodkinson	Lawrence	Much
Greenwood	Holder	Laws	Mugeli
Gresham	Holding	Lawton	Murdey
Grey	Holehouse	Lea	Mutch
Grey	Holland	Leather	Naylor
Griffin	Holme	Lee	Nellist
Groves	Holmes	Leese	Nelson
Grundy	Hope	Leigh	Nesbit
Gudgeon	Hornby	Lingwood	Newton
Hacking	Horrocks	Link	Nicholls
Haighton	Horsfield	List	Nickson
Hakami	Hoverstadt	Lloyd	Norbury
Hall	Howlett	Lofthouse	Norman
Hamilton	Hulme	Lomas	O'Brien
Hamlin	Hyatt	Longworth	O'Shaughnessy
Hammersley	Hynd	Lowe	Offen
Hammond	Icke	Lowrie	Okill
Hamnett	Ingram	Madgen	Oldroyd
Handford	Irlam	Mallion	Orr
Hardy	Jackson	March	Oxford
Harmens	James	Marland	Packham
Harradine	Jarrold	Marshall	Page
Harrison	Jepson	Martin	Parkinson
Hartell	Johnson	Mason	Parr
Hartman	Johnston	Mastin	Parrack
Hartwell	Jones	Mayer	Patton

Pearce	Robertson	Sullivan	Walton
Pearson	Robinson	Sutcliffe	Warburton
Perratt	Rochford	Sutton	Ward
Phillips	Rogers	Swain	Wardell
Pick	Rourke	Swift	Watt
Pickard	Rowbottom	Swindlehurst	Wearing
Pickering	Rowland	Tanner	Webb
Pickford	Roycroft	Taylor	Weekes
Pimlott	Ryder	Tennant	Weight
Plant	Sant	Thelwell	Welch
Plaskitt	Saunders	Thomason	Wheatley
Pointon	Scarrow	Thompson	Wheldon
Potts	Schurholtz	Thornhill	White
Preece	Scott	Thornton	Whitehurst
Pritchard	Shackleton	Thorp	Whittle
Procopi	Shardlow	Thorpe	Wilding
Provost	Shemilt	Tierney	Wilkinson
Purcell	Shenton	Todd	Williams
Radford	Sheridan	Tolliss	Willis
Ranson	Shuttleworth	Tozer	Wilson
Read	Simons	Trevor	Winstanley
Reading	Simpson	Tristram	Winter
Record	Slater	Tucker	Withers
Rectanus-Smith	Smart	Turner	Wood
Redfern	Smele	Turnock	Woodcock
Reece	Smith	Twist	Woods
Reeve	Snelson	Tyre	Worthington
Richardson	Stannard	Unsworth	Wright
Rickard	Stevenson	Vickers	Yates
Ridehalgh	Stewart	Viggars	Yeo
Rider	Stott	Vora	Young
Riley	Strudley	Wakefield	
Roberts	Stubbs	Walker	

FURTHER READING

<u>Books</u>

CHESHIRE FEDERATION OF WOMEN'S INSTITUTES

> The Cheshire Village Book
> > Countryside Books, Newbury & CFWI, Chester 1990
> Snippets of history and reminiscence from Chelford on p.55-56

COMBER, WINIFRED M; GIBSON, Lesley & HAWORTH, Dorothy (Editors)

> Cheshire Village Memories II
> > Cheshire Federation of Women's Institutes, 1961
> Similar to the preceding work but contains information not found in it.
> Chelford is covered on p.38-40

DEPARTMENT OF THE ENVIRONMENT

> List of Buildings of Special Architectural or Historic Interest.
> > Borough of Macclesfield, Cheshire. (Parishes of Chelford...
> > Withington). DOE, 1984
> Chelford is covered on p.1-5. Gives approximate date, architect where
> known, and features of merit.

DODGSON, J McN

> The Place-Names of Cheshire. Part I:
> Macclesfield Hundred
> > Cambridge University Press, 1970
> Chelford is covered on p.75-77. Useful for origins of names of places,
> fields, streets etc. For more detailed study, needs to be used in
> conjunction with Part V (place-name elements).

EARWAKER. J P

> East Cheshire: Past and Present. Volume II
> > Author, 1880
> Account of Chelford on p.360-370.

PLANT, W KEITH

Chelford: 19th Century. A Demographic and Historical Study.
  W Keith Plant, 22 Chapel Croft, Chelford, near Macclesfield,
  SK11 9SU, 1995
Statistical information from censuses, tithe apportionments and trade
directories, plus details of specific areas of the village and the families
resident there during the period.

ROYCROFT, ROGER

Reflections upon the Chelford Railway Disaster of 22nd December 1894.
  np, 1994

Extremely detailed account of the accident, inquest, inquiry and final
report. Includes details of killed and known injured.

Articles
ANON

"The Homes of Cheshire – 28. The Manor House, Chelford"
  Cheshire Life, August 1952, p.18-20 (Part I);
  September 1952, p.21-23 (Part II)
History of the building, plus description of interior, barn and gardens.

"Tales from an Edwardian Lady's Garden"
  Cheshire Life, December 1985, p.43
Brief biography of Frances Eliza Crompton, writer of books for children.
She was born at Butley and resided at Chelford.

BELL, T HEDLEY

"Mere Water: Farmwood Pool, Chelford"
  Cheshire Life, July 1977 p.42-43
The pool was formed as a result of sand extraction. The article describes
birds and other wildlife of the area, turned into a nature reserve by its
owner, Eric Crosby.

KENNETT, CECIL

"The Charm of Chelford"
  Cheshire Life, May 1965, p.61, 63

Light-hearted view of the paradox that, although Chelford figures prominently on signposts, it is surprisingly difficult to find.

O'NEILL, PATRICK

"To Market, To Market"
Cheshire Life, July 1995, p.36-36
A look at Chelford Market, the biggest market for hay, straw and calves in the country.

SHARPLEY, ROBIN

"Turn Off and Tarry: Chelford"
Cheshire Life, November 1975, p.80-81, 83-84
Profile of the village, concentrating on the Manor House, other buildings, and the market.

SKINNER, TONY

"First Class Service"
Cheshire Life, March 1995, p.150-151
Ruth and Bernard Annikin, who run the post office and general stores at Chelford.

STEAD, ROBERT

"Lawn Order"
Cheshire Link, July 1989, p.36-41
The garden at Astle Farm, which at the time of writing held the Cheshire County Farm Gardens championship.

WALSH, AUDREY CECIL & BRILL, BARBARA

"Relatively Speaking"
Cheshire Life, January 1986, p.33
Miss Walsh recounts memories of her mother, children's writer, Frances Eliza Crompton, who lived at Larchwood, Chelford.

WRIGHT, BEN

"Breeding in Cheshire"
Cheshire Life, May 1963, p.60-61,63
Visit to Mr Blair Gething of Chelford, breeder of racing pigeons.

YARWOOD, DEREK

"Sand Storm"
Cheshire Life, December 1988, p.88-91
Fight by residents of Chelford and neighbouring villages to prevent the granting of planning permission for further sand extraction in the area.

FORTHCOMING PUBLICATIONS

The Village School Log Book – 1900 to 1950
> To be published January 2000 to commemorate the official opening of the new school.

The Three Witches of Chelford

Chelford in the 19th Century – Revised Edition

Marthall in the 19th Century

Lower Withington in the 19th Century

Snelson in the 19th Century

For further information contact Keith Plant on 01625 860074.